Simplified Design
of Building Structures

Simplified Design
of Building Structures

||||||||||||||||||||||||||||||||||||||||||||||||||||||||||||||||||||

James Ambrose

Professor of Architecture
University of Southern California

A Wiley-Interscience Publication

JOHN WILEY & SONS

New York   Chichester   Brisbane   Toronto

690
A496

Library of Congress Cataloging in Publication Data:

Ambrose, James E
  Simplified design of building structures.

  "A Wiley-Interscience publication."
  Includes bibliographical references and index.
  1. Structural design. 2. Architectural design.
3. Buildings. I. Title.

TA658.A5   690   79-413
ISBN 0-471-04721-X

Printed in the United States of America

10 9 8 7 6 5 4 3 2 1

To
EDMUND F. TOTH
who taught more people than he realized
more than they realized

Preface

||||||||||||||||||||||||||||||||||||||||||||||||||||||||||||

This book is intended to fill a gap that has existed in the technical literature in the area of structural design for buildings. While the subject has usually been well covered with regard to its many topics in an incremental way, there have been relatively few books written to explain the overall process of designing a building structure; beginning with the architect's design drawings and ending with a set of structural plans and details. That is, of course, precisely what the structural designer does in the majority of building design cases, and yet the process has seldom been illustrated. The few attempts to do so have usually consisted of examples of the designer's calculations, with little explanation of the general process or of the relations between the architectural and structural design, and with a minimum of graphic illustration.

The work here consists of the illustration of the design of the structural systems for three relatively ordinary buildings: a two story residence, a one story commercial building, and a six story office building. For each building the presentation begins with a set of architectural design drawings such as would normally be developed early in the building design process. This is followed by the development of an example structural system, with sample calculations for typical elements of the system and some discussion of the alternates and options possible for various situations. For each of the second two buildings two separate structures are designed with different materials. Completing the illustration in each case is a set of typical structural plans and details.

In order to keep the work within the range of those with less than a complete training in structural engineering, calculations have been limited to simplified and approximate methods as usually presented in books written for architecture students and others with less than a thorough background in calculus and engineering physics. This means that the work is slightly below acceptable professional standards in some cases, although it is generally sufficient to obtain approximate designs that are useful for cost estimating, for development of the architectural details, and for gaining a general sense of the needs of the structure. The reader with a more rigorous training in engineering may easily pursue the analysis and design calculations to a higher level of accuracy, but will usually find that the end results are not substantially changed.

While this book is essentially intended for self-study, or for use in teaching in architecture or technical school programs, the lack of similar illustrative material should also make it of considerable value to engineering students and engineers in training. In fact, anyone who is interested in the general problem of designing structures for buildings, and who has not actually done it much, should benefit from reading this work.

Two decisions had to be made in developing this material. The first had to do with the selection of the references to be used. These were deliberately chosen to be ones that were generally available as well as being usable by the less than experienced reader. The second decision had to do with the use of English units (feet, pounds, etc.) instead of international units (metrics) which are steadily becoming more widely used in engineering work. Since the references selected all use English units, the decision was a pragmatic one—to reduce confusion for the reader. The necessity for conversion from one system to the other will simply be a way of life for designers in the coming years.

This work has been developed from my experience over some 30 years of involvement in building design, as a student, teacher, writer, and professional designer. Much is owed to the teachers, students, critics, and professional colleagues whose reactions and help have molded that experience and tempered it. I am grateful to the International Conference of Building Officials, the American Institute of Steel Construction, and the Concrete Masonry Association of California for permission to draw extensively from materials in their publications. Reading of the text drafts by my colleagues,

Harold Hauf and Dimitry Vergun, provided invaluable assistance and encouragement. Finally, I am indebted to my family for their patience and indulgence and especially to my wife, Peggy, for her faith and her important assistance.

JAMES AMBROSE

Los Angeles, California
March 1979

Contents

||||||||||||||||||||||||||||||||||||||||||||||||||||||||||||

Introduction   **1**

1   Building One   **5**

1.1   The Building   5
1.2   The Structural System   9
1.3   Design of the Roof Structure   9
1.4   Design of the Floor Structure   17
1.5   Design of the Walls and Columns   22
1.6   Design of the Foundations   26
1.7   Design for Wind   27
1.8   Design of an Alternate Roof Structure   42
1.9   Construction Drawings   47

2   Building Two   **62**

2.1   The Building   62
2.2   The Wood Structure   65
2.3   Design of the Wood Roof Structure   66
2.4   Design of the Wood Studs and Columns   70
2.5   Design of the Foundations   73
2.6   Design for Seismic Load   77
2.7   Construction Drawings—Wood Structure   87
2.8   Design of an Alternate Wood Roof   97
2.9   The Steel and Masonry Structure   99
2.10   Design of the Steel Roof Structure   100
2.11   Design of the Masonry Walls   103
2.12   Design of the Foundations   115

xi

2.13   Design for Seismic Load   116
2.14   Design of an Alternate Steel Roof Structure   123
2.15   Construction Drawings—Steel and Masonry
       Structure   126

3   Building Three   133

3.1   The Building   133
3.2   The Steel Structure   137
3.3   Design of the Steel Floor System   141
3.4   Design of the Steel Columns and Bents   146
3.5   Design for Wind   155
3.6   Second Approximation of the Columns and Bents   163
3.7   Design of the First Floor, Basement, and
       Foundations   172
3.8   Construction Drawings—Steel Structure   175
3.9   The Concrete Structure   189
3.10   Design of the Concrete Floor System   190
3.11   Design of the Concrete Columns   205
3.12   Design for Wind   216
3.13   Design of the First Floor, Basement, and
       Foundations   220
3.14   Construction Drawings—Concrete Structure   222
3.15   Alternate Floor Systems   232

References   **239**

Appendix   **241**

Index   **267**

Introduction

||||||||||||||||||||||||||||||||||||||||||||||||||||||||||

Designing structures for buildings involves the consideration of a wide range of factors. Building structural designers must not only understand structural behavior and how to provide for it adequately, but must also be knowledgeable about building construction materials and processes, building codes and standards, and the economics of building. In addition, since the structure is merely a subsystem in the whole building, they must have some understanding of the problem of designing the whole building. Structures should not only be logical in their own right, but should also relate well to the functional purposes of the building and to the other subsystems for power, lighting, plumbing, heating, and so on.

Formal education in structural design is usually focused heavily on learning the procedures for structural analysis and the techniques and problems of designing individual structural elements and systems in various materials. The whole problem of designing a structure for a building is not well documented, and learning it usually takes place primarily on the job in professional offices. While this means of learning is valuable in some ways, it does not provide a good general understanding, since it is usually limited to the highly specific situations of each design problem.

The principal purpose of the examples in this book is to illustrate the problems and processes of designing whole structural systems

1

for buildings. The procedure used in the examples is to present a general building design as a given condition, following which is the illustration of the selection and design of the various typical elements of the structural system. The buildings shown are not particularly intended as examples of good architectural design, but merely as illustrations of common structural design situations.

While most of the calculations shown are in reasonably complete form, it is assumed that the reader has previously mastered the fundamentals of analysis and design of simple structures. The word "simplified" implies some limit to the complexity of the work, and the general image for this limit is the level of complexity dealt with in the series of books originally authored by the late Harry Parker that bear titles beginning with the word simplified. The first five books in the list of references for this work are from that series and should be considered as the basic references for the structural calculations in this work. A few topics not presently covered in those books, such as the design of foundations and masonry structures and analysis and design for wind and earthquakes, are developed somewhat more thoroughly in this book.

In many relatively simple structures most structural design problems can be "solved" by the use of tabulated materials from codes, handbooks, and manufacturer's flyers. Where this is possible, from readily available sources, the examples show such use. Usually, however, longhand calculations are shown for the purpose of explaining the problems more thoroughly.

For sake of brevity the structural calculations shown are not complete, but are limited to the typical elements of the systems. In order to complete the illustrations, however, the framing plans and other drawings are usually shown in reasonably complete detail.

Construction detailing of structures and of buildings in general is subject to considerable variation, effected by the judgment of individual designers as well as by regional conditions and practices. While detailing of the construction in the examples has been developed from the recommendations of various codes, industry standards, and other sources, it is not the purpose of this book to serve as a guide for building construction detailing. Details shown are for the purpose of giving complete illustrations and should not be considered as recommended standards.

While the procedure in the examples is to begin the structural design after the general building design has been predetermined in considerable detail, it is much better practice to involve structural considerations in the earliest design work. Since it is not possible to illustrate this process without a complete presentation of the whole architectural design process, the examples should be accepted with this limitation in mind. It is assumed that there are good reasons for the situations shown in the examples, although it is pointed out occasionally how some changes in material use, in plan layouts, or in other details might result in improvement of the structure.

Since there are several model building codes and hundreds of local codes in use throughout the United States, it is difficult to deal generally with building code requirements. It is not possible, however, to show building design examples without the use of some code criteria. Because of its reasonable thoroughness, we have chosen to use the *Uniform Building Code* as a general reference for the work here. Fortunately, except for regional variations of snow, wind, and earthquake problems, structural design criteria are reasonably consistent between most building codes. The reader is cautioned, however, to use the legally enforceable code for any actual design work.

References for structural design information in general tend to be dated, and their use varies regionally. Anyone using this work as a guide for actual design problems should take care to be sure that the references are currently accepted by legally enforceable codes and regulatory agencies. The references used in this work are listed at the end of the book and note should be made of their dates.

In order to keep the work in this book within the scope of persons not fully trained in structural engineering use has been made of simplified analysis and design techniques. The reader is encouraged to not accept this simplified approach entirely, but to pursue the mastery of more exact and thorough methods where they are significant to the work. It is hoped that the learning of these simplified techniques will serve as an initial stage in an ongoing development of competency in structural design.

Design of even the simplest building structures is not entirely an automatic process. While the work in this book may appear to use some reasonably logical processes, judgment and compromise are ever present parts of the design process. With all the facts in hand, and with the ability to intelligently interpret them, the structural designer will, it is hoped, proceed logically. In the best of real situations, however, lack of time, of clear information, of experience with problems of a similar nature, and of numerous other factors will leave the designer in something short of an ideal decision-making situation. We have tried to make the examples in this book as "real" as possible, in order to present true design conditions. Designing real buildings, however, is both a little more mysterious and a lot more fun than it appears here.

1

Building One

||||||||||||||||||||||||||||||||||||||||||||||||||||||||

Building One is a two story, two family, residential building. The construction to be used is ordinary light wood framing for all of the portions of the building above grade and poured concrete for the basement walls, floor, and footings. In professional practice a complete set of structural calculations is seldom done for such a building, since the majority of structural elements are selected from code requirements, handbook tables, or manufacturer's recommendations. Even when local building regulatory agencies require a set of calculations, they are generally limited to special structural elements, such as long span beams, special foundations, and unusual lateral bracing. The analysis and design work shown in this example is therefore presented for the purpose of explaining the structure and not to illustrate what must typically be done to obtain a building permit.

1.1 The Building

The configuration of the building and the general details of the construction are shown in Figures 1.1 through 1.3. Construction materials and details for such a building vary considerably because of the wide range of weather conditions, local code requirements, the practices of local builders, and similar factors. The basic structural design is relatively common, however.

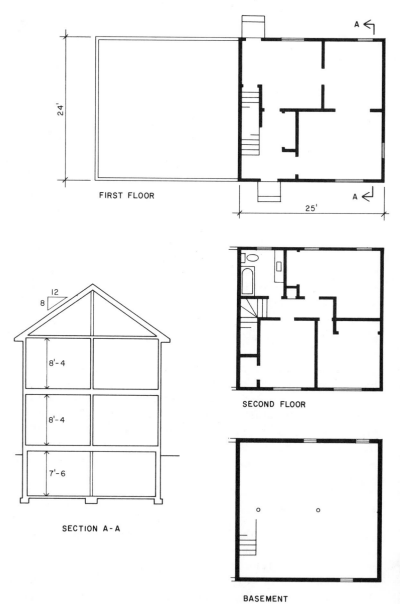

FIRST FLOOR

SECOND FLOOR

BASEMENT

SECTION A-A

FIGURE 1.1. Building One.

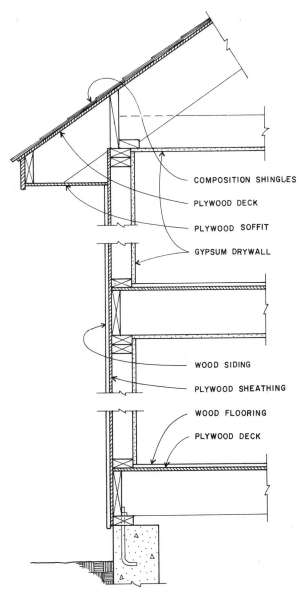

COMPOSITION SHINGLES

PLYWOOD DECK

PLYWOOD SOFFIT

GYPSUM DRYWALL

WOOD SIDING

PLYWOOD SHEATHING

WOOD FLOORING

PLYWOOD DECK

FIGURE 1.2.   Typical construction details.

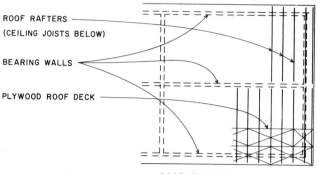

ROOF RAFTERS
(CEILING JOISTS BELOW)

BEARING WALLS

PLYWOOD ROOF DECK

ROOF FRAMING

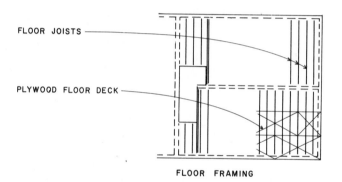

FLOOR JOISTS

PLYWOOD FLOOR DECK

FLOOR FRAMING

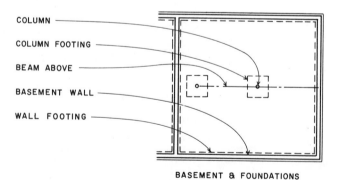

COLUMN

COLUMN FOOTING

BEAM ABOVE

BASEMENT WALL

WALL FOOTING

BASEMENT & FOUNDATIONS

FIGURE 1.3.   Structural plans.

8

Model building codes, such as the *Uniform Building Code*, usually do not cover the construction of single and two family residences. Local building codes, or special housing codes, are generally the source of design criteria for these buildings. These codes contain specifications, tables, charts, and illustrations that permit the direct selection of many structural elements for specific situations of use. In the example we have used the *Uniform Building Code* as the basic reference for structural design criteria. The results, in some cases may be slightly conservative, when compared to those that are permitted by housing codes.

1.2   The Structural System

The illustrations in Figures 1.2 and 1.3 indicate the structural system for the building. The design of the various structural elements labeled in Figure 1.3 is discussed in this section and those that follow. The materials to be used are as follows:

Joists, rafters and studs: No. 2, Douglas fir–larch.

Beams and posts: No. 1, Douglas fir–larch (4× and larger).

Roof deck, floor deck, and exterior wall sheathing: Douglas fir plywood, structural grade.

Structural steel: A36, $F_y = 36$ ksi.

Concrete: stone aggregate, $f'_c = 3000$ psi.

Some of the criteria used for the structural design are as follows:

Floor live load: 40 psf (UBC Table 23-A).

Roof live load 30 psf (snow), assumed local requirement.

Wind load: 25 psf, assumed UBC zone, 30 ft reference height, see UBC Table 23-F.

Soil: 2000 psf maximum, UBC Table 29-B for sandy gravel.

1.3   Design of the Roof Structure

The roof structure, as illustrated, consists of structural plywood sheathing on closely spaced rafters. The rafters span from the exterior bearing walls to the ridge member that is supported by the interior bearing wall, and are inclined at a slope of 8:12, or approximately 34°.

Plywood Roof Sheathing. The required thickness for the plywood depends on the grade of the plywood used, the roofing materials (for weight and attachment), the live load and wind load, and the rafter spacing. Logical spacing for rafters is some even incremental module of 8 ft: 12, 16, 19.2, 24, 32, or 48 in. For this situation the most common spacings are 16 or 24 in. Since the ceiling is not attached to the rafters, the 24 in. spacing may be used.

Many codes and handbooks have recommendations for plywood. The following examples are typical.

UBC Table 25-R-1 (see the Appendix): minimum of $\frac{3}{8}$ in., 24/0 with edges blocked.

Architectural Graphic Standards, reference 6, table on p. 257: $\frac{3}{8}$ in., 24/0, no blocking.

This selection is, of course, subject to modification when the function of the roof deck as a horizontal diaphragm is dealt with later in the design of the lateral load resistive system.

Rafters.   Design of the rafters includes the following structural considerations:

1. Bending plus axial compression due to the vector components of the gravity dead and live loads, with an increase of 15 % in allowable stresses due to the snow load.
2. Deflection due to the bending force component of the gravity loads.
3. Bending plus axial compression due to the gravity loads plus the wind load, with an increase of 33 % in allowable stresses.

There are also shear and bearing stresses, of course, but we have left them out of the calculations, since they are seldom critical in this situation.

Figure 1.4 shows the rafter geometry and the basis for determination of the loadings for the three cases mentioned. The actual length of the rafter is the hypotenuse of the triangle made by the 12 ft horizontal span and the 8 ft rise. This makes the actual length of the

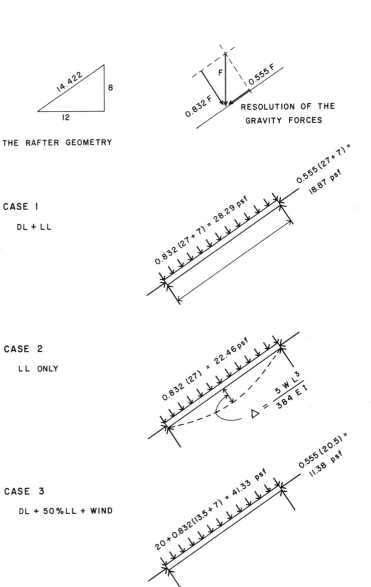

THE RAFTER GEOMETRY

RESOLUTION OF THE GRAVITY FORCES

CASE 1
DL + LL

CASE 2
LL ONLY

CASE 3
DL + 50%LL + WIND

FIGURE 1.4.   Forces on the rafter.

11

rafter approximately 14.4 ft. Tabular references usually quote rafter sizes for the horizontal span dimension, but the work that follows will use the actual rafter length and the vectors of the load forces.

Loadings for design:

Dead load:	Roofing + plywood =	5 psf
	Joists (average) =	2 psf
	Total dead load =	7 psf
Live load:	Snow load =	30 psf

UBC 2305(d) allows a reduction for the 34° slope as follows:

$$(34 - 20)(\tfrac{30}{40} - \tfrac{1}{2}) = 3.5 \text{ psf reduction}$$

The design live load thus becomes

$$30 - 3.5 = 26.5 \text{ psf (say 27 psf)}$$

Wind load: For the 34° slope the UBC requires that the full horizontal wind pressure be applied normal to the windward slope of the roof. [See UBC 2311(d).] UBC Table 23-F requires a horizontal pressure of 20 psf for height from zero to 30 ft aboveground.

On the basis of these determinations, and referring to the illustrations in Figure 1.4, we now consider the three design conditions as follows:

1. Bending plus axial compression due to the gravity loads only. As shown in the illustration, the vectors of the loads result in a bending loading of 28.29 psf and an axial compression loading of 18.87 psf. When multiplied by the rafter length and spacing these will yield the total load on one rafter.
2. Deflection due to live load. The high ratio of live to dead load makes this the critical deflection case. This loading may be used either to determine a required I value for the rafter or to check the actual deflection of a rafter that has been chosen for stress criteria. The latter procedure is used in the example.
3. Bending plus axial compression due to gravity plus wind. UBC 2311(j) requires that 50 % of the live load be included in this loading. Although a complete analysis of cases 1 and 3 should be done in order to determine which is critical, an

approximate determination can sometimes be made as follows. Note that with the 15 and 33% increases in allowable stress for the two cases, case 3 will not be critical unless the loads exceed those in case 1 by a ratio of 1.33/1.15, or approximately 1.16. Referring to the numbers in Figure 1.4, these ratios are:

$$\text{for bending:} \frac{\text{wind} + \text{gravity}}{\text{gravity only}} = \frac{41.33}{28.29} = 1.46$$

$$\text{for axial compression:} \frac{11.38}{18.87} = 0.603$$

This is somewhat inconclusive in the example, since the ratio for bending indicates case 3 to be critical while the ratio for compression indicates the opposite. As will be shown later, bending is by far the major consideration in this example. We thus proceed with the analysis for case 3 for the rafter design. However, only a complete analysis of both cases would conclusively demonstrate the wisdom of the judgment.

In the design of the rafter for the case 3 loading, from UBC Table 25-A-1 the allowable stresses are as follows for No. 2, Douglas fir–larch, 2 × 6 and wider:

$$F_b = 1450 \text{ psi (repetitive use member)}$$
$$F_c = 1050 \text{ psi}$$
$$F_v = 95 \text{ psi}$$

With rafters on 24 in. centers the load per rafter is

$$w = 2(41.33) = 82.66 \text{ lb/ft}$$

The maximum bending moment is thus

$$M = (\tfrac{1}{8})(w)(L)^2 = (\tfrac{1}{8})(82.66)(14.42)^2 = 2148.5 \text{ lb-ft}$$

for which the required section modulus is

$$S = \frac{M}{F_b} = \frac{2148.5(12)}{1.33(1450)} = 13.37 \text{ in.}^3$$

This is just slightly over the value for a 2 × 8, indicating that a 2 × 10 or 3 × 8 is required. We will try the 2 × 10, for which the following properties exist:

$$S = 21.39 \text{ in.}^3, \qquad A = 13.88 \text{ in.}^2, \qquad I = 98.93 \text{ in.}^4$$

Although it is seldom critical, the shear stress may be checked as follows:

$$\text{maximum } V = 82.66(7) = 579 \text{ lb (critical at } d \text{ distance from end)}$$

$$\text{critical } F_v = \left(\frac{3}{2}\right)\left(\frac{V}{bd}\right) = \left(\frac{3}{2}\right)\left(\frac{579}{13.88}\right) = 62.6 \text{ psi}$$

This is considerably less than the allowable of 1.33(95) psi.

We next proceed to check for the bending and compression as combined forces:

$$\text{axial compression} = 2(11.38)(14.42) = 328 \text{ lb}$$

$$\frac{L}{d} = \frac{14.42(12)}{9.25} = 18.7$$

$$F'_c = \frac{(0.3)(E)}{(L/d)^2} = \frac{(0.3)(1,700,000)}{(18.7)^2} = 1458 \text{ psi}$$

Since this is greater than the limit for F_c, we use the lower F_c value of 1050 psi.

Then the combined stress check is made as follows:

$$\frac{P/A}{F'_c} + \frac{M/S}{F_b} = \frac{328/13.88}{1.33(1050)} + \frac{2148.5(12)/21.39}{1.33(1450)}$$

$$= 0.017 + 0.625 = 0.642$$

This indicates that the 2 × 10 is quite conservative. Note that the axial compression ratio of 0.017 is very low, which verifies the earlier assumption that it is not a critical consideration in this particular example. We have, of course, used the least d as 9.25 for the L/d ratio, which assumes that the plywood deck serves to brace the rafters on their weaker axis.

Deflection of the 2 × 10 may be checked as follows, using the case 2 loading from Figure 1.4.

$$\text{total load} = 14.42(2)(22.46) = 648 \text{ lb}$$

$$\text{maximum deflection} = \frac{5WL^3}{384EI} = \frac{5(648)(14.42 \times 12)^3}{384(1,700,000)(98.3)} = 0.26 \text{ in.}$$

Since the ceiling is not attached to the rafters, the maximum permitted live load deflection is usually 1/240 of the span. Thus:

$$\text{allowable deflection} = \frac{14.42(12)}{240} = 0.72 \text{ in.}$$

By calculation, therefore, the 2 × 10 is quite adequate. Comparison may be made with the recommendations of tabulated rafter loadings. UBC Table 25-T-R-14 (see the Appendix) indicates that a 2 × 8 is permitted for a horizontal span of up to 15 ft or so. However, this table does not account for the combined wind and gravity loading, and it also generalizes on the actual rafter slope and length as being merely "over 3 in 12." Our rafter is considerably steeper and longer.

The tables on page 220 of *Architectural Graphic Standards* (reference 6) give allowable spans for rafters and floor joists with 30 psf live load. The tables do not include 24 in. spacing, however. Furthermore, since this edition was published before the standard lumber sizes were reduced, the section properties used in making the tables are slightly off. Nevertheless, a scan of the tables would seem to indicate that a 2 × 8 is close to being accurate. Again, the wind is not included and the actual rafter length is not considered.

Actually, our calculations would indicate that a 2 × 8 is only slightly overstressed, and if used would not really constitute an unsafe design. Nevertheless, based on our analysis, we would recommend the use of the 2 × 10 rafters at 24 in. spacing.

Ceiling Joists.   Design of the ceiling joists is somewhat arbitrary. Some of the considerations are:

1. Deflection should not be such as to cause visible sag. The straightness of the lumber is probably actually more critical in this regard. "Visible" sag is hard to put a number on.

2. If the crawl space is accessible, it should be assumed that someone may enter it or store materials in it. An old rule is to design for a maximum live load deflection of $L/360$ in order to prevent cracking of the ceiling, especially if it is plastered. An arbitrary uniform or concentrated load may be used. UBC Table 23-B requires a uniform load of 10 psf. UBC Table 25-T-J-6 (see the Appendix) indicates that a 2 × 4 at 16 in. spacing is barely adequate. (Note that the clear span from the outside to inside walls is approximately 11.5 ft.) The UBC tabulated loading is also based on a deflection of $L/240$ under the live load. A lightly more conservative design would be to allow for a maximum deflection of $L/360$ under the weight of a single person (assumed at 200 lb) at the center of the span. Thus:

$$\text{maximum } M = \frac{PL}{4} = \frac{200(12)}{4} = 600 \text{ lb-ft}$$

$$\text{required } S = \frac{M}{F_b} = \frac{600(12)}{1250} = 5.76 \text{ in.}^3$$

$$\text{maximum permitted deflection} = \frac{L}{360} = \frac{144}{360} = 0.4 \text{ in.}$$

$$\text{required } I = \frac{PL^3}{48E\Delta} = \frac{(200)(144)^3}{(48)(1,700,000)(0.4)} = 18.29 \text{ in.}^4$$

A 2 × 6, with $S = 7.563$ in.^{3} and $I = 20.797$ in.^{4}, will satisfy these criteria.

Another potential structural function for the ceiling joists is to serve to tie the tops of the walls against the outward thrust of the sloping rafters. (See Figure 1.5.) This is not the case in this building, since the central bearing wall supports the inside ends of the rafters.

A final consideration for the rafters is the required detailing for the ceiling surface material. In this example the construction might be simpler if the rafters and ceiling joists were at the same spacing. The 24 in. spacing is somewhat high for drywall ceilings, however. Thus the whole interactive relationship of the roof deck, rafters, ceiling joists, and ceiling surface must be considered.

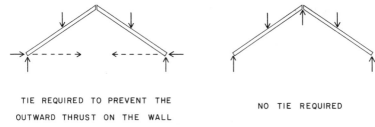

TIE REQUIRED TO PREVENT THE
OUTWARD THRUST ON THE WALL

NO TIE REQUIRED

FIGURE 1.5.   Stability of the sloped rafters.

Assuming the construction detailing problems to be solvable, we will settle for ceiling joists of 2 × 6 at 16 in.

1.4   Design of the Floor Structure

The typical floor construction will consist of 2× joists at 16 in. centers. The structural floor deck will consist of plywood sheets. These are sometimes available with tongue-and-groove edges; otherwise the edges perpendicular to the joists will be supported by 2× wood blocking. Joists should be doubled at openings, such as for the stair, and under partitions parallel to the joists.

Floor Deck.   Selection of the plywood grade and thickness depends on the type of flooring used and on the direction of the plywood face grain with respect to the joists. The face grain is normally in the 8 ft direction of the sheets and the sheets are slightly stronger and stiffer in that direction. However, placing them with the 8 ft direction perpendicular to the joists requires more blocking (every 4 ft.).

On the basis of UBC Table 25-R-1 (see the Appendix) the minimum plywood would be $\frac{1}{2}$ in., C-D grade or better, index 32/16 with the face grain perpendicular to the joists.

Floor Joists.   The usual practice for the joists would be to size the joist for the maximum span condition and use this size throughout the floor for all joists, headers, and blocking. This provides a level underside for the attachment of the ceiling and allows the top plates of all the stud bearing walls to be at a common height.

For the typical 12 ft span joist the design loading is:

Dead load: Finish floor $= 3$ psf (hardwood strip)
            $\frac{1}{2}$ in. plywood $= 1.4$
            $\frac{5}{8}$ in. drywall $= 2.5$
            Joists (average) $= \underline{2.6}$
            Total dead load $= 9.5$ psf
Live load: 40 psf, or $(\frac{16}{12})(40) = 53.3$ lb/ft of joist
Total load: 49.5 psf or $(\frac{16}{12})(49.5) = 66$ lb/ft of joist

We now proceed to determine the three section properties required:
A for shear, S for bending, and I for deflection:

$$\text{maximum } M = \frac{wL^2}{8} = \frac{66(12)^2}{8} = 1188 \text{ lb-ft}$$

$$\text{required } S = \frac{M}{F_b} = \frac{1188(12)}{1450} = 9.83 \text{ in.}^3$$

Assuming a 2×8 for critical shear distance from the end:

$$\text{maximum } V = w\left[\left(\frac{L}{2}\right) - d\right] = 66(6 - 0.67) = 352 \text{ lb}$$

$$\text{required } A = \left(\frac{3}{2}\right)\left(\frac{V}{F_v}\right) = \left(\frac{3}{2}\right)\left(\frac{352}{95}\right) = 5.56 \text{ in.}^2$$

$$\text{allowable live load deflection} = \frac{L}{360} = \frac{144}{360} = 0.4 \text{ in.}$$

$$\text{required } I = \frac{5WL^3}{384E\Delta}$$

$$= \frac{5(53.3 \times 12)(144)^3}{384(1,700,000)(0.4)}$$

$$= 36.57 \text{ in.}^4$$

These requirements are sufficiently met by a 2×8 with $S = 13.14$ in.^{3}, $A = 10.875$ in.^{2}, and $I = 47.63$ in.^{4}.

Floor Beam at First Floor.   This beam carries the inside end of the first floor joists and also supports the stud bearing wall that carries the second floor joists, the ceiling joists, and the rafters. The exact dimensions of the beam depend somewhat on the construction details. For simplicity we will assume the beam to have two equal spans of 11 ft each. The two span beam will be supported by posts at the center and one end and by the basement wall at the other end.

Since the beam supports considerable total floor area, some reduction of live load is appropriate. UBC 2306 permits a reduction of 0.08 %/ft² for beams supporting 150 ft² or more. On this basis, using the 11 ft beam span and the 12 ft joist span, the reduction allowable is:

$$R = rA = 0.0008(11 \times 12 \times 2) = 21\% \text{ (say } 20\%)$$

The calculations for the beam loading are shown in Table 1.1. The shear, moment and deflection diagrams for the two span beam are shown in Figure 1.6. Assuming a solid timber beam of Douglas fir–larch, No. 1 grade, the allowable stresses from UBC Table 25-A-1 (see the Appendix) are as follows:

$$F_b = 1300 \text{ psi}, \qquad F_v = 85 \text{ psi}, \qquad E = 1,600,000 \text{ psi}$$

TABLE 1.1   Loads on the Beam

| | | Load: lb/ft of Beam | | |
Source	Determination	LL	DL	LL + DL
Roof	$LL = 30$ psf $\times$ 12 ft span	360		
	$DL = 7$ psf $\times$ 14.42 ft rafter		101	461
Second floor ceiling	$DL = 5$ psf $\times$ 12 ft span ^{z}		60	60
Second floor	$LL = (0.80)(40)$ psf $\times$ 12 ft span	384		
	$DL = 9.5$ psf $\times$ 12 ft span		114	498
First floor	$LL = (0.80)(40)$ psf $\times$ 12 ft span	384		
	$DL = 7$ psf $\times$ 12 ft span		84	468
Wall	First and second floor, $\frac{5}{8}$ in. gyp			
	$DL = 10$ psf $\times$ 16 ft total height		160	160
	Stub wall to rafters			
	$DL = 5$ psf $\times$ 8 ft height		40	40
Beam	Assume weight		25	25
Total design loads		1128 plf		1712 plf

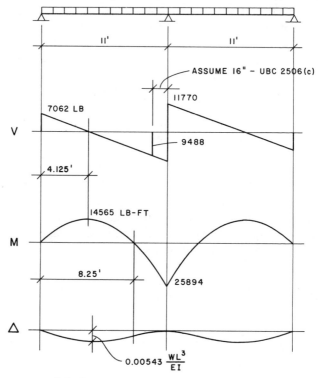

FIGURE 1.6.   Analysis of the first floor beam.

Using these stresses and the calculated critical values for V, M, and deflection, we determine the required section properties:

$$\text{required } A = \left(\frac{3}{2}\right)\left(\frac{V}{F_v}\right) = \left(\frac{3}{2}\right)\left(\frac{9488}{85}\right) = 167 \text{ in.}^2$$

$$\text{required } S = \frac{M}{F_b} = \frac{25{,}894(12)}{1300} = 239 \text{ in.}^3$$

$$\text{maximum live load deflection} = \frac{132}{360} = 0.367 \text{ in.}$$

$$\text{required } I = \frac{0.00543(WL^3)}{E\Delta}$$

$$= \frac{0.00543(1128 \times 11)(132)^3}{(1,600,000)(0.367)}$$

$$= 264 \text{ in.}^4$$

The potential solid timber choices are shown in Table 1.2. All are somewhat massive and would involve intrusion on the headroom in the basement. It would be wise to consider a glue laminated beam which has considerably higher shear and bending stresses allowable.

TABLE 1.2. Choices for the Beam

Required properties	Optional Choices and Their Properties		
	8×24	10×20	12×16
$A = 167 \text{ in.}^2$	176	185	178
$S = 239 \text{ in.}^3$	690	602	460
$I = 264 \text{ in.}^4$	8111	5870	3568

From UBC Table 25-C-1, a Douglas fir–larch beam of 24F grade has allowable bending stress of 2400 psi and allowable shear of 165 psi. This reduces the A and S property requirements to

$$A = 167\left(\frac{85}{165}\right) = 86.0 \text{ in}^2$$

$$S = 239\left(\frac{1300}{2400}\right) = 129 \text{ in.}^3$$

This would require a $6\frac{3}{4} \times 13.5$ or a $8\frac{3}{4} \times 10.5$ section.

It would also be possible to use a steel beam. This would entail the use of a $2 \times$ nailer on the top of the steel beam, adding slightly to its depth.

We will select the $8\frac{3}{4} \times 10.5$ beam. Since the bending stress is still not critical for this section, it could drop in grade to a 20F.

1.5 Design of the Walls and Columns

The vertical load elements consist of the stud walls above grade and the concrete walls and steel columns below grade. For ordinary situations the details of the wall construction will usually be covered by the specifications of the building code that applies to this type of building.

Basement Column. The column in the center of the beam carries the larger load from the beam. (See Figure 1.6.) The column at the stair carries loads from the stair framing, including the weight of the walls above, so that the loads are probably close enough to require the same size column and footing. For brevity we will design only the center column.

From the beam analysis the column load is approximately 26 kips. For calculation we assume the unsupported height to be 7 ft, from the bottom of the beam to the top of the basement floor slab.

From UBC Table 25-A-1 (see the Appendix) the allowable stress and modulus of elasticity are

$$F_c = 1000 \text{ psi}, \qquad E = 1,600,000 \text{ psi}$$

Assuming a nominal $4 \times$ member with least d of 3.5 in.:

$$\frac{L}{d} = \frac{84}{3.5} = 24$$

Then the allowable compression based on L/d is

$$F'_c = \frac{(0.3)E}{(L/d)^2} = \frac{(0.3)(1,600,000)}{(24)^2} = 833 \text{ psi}$$

The required area for a $4 \times$ member is thus

$$A = \frac{P}{F'_c} = \frac{26,000}{833} = 31.21 \text{ in.}^2$$

This would require a 4×10, with $A = 32.375$ in.^{2}, which hardly seems reasonable. Trying a larger d: if $d = 5.5$,

$$\frac{L}{d} = \frac{84}{5.5} = 15.3, \qquad F'_c = 2050 \text{ psi}$$

Since this value is higher than the value for F_c, we use the lower F_c value to find the required area for a $6 \times$ member.

$$A = \frac{26,000}{1000} = 26 \text{ in.}^2$$

This would permit the use of a 6×6, with $A = 30.25$ in.^{2}.

If a steel post is desired, the usual choice would be a round pipe column. This can be selected from the AISC Manual (reference 8) using the column allowable load tables in section 3. For this load and height, with F_y of 36 ksi for the steel, a $2\frac{1}{2}$ in. standard steel pipe is adequate.

Although either column may be used, the steel column provides for slightly better details at the footing and the beam bearing, so we have shown it in the construction details.

Stud Bearing Walls. UBC 2518 has numerous requirements and limits for stud wall construction. For this height a 2×4 stud is permitted with a maximum spacing of 24 in. Normal procedure would be to check the 2×4 studs at 16 in. centers for the heaviest loading condition. If they are not adequate, we would increase them for that wall, work backward to find the heaviest wall loading for which they are adequate, and then use them for all the rest of the walls.

From the beam load tabulation in Table 1.1 we may observe that the first floor stud wall over the beam carries the beam load less the first floor joists and the beam. This is a load of 1219 lb/ft from the tabulation. At 16 in. centers, one stud carries a load of

$$P = 1219\left(\frac{16}{12}\right) = 1625 \text{ lb}$$

With Douglas fir–larch No. 2 studs, we determine from UBC Table 25-A-1 (see the Appendix):

$$F_c = 1000 \text{ psi}, \qquad E = 1,700,000 \text{ psi}$$

For the individual stud/column the critical d dimension for buckling will be 3.5 in., since the wall surfacing serves to brace the studs on the weaker 1.5 in. axis. The allowable load on the 2 × 4 with an unsupported height of 8 ft 4 in. is therefore:

$$\frac{L}{d} = \frac{100}{3.5} = 28.6$$

$$F'_c = \frac{(0.3)(1,700,000)}{(28.6)^2} = 623.5 \text{ psi}$$

Allowable $P = (F'_c)(\text{area of } 2 \times 4) = (623.5)(5.25) = 3273 \text{ lb}$

Since this is twice the required load, and the heaviest loaded wall, we may safely use the 2 × 4 studs at 16 in. centers for all the walls.

Basement Wall.   Depending on local codes and practices, these walls may be of solid poured concrete or of concrete masonry units. We will show the design for poured concrete walls. UBC Table 29-A requires a minimum 8 in. wall thickness for either type of construction.

It is not uncommon for these walls to be built with little or even no reinforcement. We recommend a minimum of reinforcement to be a continuous horizontal #4 bar at the top and bottom of the walls. For the best construction it is also recommended that the minimum vertical and horizontal temperature and shrinkage reinforcement be provided as recommended by the ACI code (reference 9).

The typical exterior basement wall is under a combination of loads due to the vertical loads from the construction above and the

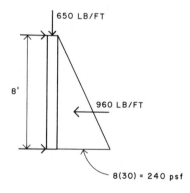

FIGURE 1.7.   Forces on the basement wall.

horizontal pressure from the soil. This results in a combination of axial compression plus bending. For the concrete the critical stress condition will be the net tension stress, which will be the greatest when the axial compression is the least. We therefore look for the outside wall with the least load from the building above. In our example this will be the end walls, since the rafters and floor joists are parallel to them.

Figure 1.7 shows the assumed loading for the end wall. Since the bending will produce a maximum moment at approximately midheight of the wall, we have used the axial compression load at midheight for the determination of the maximum tension stress. On this basis the load is as follows:

Stud wall, approximately 20 ft at 10 psf	= 200 lb/ft
4 ft of basement wall at 100 psf	= 400
Portion of roof and floor, say	= 50
Total load at midheight	= 650 lb/ft

The soil pressure is taken as equal to the pressure in an equivalent fluid with density of 30 pcf. This is the minimum pressure which is usually required by codes, and may be higher if the soil type or the groundwater conditions are more severe.

We now proceed to find the net tension stress due to the combined loading using a 12 in. wide strip of wall. The maximum moment due to the triangular distributed loading can be found from the beam diagrams in section 2 of the AISC Manual (reference 8) or from other handbooks:

$$\text{maximum } M = 0.1283WL = 0.1283(960)(8) = 985 \text{ lb-ft}$$

The section modulus for the 8 × 12 in. wall portion is

$$S = \frac{bd^2}{6} = \frac{(12)(8)^2}{6} = 128 \text{ in.}^3$$

The maximum bending stress is then

$$F_b = \frac{M}{S} = \frac{985(12)}{128} = 92.3 \text{ psi}$$

The compressive stress due to the gravity load is

$$F_c = \frac{P}{A} = \frac{650}{96} = 6.8 \text{ psi}$$

The net tension stress is therefore

$$F_t = 92.3 - 6.8 = 85.5 \text{ psi}$$

For the concrete with F_c' of 3000 psi this is slightly less than 3 % of the ultimate compressive strength, which is not usually considered critical. The wall is therefore theoretically adequate without vertical reinforcing.

1.6   Design of the Foundations

For this construction a strip footing would normally be provided under the basement walls to serve as a foundation as well as a platform for the construction of the wall. For the latter purpose it would normally be made a few inches wider than the wall. For the 8 in. wall we would usually use a minimum 14 in. wide footing for this purpose. UBC Table 29-A requires a minimum 15 in. wide by 7 in. thick footing for the two story building.

The heaviest loaded walls are the front and rear walls that carry the ends of the rafters and floor joists. The tabulation of the load for this wall is shown in Table 1.3. With the allowable soil pressure of 2000 psf the 15 in. wide footing will carry a load of

$$w = 2000\left(\frac{15}{12}\right) = 2500 \text{ lb/ft}$$

The minimum footing is therefore adequate for the heaviest wall load.

Column Footing.   From the column design calculations, the center column will place a total load of approximately 27 kips on the footing. If we deduct from the allowable soil pressure for the weight of a 10 in. thick footing, the required area for this load will be

$$A = \frac{27,000}{1875} = 14.4 \text{ ft}^2$$

A 3 ft 10 in. square footing will provide $A = 14.7 \text{ ft}^2$.

TABLE 1.3.   Load on the Front Wall Footing

	Loads: lb/ft of Wall Length		
Load Source	DL	LL	Total
Rafters and second floor ceiling	86	180	266
Floor joists (with 100% LL)	99	480	579
Stud wall: 20 ft at 12 psf	240		240
Basement wall: 8 ft at 100 psf	800		800
Footing (estimate)	110		110
Total load on footing	1335	660	1995

Although calculations can be performed for the footing, there are tabulated designs in various handbooks from which the footing width and thickness and the reinforcing can be determined once the total load and allowable soil pressure are known.

1.7   Design for Wind

There are various problems to be considered in design for wind force on the building. The following discussion deals separately with the issues relating to the three principal building elements involved in wind resistance: the roof, the floors, and the walls.

The Roof.   The roof must resist inward and outward pressures. The effect of the inward pressure, as additive to the gravity loads, was treated in the design of the rafters. With the relatively light construction and roofing the upward wind pressure is often larger than the roof dead load in these buildings. Minimum code requirements for the attachment of the rafters to the stud walls will provide some anchorage, but it is usually best to provide more positive anchorage by the use of nailed sheet metal connectors, such as that shown in the construction details. (See Figure 1.21.)

The roof also acts as a horizontal diaphragm (even though it is sloped) that transfers the wind force to the vertical bracing elements; in this case to the shear walls. Wind force on the long side of the building applies force as a uniform load to the edge of the roof. The load area for this pressure, as shown in Figure 1.8, is one half the

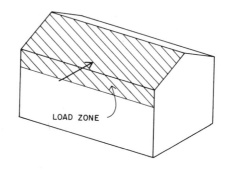

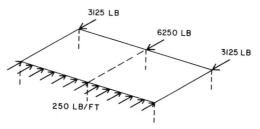

FIGURE 1.8. Wind load to the roof diaphragm.

second story height plus the roof height. The load per foot of roof edge is thus

$$w = (20 \text{ psf})\left[\left(\frac{9}{2}\right) + 8\right] = 250 \text{ lb/ft}$$

The roof spans to transfer this load to the two end walls and the center dividing wall, as shown in Figure 1.8. Considering these as two simple spans, the load delivered to the end walls is thus

$$V = (250)\left(\frac{25}{2}\right) = 3125 \text{ lb}$$

The load on the center wall is twice this.

Considering the roof diaphragm as a horizontal element, its action is as shown in Figure 1.9. The unit shear stress in the plywood

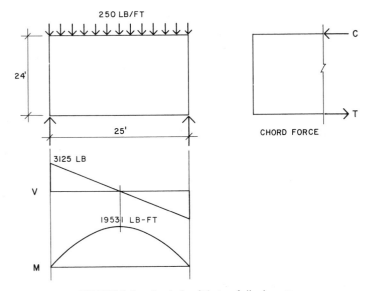

FIGURE 1.9.   Analysis of the roof diaphragm.

is a maximum at the ends and is equal to the total end shear divided by the plywood edge length. The latter is actually twice the true length of the rafter, so the calculation is as follows:

$$v = (3125)/(2 \times 14.42) = 108 \text{ lb/ft}$$

Referring to UBC Table 25-J (see the Appendix) this value is less than the lowest rated value for $\frac{3}{8}$ in. plywood, even with unblocked edges for the plywood sheets. The minimum code required nailing of 6 in. spacing at panel edges and 12 in. spacing at intermediate supports (not at the edge of a plywood sheet) is adequate for the roof sheathing.

The chord forces in the framing at the front and rear edges of the roof (actually at the top of the wall) must resist the moment shown in Figure 1.9. Since the two halves of the gable roof actually act like two separate diaphragms in tandem, there are actually two elements each 12 ft deep, rather than one 24 ft deep. However, the numerical result is the same if we divide the moment in two and use the d of 12 ft or use the whole moment with a d of 24 ft. Thus

$$C = T = \frac{M}{d} = \frac{19,531}{24} = 814 \text{ lb}$$

Referring to Figure 1.21, it may be seen that the edge force from the roof is transferred through the blocking to the top plates of the stud wall. These continuous elements will actually serve as the edge chord for the roof. From UBC Table 25-A-1 (see the Appendix) the allowable compression for the No. 2 2 × 4 members is 1000 psi. Thus the required area for the chord is

$$A = \frac{C}{F_c} = \frac{814}{(1.33)(1000)} = 0.612 \text{ in.}^2$$

This is less than the area of one 2 × 4, so the plates can easily serve as chords if their continuity is assured. Specifications usually require that the splices of the two plates be staggered a minimum of 4 ft. If this is done, the normal nailing of the plates to each other plus the nailing of the exterior plywood and the interior drywall will provide a reasonable continuity for the plate/chord in this case. Some designers (and some building regulatory agencies) would prefer to ensure a more positive continuity by specifying that the chords be bolted on each side of all splices. If the continuity of only one plate member is required, as in this case, the plates would be simply bolted to each other with sufficient bolts to develop the chord force. If the continuity of both plates is required, a metal plate would be added to the splice.

From UBC Table 25-F a $\frac{1}{2}$ in. bolt in single shear in the 2 × member is good for 650 lb, which may be increased by one third to 867 lb for wind. The number of bolts required is thus

$$N = \frac{C}{p} = \frac{814}{867} = 0.939$$

or one bolt on each side of the splice.

Splicing of the ridge is not necessary, since in the tandem action it acts simultaneously as a tension chord for one diaphragm half and a compression chord for the other.

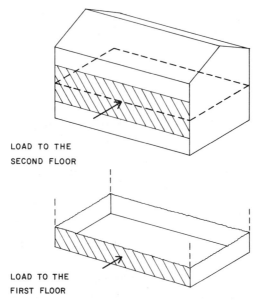

LOAD TO THE
SECOND FLOOR

LOAD TO THE
FIRST FLOOR

FIGURE 1.10.   Wind loads to the floor diaphragms.

Transfer of the roof diaphragm forces into the walls is discussed in the wall design and in the development of the construction details.

The Floors.   The second floor acts as a horizontal diaphragm similar to the roof. In this case the load zone, as shown in Figure 1.10, is from midheight of the first story to midheight of the second story, or approximately 9 ft. The load per foot on the edge of the diaphragm is thus

$$w = (20 \text{ psf})(9 \text{ ft}) = 180 \text{ lb/ft}$$

The maximum shear at the ends of the diaphragm is

$$V = (180)\left(\frac{25}{2}\right) = 2250 \text{ lb}$$

The maximum stress in the diaphragm at the building ends will be

$$v = \frac{2250}{24} = 94 \text{ lb/ft}$$

At the center dividing wall the diaphragm is reduced in net width by the stair opening. Assuming a hole of 10 ft length, the net width is thus 14 ft and the stress is

$$v = \frac{2250}{14} = 161 \text{ lb/ft}$$

Referring to UBC Table 25-J (see the Appendix) this is still not critical for the $\frac{1}{2}$ in. plywood, so minimum nailing may also be used for the second floor deck.

The first floor deck acts as a horizontal diaphragm, transferring the load from the lower half of the first story wall to the basement walls. Since this is only half the load on the second floor deck, it will not be critical.

The Walls.   The exterior stud walls have two conditions to consider. The first is a combination of vertical compression due to gravity plus bending due to the direct wind pressure on the wall with the wall spanning vertically, as shown in Figure 1.11. The studs must be checked for this combined load condition. We will assume a design load of wind plus dead load plus one half live load for this condition. The gravity load on the first story studs on this basis is approximately 1100 lb/stud.

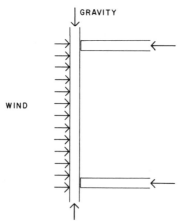

FIGURE 1.11.   Forces on the exterior walls.

The wind load on the studs is

$$w = (20)\left(\frac{16}{12}\right) = 26.7 \text{ lb/ft}$$

Assuming the studs to span 9 ft in simple span from floor to floor, the maximum moment is

$$M = \frac{wL^2}{8} = \frac{(26.7)(9)^2}{8} = 270.3 \text{ lb/ft}$$

The allowable compression stress, as calculated earlier for the interior wall, is 623.5 psi. From UBC Table 25-A-1 (see the Appendix) the allowable bending stress for the No. 2 2 × 4 stud is 1650 psi for a repetitive stress member. The interaction of compression plus bending is thus considered as follows:

$$\frac{P/A}{F_c'} + \frac{M/S}{F_b} = \frac{1100/5.25}{1.33(623)} + \frac{270.3(12)/3.063}{1.33(1650)}$$

$$= 0.253 + 0.483 = 0.736 < 1.0$$

The second condition for the wall involves its function as a shear wall for transfer of the loads from the roof and floor to the basement. The highest stressed wall is the first story end wall, that carries the edge loads from the roof and second floor, as shown in Figure 1.12. The total shear force in the wall is 5375 lb, and if the wall is a continuous surface the average shear is:

$$v = \frac{5375}{24} = 224 \text{ lb/ft}$$

If the wall has an opening, as shown in Figure 1.12, there are several approaches to its design. One alternative would be to ignore all but the 17 ft long solid portion of the wall and consider it as a single panel for resistance of the entire force on the wall. The unit shear would thus be

$$v = \frac{5375}{17} = 316 \text{ lb/ft}$$

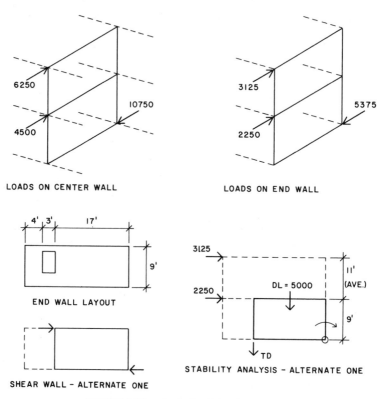

FIGURE 1.12. Analysis of the shear walls.

Referring to UBC Table 25-K (see the Appendix) the possible options for the wall are the following:

$\frac{1}{2}$ in., Structural I plywood with 6 in. edge nailing.
$\frac{1}{2}$ or $\frac{3}{8}$ in. C-D or Structural II plywood with 4 in. edge nailing.

In addition to the shear stress, the wall must be investigated for sliding and overturn. For the overturn analysis the loads must be considered at their points of application; that is, the roof load at the roof level and the second floor load at the second floor level. The overturning moment on the wall due to these forces must be resisted by the dead load on the wall with a safety factor of 1.5. Estimating the dead load at 5000 lb, due to the weight of the wall plus a small portion of the roof and floor, the analysis is as follows:

Overturning M: $3125 \times 20 = 62,500$ lb/ft
$2250 \times 9 = \underline{20,250}$
Total $= 82,750$ lb/ft
Resisting M: $5000 \times 8.5 = 42,500$ lb/ft

Since the safety factor against overturn is clearly less than 1, an anchorage force, called a tiedown, is required. The required magnitude for this force is found as follows:

Overturning $M \times$ safety factor: $82,750 \times 1.5 = 124,125$ lb/ft
Deducting for dead load moment $= 42,500$
Net required M for tiedown $= 81,625$ lb/ft
Required tiedown force: $\dfrac{81,625}{17} = 4,802$ lb

For a conservative design an anchorage device, such as that shown in Figure 1.13, would be provided at each end of the shear wall panel. This consists of a braced metal angle that is bolted to a $4 \times$ or double $2 \times$ member at the shear panel edge and is secured by an anchor bolt in the foundation; in this case the basement wall.

Anchorage is also provided by the sill bolts ordinarily used to secure the stud wall sill member to the concrete. UBC 2907(e) calls for these bolts to be a minimum of $\frac{1}{2}$ in. bolts at 6 ft centers, with one bolt not more than 12 in. from each end of the sill. The use of these bolts for overturn resistance is not generally permitted at the present, however, since the stress condition involves cross-grain bending in the sill.

At the building corner the plywood on the two intersecting wall surfaces will be nailed to a common framing member. This means that the overturn of one wall requires the lifting of the end of the other wall. If the nailing at the corner is sufficient to develop this interaction of the two surfaces, it is probably redundant to provide an anchorage device for the tiedown force at this point. If we con-

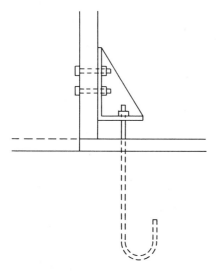

FIGURE 1.13. Typical hold down device.

sider the two story wall, approximately 18 ft high, the total tiedown force produces an average shear stress at the corner of

$$v = \frac{4802}{18} = 267 \text{ lb/ft}$$

If the plywood previously determined is used, this is within the capacity of the edge nailing.

A second alternative for the first story end wall is to consider the short 4 ft long section to act in tandem with the longer 17 ft panel. This will slightly reduce the load on the 17 ft panel, but will produce considerable overturn for the 4 ft panel. The result would be to add more anchorage to the wall with only a slight reduction in the plywood shear stress. See Figure 1.14.

A third alternative is to consider the entire 24 ft long wall as a single panel and to develop the necessary stresses around the hole. The main requirement for this would be to add horizontal blocking at the level of the top and bottom of the window with metal straps to carry the force into the solid wall portions. The additional framing and metal ties would be a trade-off against the close nail

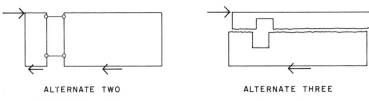

ALTERNATE TWO   ALTERNATE THREE

FIGURE 1.14.   Alternate design assumptions for the end shear wall.

spacing and the tiedowns required for the first alternative. Of the three alternatives the first is probably the simplest for construction and the most economical.

From the earlier analysis, it was determined that the center dividing wall must resist shear forces twice those in the end walls. Assuming a continuous uninterrupted wall, the shear stresses will be (see Figure 1.12 for loading)

$$v = \frac{6250}{24} = 260 \text{ lb/ft at the second story}$$

$$v = \frac{10{,}750}{24} = 448 \text{ lb/ft at the first story}$$

Design of this wall must include the consideration that it is required to provide good acoustic separation between the two housing units. One solution for this is to supply two separate, complete stud framing systems with a small separation between them. In effect, this provides two walls, although the construction at the floors and the second floor ceiling will generally give sufficient tying to consider them as a single structural wall. Assuming this construction, and the shear stresses just determined, some alternatives for the wall surfacing are as follows:

1.   Gypsum wallboard (drywall) on both sides. UBC Table 47-I (see the Appendix) permits a shear of 125 lb/ft on $\frac{1}{2}$ in. drywall with $5d$ nails at 7 in. spacing. This is just a little short, so it would be necessary to use 4 in. nail spacing, for which the table allows 150 lb/ft. The total resistance for the wall is thus 300 lb/ft, which is sufficient for the second story, but not for the first.

2. A $\frac{7}{8}$ in. cement plaster on metal lath. The UBC allows 180 lb/ft for this, making the total for the wall 360 lb/ft. Again, this is adequate for the second story, but not for the first.

3. Plywood on one or both sides is an alternative for the second floor and the only choice for the first floor. Note that UBC 4713(a) states that when different materials are applied to the same wall their shear resistance is not cumulative. Thus if plywood is used, its shear resistance cannot be added to that of the finish materials placed over it.

On the basis of these considerations, we would recommend the following construction for the center wall.

At the second floor: $\frac{1}{2}$ in. drywall with 5d nails at 4 in. spacing on both sides of the wall.

At the first floor: $\frac{3}{8}$ in. C-D plywood with 8d nails at 6 in. spacing at edges on both sides of the wall, with drywall applied as a finish.

Transfer of the shear force from level to level is relatively simple at the end walls, since the plywood on the exterior is continuous from top to bottom of the wall. Assuming ordinary platform type construction, this continuity does not exist at the center wall, making some special consideration for the transfer necessary.

Figure 1.15 shows details of the floor and wall framing at the center dividing wall. The routing of the wind shear from the second floor to the basement is as follows:

The second floor wall surfacing is nailed to the sill.

The sills are nailed to the continuous joists.

The joists are nailed to the spreader block.

The spreader block is nailed to the top plates of the first story wall.

The first floor wall surfacing is nailed to the top plates and the sill.

The sill is nailed to the first floor joists.

The joists are nailed to the spreader.

The spreader is bolted through the sill to the basement wall.

The nailing of the framing members at the second floor level must transfer the total load of 6250 lb from the second floor shear wall to

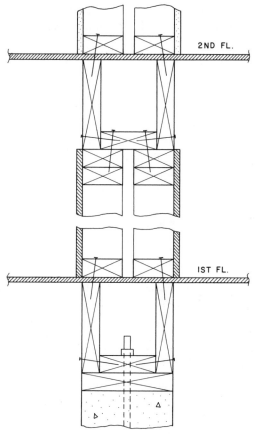

FIGURE 1.15.   Details of the center dividing wall.

the first floor shear wall. If 16*d* common nails are used, the required spacing is determined as follows.

UBC Table 25-G gives an allowable load of 107 lb nail. This may be increased by one third for the wind loading. Then

$$\text{required number} = \frac{6250}{(1.33)(107)} = 44, \text{ or 22 on each side}$$

$$\text{required spacing} = \frac{(24 \times 12)}{22} = 13.1 \text{ in.}$$

At the first floor the nails and bolts must transfer the total force of 10,750 lb to the basement wall. The required nailing is thus

$$N = \frac{10,750}{(1.33)(107)} = 76$$

$$S = \frac{(24 \times 12)}{38} = 7.58 \text{ in. maximum}$$

If $\frac{3}{4}$ in. bolts are used, UBC Table 25-F gives an allowable load of 1350 lb/bolt on the $2\times$ sill in single shear. This should also be checked against the load values in UBC Table 26-G which are for the bolt loads in the concrete wall. In this case, with the f_c' value of 3000 psi for the concrete, the allowable load is 1780 lb, so the wood limit is critical. The number of bolts required is thus

$$N = \frac{10,750}{(1.33)(1350)} = 6$$

Various details of the horizontal diaphragms and shear walls are shown in the construction details that follow. While there is some standardization by codes and industry recommendations, there is room for considerable variation in these details because of local practices and the judgment of individual designers.

Wind in the east–west direction produces slightly less than half the total load on the building as that in the north–south direction. This will not be critical for stress in the horizontal diaphragms, although attention should be given to the transfer of the edge loads into the chords and shear walls. Stresses in the shear walls will depend on the size and arrangement of openings in the walls. Since the openings will not be the same on the two walls, some consideration may be necessary for the torsional stresses due to the eccentricity of the lateral load from the center of stiffness of the shear walls. An example of this type of analysis will be shown in the design of Building Two for lateral loads.

Building Overturn and Sliding.   The total wind load on the building may tend to tip it over (called the overturn effect) or to slide it off its foundations, as shown in Figure 1.16. The dead load of the building will serve as a resistive force to both of these effects.

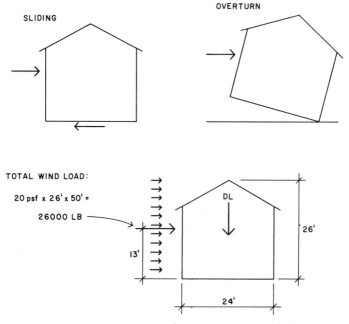

FIGURE 1.16.   Sliding and overturn of the building.

Building codes generally require that the dead load restoring moment resist the overturn moment with a safety factor of 1.5. See UBC 2311(i). The sill anchor bolts and tiedowns will add to the resistance to overturn, but it is not a critical concern, as the following analysis will show.

The total dead load of the building is approximately determined in Table 1.4. Assuming this total load to be approximately centered in the building mass, the dead load restoring moment thus becomes

$$(87,000)(12) = 1,044,000 \text{ lb/ft}$$

The total wind load on the long side of the building is 26,000 lb, as shown in Figure 1.16, and the overturn moment is thus

$$(26,000)(13) = 338,000 \text{ lb/ft}$$

TABLE 1.4.   Total Building Dead Load

Load Source	Load (lb)
Roof: 1600 ft^2 at 7 psf	11,200
Second floor ceiling: 1200 ft^2 at 4	4,800
Second floor: 1200 ft^2 at 9.5	11,400
First floor: 1200 ft^2 at 7	8,400
Exterior Walls: 2600 ft^2 at 12	31,200
Interior walls: 2000 ft^2 at 10	20,000
Total dead load (above basement)	87,000

The actual safety factor against overturn is thus

$$SF = \frac{1,044,000}{338,000} = 3.09$$

Friction due to the building dead load also offers resistance to sliding. In this example, assuming the total dead load to help in developing friction, the minimum average friction factor required to resist sliding would be:

$$\frac{26,000}{87,000} = 0.299$$

Since the actual friction between the wood and concrete is probably higher than this, sliding does not seem to be a major problem for this building. The shear wall design, however, assumes that the total wind load is taken by the three shear walls; at the center and the two ends. For a conservative design of these walls, the anchor bolts are usually sized to take the entire shear force, ignoring the friction at the bottom of the wall. The anchor bolts for the center wall, as shown in Figure 1.15, were designed on this basis.

1.8   Design of an Alternate Roof Structure

The rafter and ceiling joist system previously designed could be replaced by a truss system in which the top chords of the truss provide the roof framing and the bottom chords provide the second floor ceiling framing. The trusses would span the full width of the building, shifting some additional load to the outside walls, but reducing slightly the load on the first floor beam.

For this span the truss members would consist of single 2× pieces arranged in a single plane with gussets of either plywood or metal. The trusses would usually be factory assembled and may use a patented jointing system. In many areas these trusses could be selected from the stock designs of a manufacturer, reducing the building designer's work to determining the span and load. The calculations that follow illustrate the design based on the truss member arrangement shown in Figure 1.17. Analysis is shown for

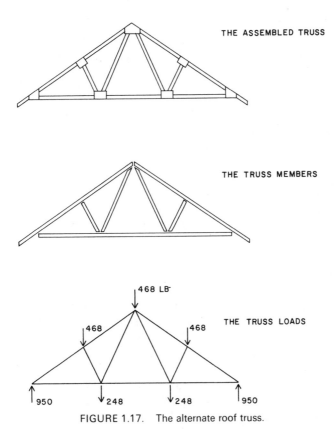

THE ASSEMBLED TRUSS

THE TRUSS MEMBERS

THE TRUSS LOADS

468 LB

468

468

950   248   248   950

FIGURE 1.17.   The alternate roof truss.

the load condition of dead load plus live load only, assuming this to be critical for design.

The loads on the trusses consist of the dead load of the truss plus the dead and live loads of the roof and ceiling. The roof load is actually applied as a uniform load on the top chord, while the ceiling is applied as a uniform load on the bottom chord. These loads are translated into panel, or joint, loadings for the truss analysis, as shown in Figure 1.17. The design of the chord members, however, must consider the truss axial forces plus the bending due to the actual uniform loading.

With the trusses at 24 in. centers, the loadings are as follows:

Roof live load:	30 psf(2 ft) = 60 lb/ft on the chord.
	60(6 ft) = 360 lb on the top chord joints.
Roof dead load:	5 psf(2) = 10 psf(1.2) = 12 psf/horizontal ft.
	12(6) = 72 lb on the top chord joints.
Ceiling live load:	10 psf(2) = 20 lb/ft on the chord.
	20(8) = 160 lb on the bottom chord joints.
Ceiling dead load:	2.5 psf(2)(8) = 40 lb on the bottom chord joints.

Assuming the trusses to weigh approximately 12 lb/ft of span, a load is added to the joints as follows:

$$6 \text{ plf}(6 \text{ ft}) = 36 \text{ lb at the top chord joints}$$

$$6 \text{ plf}(8 \text{ ft}) = 48 \text{ lb at the bottom chord joints}$$

The totals of these loadings are shown as the truss loads on Figure 1.17. The equilibrium diagrams for the individual joints of the truss are shown in Figure 1.18. Since the truss and the loads are symmetrical, only half of the truss is shown. Forces in the members are first found as vertical and horizontal components, using the typical solution by joints. These are then translated into the actual vector forces in the members as shown between the joints. T is used to disignate a tension member and C is used for compression.

The top chord must be designed for the maximum compression force of 1712 lb plus the bending due to the uniform load of the roof.

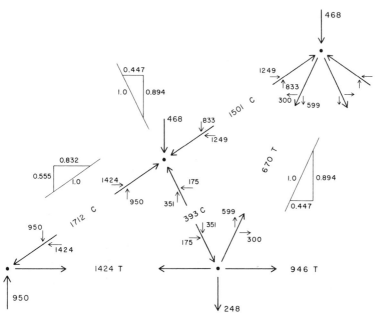

FIGURE 1.18.   Force analysis for gravity loads on the truss.

The roof load may be taken from case 1 in Figure 1.4, where it was found for the rafter design. With the trusses at 24 in., this load becomes

$$2(28.29) = 56.6 \text{ lb/ft}$$

The span is the true member length which is 1.2 times the 6 ft horizontal dimension, or 7.2 ft. For the continuous two span chord member the maximum moment is thus

$$M = \frac{wL^2}{8} = \frac{(56.6)(7.2)^2}{8} = 366.8 \text{ lb/ft}$$

With a 2 × 4 of No. 1 Douglas fir–larch, UBC Table 25-A-1 (see the Appendix) specifies:

$$F_b = 2050 \text{ psi}, \qquad F_c = 1250 \text{ psi}, \qquad E = 1,800,000 \text{ psi}$$

Since the roof deck braces the weak axis, $L/d = 7.2(12)/3.5 = 24.7$. The allowable compressive stress is thus

$$F'_c = \frac{(0.3)(1,800,000)}{(24.7)^2} = 885 \text{ psi}$$

The combined compression and bending is thus

$$\frac{P/A}{F'_c} + \frac{M/S}{F_b} = \frac{1712/5.25}{885} + \frac{(366.8)(12)/3.06}{2050}$$

$$= 0.368 + 0.702 = 1.070$$

Since this is over 1.0, the 2 × 4 is theoretically not adequate. However, the overstress is only 7% and a more accurate analysis may show it to be less. The true truss span is slightly less than 24 ft, and the gussets tend to reduce the actual unbraced length of the members. For a conservative design the member size may be increased to a 2 × 6 or the stress grade raised by using a higher quality wood.

The bottom chord must be designed for the maximum tension force of 1424 lb plus the bending due to the ceiling load. The load for bending will be $2(12.5) = 25$ lb/ft. Thus

$$M = \frac{wL^2}{8} = \frac{(25)(8)^2}{8} = 200 \text{ lb/ft}$$

Trying a 2 × 4 as before, we may use the previous data, adding that the allowable tension stress (F_t) from Table 25-A-1 is 1050 psi. Then

$$\frac{P/A}{F_t} + \frac{M/S}{F_b} = \frac{1424/5.25}{1050} + \frac{200(12)/3.06}{2050}$$

$$= 0.258 + 0.383 = 0.641$$

The stresses are very low on the interior members, since no bending is involved. For connection purposes these need to be 2 × members and would probably be 2 × 3 or 2 × 4 for development of the joint forces at the gussets.

One disadvantage of the trusses is that the second floor ceiling drywall would have to be heavier to span the 24 in. distance. Also the attic space becomes less functional for storage space when it is filled with the forest of truss members.

1.9 Construction Drawings

The structural designer ordinarily documents the design in the form of three elements: the structural calculations, the structural working (or construction) drawings, and the written specifications. The calculations should be written in reasonably readable form, since they must often be submitted for review when obtaining a building permit. The specifications are written in fairly legal form, since they are actually parts of a contract. For a building of this type the construction drawings for the structure are often incorporated in the general architectural drawings with a minimum of separate, purely structural, details. Many of the items usually covered by lengthy specifications in larger buildings are often covered with abbreviated notes on the construction drawings for this type of building.

The drawings that follow are typical "structural" details and are primarily intended to illustrate the design of the systems just discussed. They are not intended as models for construction drawings, although that style is used in the illustrations. They do not, in most cases, show the complete architectural details in terms of the finish materials, since the focus has been on the structure.

Basement and Foundation Plan. (Figure 1.19.) This is the conventional form for this type of plan, showing the footings, the floor slab, and the walls and columns. The footings are seen in dotted line where they are beneath the floor slab and in solid line where they extend outside the walls and are covered only by the soil.

First Floor Framing Plan. (Figure 1.19.) This is one convention for this type of drawing. Individual joists or beams are shown in solid line, indicating their approximate location in plan. Some of the members in a repetitive series are often omitted to simplify the drawing, with the extent of the series shown by including at least the end members on the drawing. Beams and headers are sometimes shown by a heavier line or by a broken line of some form to make them more obvious.

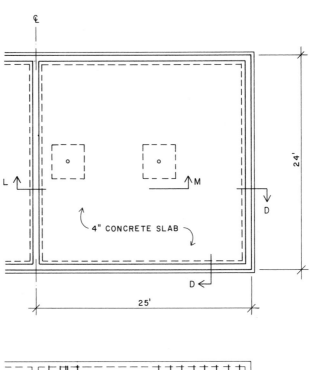

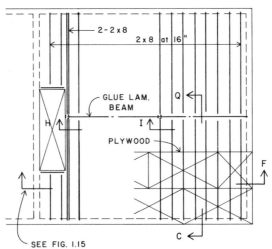

FIGURE 1.19. Structural plans: basement and first floor.

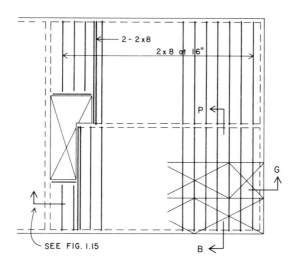

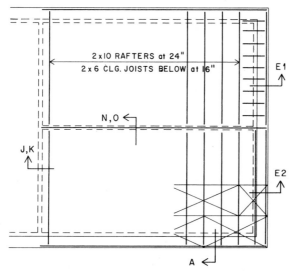

FIGURE 1.20. Structural plans: second floor and roof.

Openings are normally shown with an X. The floor sheathing is shown in terms of the arrangement of the 4 ft by 8 ft plywood sheets. The staggering shown slightly increases the strength and stiffness of the horizontal diaphragm.

Walls below the framing level, especially bearing walls, are usually shown by dotted lines.

Note that the joists are doubled at the edge of the stair opening. They would also be doubled under the partitions that are parallel to the joists.

Second Floor Framing Plan.   (Figure 1.20.) This is essentially similar to the first floor plan, except for the slightly different stair opening and the lack of the beam at the center.

Roof Framing Plan.   (Figure 1.20.) This shows the rafter and roof deck layout. The ceiling joists are covered by a note, since their arrangement is similar to the rafters, except for spacing. Two options are shown for the extended gable end in the two variations of Detail E.

Detail A.   (Figure 1.21.) This shows the typical roof edge condition at the front and rear. The rafter is notched to provide full bearing on top of the plate and is normally toenailed to the plates. The sheet metal tie shown is one type that may be used for a more positive anchorage of the roof to the walls.

The vertical blocking is used to transfer the roof wind load into the wall. The horizontal blocking on top of the plates serves two purposes. It assists in the transfer of wind shear from the vertical blocking and also provides a backup for the edge of the ceiling drywall.

The roof edge, facia, and soffit have many variations, depending on the desired architectural detailing.

Detail B.   (Figure 1.22.) This shows the typical condition at the edge of the second floor at the front and rear. Note the transfer of shear from the floor plywood through the continuous header and into the wall plywood. The block on type of the plate is strictly for backup of the drywall in this case.

Detail C.   (Figure 1.22.) This is the typical detail at the edge of the first floor. The wind load transfer is primarily from the exterior plywood to the sill and into the concrete through the bolts. In this

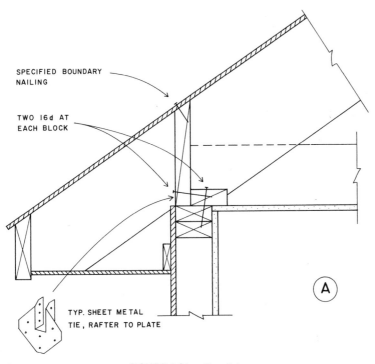

SPECIFIED BOUNDARY
NAILING

TWO 16d AT
EACH BLOCK

TYP. SHEET METAL
TIE , RAFTER TO PLATE

Ⓐ

FIGURE 1.21.   Detail A.

structure there is no wind load on the first floor diaphragm, although the wall plywood should be nailed to the continuous edge header as a positive tie to the floor. At the walls parallel to the joists this header should be doubled to provide support for the wall above.

Most codes require that the wood construction be kept some distance above the exterior grade; usually a minimum of 6 in.

Detail D.   (Figure 1.22.) Some codes have minimum requirements for this footing, as well as for the minimum wall and basement floor slab thicknesses. The need for various waterproofing details will depend on the specific site conditions. Reinforcing is not shown, although we recommend a minimum of one layer of wire fabric in the slab and the minimum wall reinforcing as discussed in the calculations.

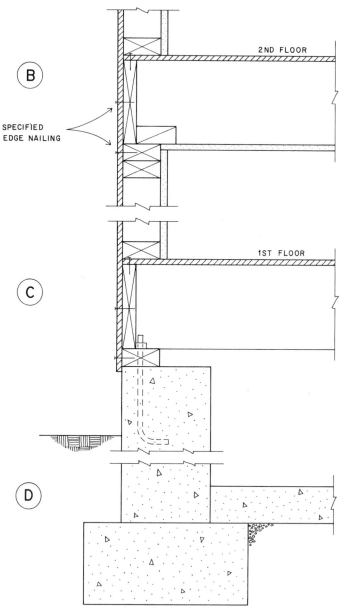

B

SPECIFIED
EDGE NAILING

2ND FLOOR

C

1ST FLOOR

D

FIGURE 1.22.   Details B, C, and D.

Detail E.   (Figure 1.23.) At the low edge of the roof the rafters can simply be cantilevered to form an overhang, as shown in Detail A. At the gable end the only cantilevered parts of the construction are the roof plywood, the ridge member, and the facia. If an overhang is desired, two possible ways of achieving it are shown in Figure 1.23.

Detail E1 illustrates the use of outriggers that rest on the top of the wall and are carried back to the first spanning rafter. The rafter that forms the roof edge is carried on the cantilevered ends of these outriggers. The blocking shown is used to carry the wind load from the roof plywood into the shear wall.

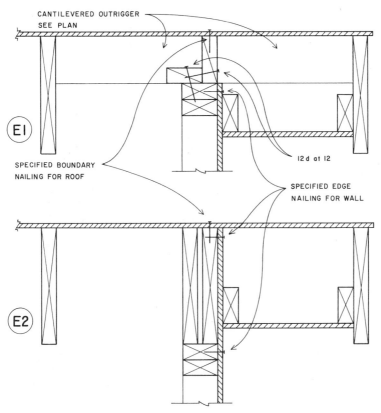

FIGURE 1.23.   Two alternates for Detail E.

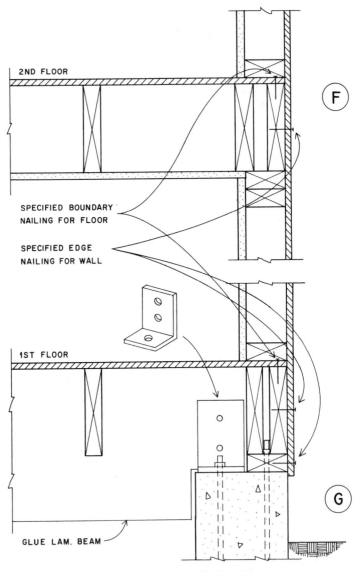

2ND FLOOR

SPECIFIED BOUNDARY
NAILING FOR FLOOR

SPECIFIED EDGE
NAILING FOR WALL

1ST FLOOR

GLUE LAM. BEAM

F

G

FIGURE 1.24.   Details F and G.

54

Detail E2 shows the condition if the roof edge rafter is made to span from the ridge to the facia. This assumes that the ridge member shown in Detail P and the facia member shown in Detail A are both cantilevered to hold the ends of the rafter. The wall is then literally built up to the underside of the roof deck. This may be done as shown or in other ways, depending on the soffit details, the wall finish, and so on.

The choice of one of these options, or of others, is usually primarily dependent on considerations of architectural detailing, rather than on structural necessity.

Detail F.   (Figure 1.24.) This is the second floor edge condition at the wall that is parallel to the joists. Since the floor plywood transfers its edge load into the edge joist that rests on the wall, the wall plywood should also be edge nailed to this member. Although we have not shown it, there is also a joint in the wall plywood here somewhere, depending on the sheet size used.

The second joist on top of the wall helps to support the wall above and is offset slightly to provide a backup for the ceiling drywall.

Detail G.   (Figure 1.24.) This shows the floor edge detail and the support for the end of the floor beam. The wind load transfer from the wall plywood to the basement concrete wall is essentially the same as in Detail C. As in Detail F, the second joist at the edge is used to support the wall above.

The end of the beam must be supported for vertical load as well as held in place during construction. This is usually achieved by using a steel member of some kind to facilitate the connection of the wood beam to the concrete. A simple pair of angles may be used as shown, or a single horizontal plate may be welded to two vertical plates to form a double T. Since the top of the wall is higher than the bottom of the beam, the beam must be notched as shown, or the wall must be pocketed. The latter is probably simpler for construction, and is only dependent on the ability of the reduced cross-section to take the end shear in the beam.

Detail H.   (Figure 1.25.) Details H and I show the connections of the floor beam to the steel pipe columns using a U-shaped, bent steel plate. A similar connection could be used with wood columns, with

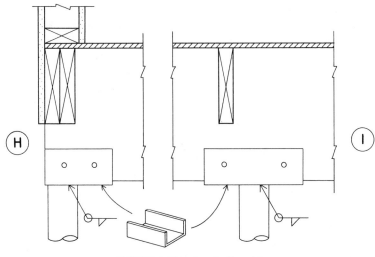

FIGURE 1.25.   Details H and I.

plates welded to the bottom of the U-shaped plate for attachment to the wood column.

Details J and K.   (Figure 1.26.) This shows the cripple wall that sits on top of the double-stud dividing wall. It serves to divide the space in the attic for the two housing units and also carries the roof diaphragm wind load down to the dividing wall. The remainder of this wall, showing the details from the second floor down to the basement, was illustrated in Figure 1.15.

Detail L.   (Figure 1.27.) This shows two options for the wall footing for the basement wall at the dividing wall. The difference between the two has to do with the sequence of construction of the wall and floor slab. The upper detail would be used if the wall is poured first. This is sometimes done to protect the slab during construction; delaying the pour until the first floor is in place. If the slab is poured first, the lower detail could be used, in which the footing and slab are poured together.

Detail M.   (Figure 1.27.) This shows the base detail for the steel column. A steel base plate is welded to the bottom of the column and

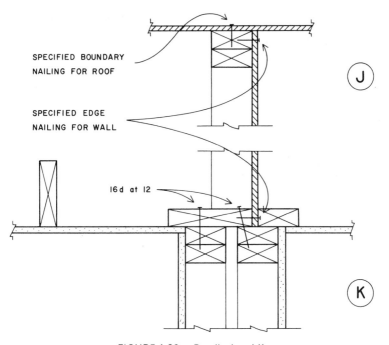

SPECIFIED BOUNDARY
NAILING FOR ROOF

SPECIFIED EDGE
NAILING FOR WALL

16d at 12

FIGURE 1.26.   Details J and K.

rests on a grout bed on top of the footing. The anchor bolts may be
minimal in size, as they merely serve to hold the column in position
during construction. If the slab and footing are poured at the same
time, as in the lower illustration for Detail L, a pocket would be provided in the top of the footing so that the base plate and anchor bolts
may be kept below the top of the slab.

Detail N.   (Figure 1.28.) This shows the typical ridge detail for
the roof. The ridge member is used to facilitate the joining of the
rafters as well as to provide edge nailing for the plywood. The rafters
are normally toenailed to the ridge. The strap shown is used to tie
the rafters together and provide for some resistance to uplift. An
alternative to the strap would be to use a 2 × 4 just under the plate
of the wall and nailed to the rafter on each side.

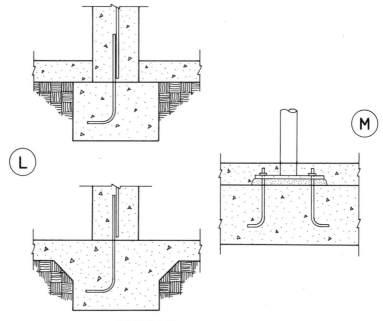

FIGURE 1.27.   Details L and M.

Detail O.   (Figure 1.28.) This shows the seating of the attic cripple wall on top of the center partition wall below. Since the cripple wall serves only for vertical load transfer, it could be an open stud wall with no surfacing. If so, the studs should be braced, possibly with 1 × 4 diagonal braces nailed to the studs, plates, and sill.

Although it is theoretically not required that the ceiling joists serve to tie the building against the thrust of the rafters (see Figure 1.5), it adds generally to the structural integrity of the building if they do so. This may be done by lapping them or using metal straps, as shown in the sketches.

Detail P.   (Figure 1.29.) This shows the floor at the center wall. The blocking serves the dual purpose of vertical support and backup for the ceiling drywall. The floor joists may be lapped or tied, as with the ceiling joists. However, the floor plywood serves adequately for tie purposes at this location.

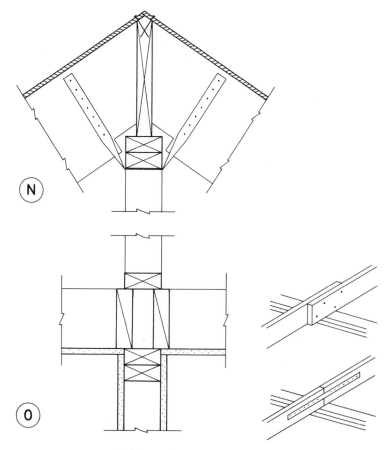

FIGURE 1.28.   Details N and O.

Detail Q.   (Figure 1.29.) This shows the floor beam at the center wall. Since the top of the floor joists is at the same level as the top of the beam, the ends of the joists would be supported with metal joist hangers or a ledger bolted to the side of the beam.

Diaphragm Nailing.   Figure 1.30 shows a typical schedule for the nailing of the wall and floor paneling to the framing for diaphragm

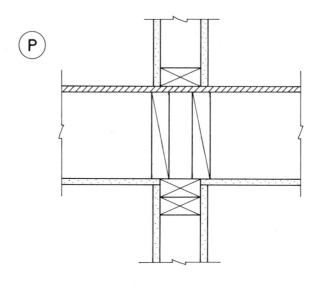

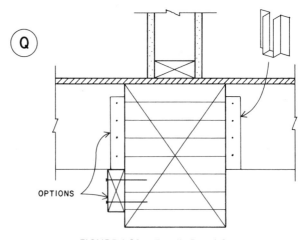

FIGURE 1.29. Details P and Q.

SHEAR WALL AND HORIZONTAL DIAPHRAM NAILING SCHEDULE					
LOCATION	SURFACING	NAILS	NAIL SPACING AND LOCATION		
			AT BOUNDARIES	AT OTHER EDGES	AT INTERMEDIATE SUPPORTS
ROOF	3/8" C-D PLYWOOD	6 d COMMON	6	6	12
FLOORS	1/2" C-D PLY.	8 d COM.	6	6	12
WALL A	1/2" C-D PLY.	8 d COM.	6	6	12
WALL B	3/8" C-D PLY.	6 d COM.	6	6	12
WALL C	1/2" GYP. DRYWALL	5 d COOLER	4	4	4
WALL D	1/2" GYP. DRYWALL	5 d COOLER	7	7	7

FIGURE 1.30.   Nailing for the Building One diaphragms.

action. Because of the relatively low shear stresses in most cases, the nail spacing shown is the minimum code required nailing for most of the diaphragms. Shear walls are usually labeled as such on the plans with number or letter designations for identity in the schedule.

2

Building Two

||||||||||||||||||||||||||||||||||||||||||||||||||||||||||

Building Two is a simple box—a single story, flat-roofed, single space building. The possible variations for the structural system and for the materials and details of individual components are quite extensive. If the building is built essentially for investment purpose, dictates of economy, local codes, and available local materials would probably narrow the range of choice. We will show the design for two different solutions. The first is an all wood structure. The second is a structure with masonry walls and a steel framed roof.

2.1 The Building

The general configuration of the building is shown in Figures 2.1 and 2.2. For maximum flexibility in the arrangement of interior walls, it is desired that there be no interior structural walls or columns. The roof therefore requires a clear span of 60 ft.

For the 9000 ft² building the UBC requires a one hour fire rating for the walls and roof. This could be eliminated if a fire resistive partition is used to divide the interior, but we assume that this is not desired.

Some of the design criteria are:

Roof live load: 20 psf (reduced as per the UBC).
Lateral loads: 25 psf wind zone, seismic zone 4 (UBC).
Soil capacity: 2000 psf maximum for shallow, spread footings.

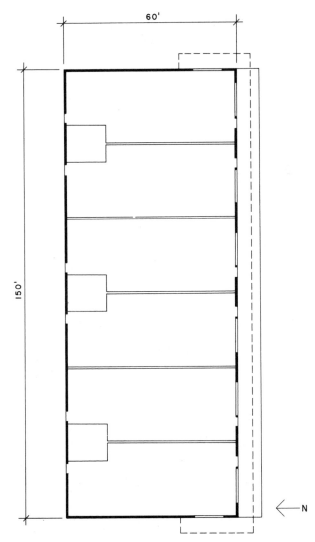

FIGURE 2.1. Floor plan: Building Two.

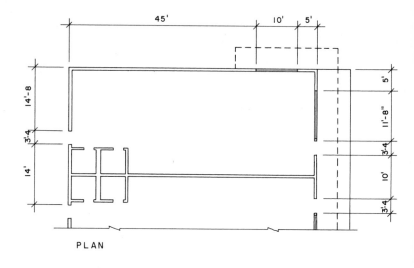

PLAN

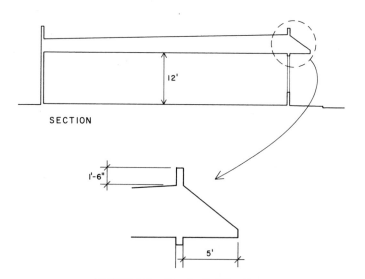

SECTION

FIGURE 2.2.   Details: Building Two.

2.2   The Wood Structure

The plans in Figure 2.3 show the layout for the wood structure, consisting of plywood roof deck, wood roof joists, glue laminated girders, and wood stud walls. Girder spacing relates to the module of the plan and not necessarily to any structural optimization.

The following materials will be used:

2 × and 3 × framing: No. 2 Douglas fir–larch.

4 × framing and larger: No. 1 Douglas fir–larch.

Glue laminated members: Douglas fir–larch, 2400f grade.

Structural steel: A36, $F_y = 36$ ksi.

Concrete: $F_c' = 3000$ psi.

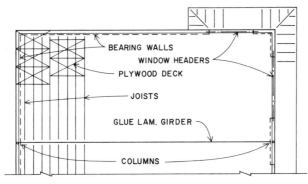

ROOF FRAMING

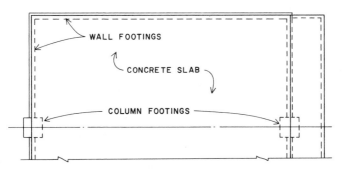

GROUND FLOOR & FOUNDATIONS

FIGURE 2.3.   Structural plans for the wood structure.

2.3   Design of the Wood Roof Structure

Dead load on the structure consists of

> Roofing: tar and gravel at 6.5 psf.
> Insulation, lights, ducts, and so on: assume 5 psf average.
> Ceiling: assume 10 psf total, finish plus suspension system.
> Total dead load: 21.5 psf plus structure.

Roof Deck.   UBC Table 25-R (see the Appendix) permits $\frac{1}{2}$ in. plywood for joists at 24 in. centers. Grade and nailing will be part of seismic design.

Roof Joists.   Allowable stresses for the joists depend on their size. Our procedure is to make an initial size assumption, perform the analysis and size the joist, and verify the initial assumption. Note that UBC 2504(c)4 permits a 25 % increase in allowable stress for roof loads.

From UBC Table 25-A-1, for 2 × 6 and larger (see the Appendix):

$$F_b = 1450 \text{ psi (repetitive member use)}$$

$$E = 1,700,000 \text{ psi}$$

Loads:

> Live load: 20 psf
> Dead load: Applied   = 21.5 psf
> $\frac{1}{2}$ in. deck   =   1.5
> Joists + blocking =   4.0 (estimate)
> Total dead load   = 27.0 psf

With the joists at 24 in. spacing, the total design load is

$$2(20 + 27) = 94 \text{ lb/ft of joist}$$

Then

$$\text{maximum } M = \frac{wL^2}{8} = \frac{94(24)^2}{8} = 6788 \text{ lb/ft}$$

$$\text{required } S = \frac{M}{F_b} = \frac{6768(12)}{(1.25)(1450)} = 44.81 \text{ in.}^3$$

This requires a 3 × 12 joist. If the stress grade is increased to No. 1, the allowable F_b is 1750 psi and the required S is

$$S = \frac{6768(12)}{(1.25)(1750)} = 37.13 \text{ in.}^3$$

This permits a 2 × 14 joist. The choice is somewhat arbitrary and would probably be made on the basis of lumber prices and availability of sizes and lengths.

Allowable total load deflection is 1/180 of the span, or

$$\frac{24(12)}{180} = 1.60 \text{ in.}$$

With the 3 × 12 the deflection will be

$$\Delta = \frac{5WL^3}{384EI} = \frac{5(94 \times 24)(24 \times 12)^3}{384(1,800,000)(297)} = 1.31 \text{ in.}$$

The I of the 2 × 14 is approximately the same, so deflection is not critical for either choice.

UBC 2506(g) requires that the ends of these joists be adequately blocked, which must be considered in the construction detailing. No bridging or intermediate blocking is required by the code, although some designers prefer to use it for all long span joists.

Since the tops of these joists will be at the same level as the tops of the glue laminated girders that support them, metal joist hangers or wood ledgers must be provided.

The Glue Laminated Girder.   From UBC Table 25-C-1, for DF-L, 24f grade (see the Appendix)

$$F_b = 2400 \text{ psi}, \quad F_v = 165 \text{ psi}, \quad E = 1,800,000 \text{ psi}$$

For the girder load area of 1500 ft² UBC Table 23-C permits a reduction of the live load to 12 psf. The girder design load is thus

$$(25 \text{ ft})(12 + 27) = 975 \text{ lb/ft} + \text{the girder weight}$$

Assuming a total load of 1075 lb/ft:

$$\text{maximum } M = \frac{wL^2}{8} = \frac{1075(60)^2}{8} = 483{,}750 \text{ lb/ft}$$

$$\text{required } S = \frac{M}{F_b} = \frac{483{,}750(12)}{(1.25)(2400)} = 1935 \text{ in.}^3$$

Options are:

$8\frac{3}{4} \times 39$, $C_f = 0.88$,   effective $S = 0.88(2218) = 1952$ in.^{3}

$10\frac{3}{4} \times 36$, $C_f = 0.88$,   effective $S = 0.88(2322) = 2043$ in.^{3}

$12\frac{3}{4} \times 33$, $C_f = 0.89$,   effective $S = 0.89(2223) = 1978$ in.^{3}

Checking the shear for the narrowest beam with the least area in cross-section:

$$\text{maximum } V = \frac{wL}{2} = \frac{1075(60)}{2} = 32{,}250 \text{ lb}$$

$$\text{maximum } F_v = \frac{3V}{2A} = \frac{3(32{,}250)}{2(341.3)} = 141.7 \text{ psi}$$

which is less than the allowable of 165 psi.

Allowable total load deflection is $L/180 = 60(12)/180 = 4$ in.

Deflection calculations will show that all the optional sections previously listed will deflect slightly more than this. Our procedure therefore is to use the deflection formula to derive the I value required for a deflection of 4 in. Thus

$$\text{required } I = \frac{5WL^3}{384E\Delta} = \frac{5(1075 \times 60)(60 \times 12)^3}{384(1{,}800{,}000)(4.0)} = 43{,}530 \text{ in.}^4$$

The lightest section with this I is a $8\frac{3}{4} \times 40.5$, which would be used unless headroom is critical and justifies a heavier, shallower section.

The seismic design will show the necessity for providing nailing support at all edges of the plywood sheets. Additional framing will be required between the joists to provide this. As shown in Figure 2.4, this is accomplished by adding blocking in continuous rows.

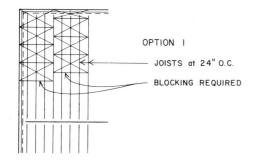

OPTION 1

—— JOISTS at 24" O.C.

—— BLOCKING REQUIRED

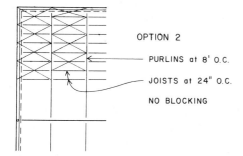

OPTION 2

—— PURLINS at 8' O.C.

—— JOISTS at 24" O.C.

NO BLOCKING

FIGURE 2.4.   Optional roof systems.

An alternative, as shown in Figure 2.4, consists of a three part system that provides for full edge nailing of the plywood without the use of blocking. The 8 ft span joists for this system may be 2 × 4's at 24 in. centers. The purlins would be as follows.

Purlins.   Loading for the purlins is approximately four times that for the previous joists, which jumps the member into another stress category.

From UBC Table 25-A-1, for beams and stringers (see the Appendix), for No. 1, Douglas fir–larch:

$$F_b = 1300 \text{ psi}$$

$$\text{maximum } M = 4(6768) = 27,072 \text{ lb/ft}$$

$$\text{required } S = \frac{27,072(12)}{(1.25)1300} = 200 \text{ in.}^3$$

This requires a 6 × 16. An alternative glue laminated member of 24f grade would require

$$S = \frac{27,072(12)}{(1.25)(2400)} = 108 \text{ in.}^3$$

$$I = \frac{5(376 \times 24)(24 \times 12)^3}{384(1,800,000)(1.60)} = 975 \text{ in.}^4$$

Select:

$5\frac{1}{8} \times 13.5,$ $S = 0.99(155.7) = 154 \text{ in.}^3$ effective, $I = 1050.8 \text{ in.}^4$

2.4   Design of the Wood Studs and Columns

Studs.   The end walls of the building carry the ends of the 25 ft span joists or purlins. Because of the sloping roof surface, it is easier for construction to make these studs continuous to the top of the parapet and to carry the joists or purlins on a ledger bolted to the face of the studs. The unbraced height of the studs is thus the distance from the floor to the bottom of the ledger. With the roof slope, this distance varies 15 in. from front to rear of the building. In order to attain the desired 12 ft clear ceiling height under the deep girder, the bottom of the joists at the front of the building will be at approximately 15.5 ft above the floor. For this height UBC 2518(g)2 requires that the studs be 2 × 6.

The studs should be checked for the combined compression plus bending due to the wind load and gravity load.

Gravity load equals:

Roof:	12.5 ft(20 + 27) = 588 lb/ft of wall	
Canopy:	Assume	= 100
Total $DL + LL$		= 688 lb/ft
Or:	688(1.33) = 915 lb/stud at 16 in. centers	

For the 15.5 ft high stud, $h/t = 15.5(12)/5.5 = 33.8$

$$F_c' = \frac{(0.3)(1,700,000)}{(33.8)^2} = 446 \text{ psi}$$

With the wind load the allowable load/stud is thus

$$\text{load} = 446(8.25)(1.33) = 4894 \text{ lb}$$

With wind pressure of 20 psf on the wall, the moment is

$$M = \frac{wL^2}{8} = \frac{20(1.33)(15.5)^2}{8} = 799 \text{ lb/ft}$$

The combined effect is thus

$$\frac{P/A}{F_c'} + \frac{M/S}{F_b} = \frac{915}{4894} + \frac{799(12)/7.56}{1.33(1450)}$$

$$= 0.187 + 0.658 = 0.845 < 1$$

Since the canopy is cantilevered from the wall, the studs should also be checked for this load, unless the cantilever forces are carried directly back into the roof construction with struts and ties. Since we are not detailing the canopy construction, we will assume the 2 × 6's to be adequate for this condition.

We have checked the heaviest loaded stud, so that we may safely use the 2 × 6's for the other walls. Actually, 2 × 4's can probably be used for the shorter rear wall.

Columns.   The girder ends bring large concentrated loads to the front and rear walls, making it desirable to build a column into the wall at this location. Three options are possible: multiple 2 × 6 studs, a solid 6 × member, or a steel post inserted in the hollow wall space. From the girder calculations the end load is approximately 32 kips. At the front wall the column height is approximately 13.5 ft to the bottom of the girder.

For No. 2 2 × 6 studs, UBC Table 25-A-1 gives (see the Appendix)

$$F_c = 1050 \text{ psi}, \qquad E = 1,700,000 \text{ psi}$$

Then

$$\frac{h}{t} = \frac{13.5(12)}{5.5} = 29.45$$

$$F_c' = \frac{(0.3)(1,700,000)}{(29.45)^2} = 588 \text{ psi}$$

$$\text{required area} = \frac{32,000}{588} = 54.4 \text{ in.}^2 \text{ (or seven } 2 \times 6\text{'s)}$$

If a solid timber is used, E drops to 1,600,000 psi and a 6×12 would be required. If a steel column is used, options are a 4 in. standard round pipe or a 4 in. square tube with $\frac{1}{4}$ in. wall thickness, both of which will fit in the wall space.

Design of the wall details and of the girder connection and the foundations may determine the desirability of one of these options over the other.

Header at Wall Opening. Load on the headers consists of the weights of the wall and canopy and part of the roof load. With the purlin system the load on the front wall headers will be:

Roof $DL + LL$: $4(47) =$ 188 lb/ft
Wall and parapet: $5(15) =$ 75
Canopy (estimate) $=$ 100
Header (estimate) $=$ 25
Total load $=$ 388 lb/ft

At the front wall the header will span approximately 16 ft, the exact dimension depending on the construction details:

$$\text{maximum } M = \frac{wL^2}{8} = \frac{(388)(16)^2}{8} = 12,416 \text{ lb/ft}$$

If a solid $6 \times$, No. 1, Douglas fir–larch, with $F_b = 1300$ psi is used

$$\text{required } S = \frac{M}{F_b} = \frac{(12,416)(12)}{1300} = 114.6 \text{ in.}^3$$

A 6 × 12 can be used to provide this section modulus. Since the percentage of live load is small, deflection should not be critical for the window construction detailing. The true loading and span conditions should be verified when the final details of the construction are developed. The actual span will be from center to center of the posts, if a direct bearing is used for the end connection of the header. If the header spans from face to face of the posts, the span will be slightly less.

The header at the end wall carries more roof load because of the purlin span. This higher load on the shorter span will probably result in approximately the same size header.

Checking shear for the 16 ft span:

$$\text{maximum } V = 388(7) = 2716 \text{ lb (approximately critical shear)}$$

$$F_v = \frac{3V}{2A} = \frac{3(2716)}{2(63.25)} = 64.4 \text{ psi} < 85 \text{ psi}$$

2.5   Design of the Foundations

Stud Wall Foundation.   At the solid end wall this load is approximately as follows:

Roof dead load:	27 psf × 12 ft =	324 lb/ft
		of wall
Wall:	20 psf × 17 ft =	340
Grade wall and footing (estimated)	=	450
Total dead load	=	1114 lb/ft
Roof live load:	20 psf × 12 ft =	240 lb/ft
Total $DL + LL$	=	1354 lb/ft

With the allowable pressure of 2000 psf this requires less than a foot of width. Depending on the depth required for frost or for adequate soil bearing, there are several options for detailing of the grade wall and footing. We will assume that a depth of 3 ft is required and will design for a separate wall and footing, as shown in the construction details.

This footing should be slightly wider than the wall for construction purposes. If a 14 in. wide footing is used, the dead load pressure will be slightly less than 1000 psf. To equalize settlements the rest of the footings should be designed for this dead load pressure, rather than for the maximum total load limit of 2000 psf.

Column Footing.   Since the column occurs in the wall, there are several options for this footing. As shown in Figure 2.5, three possibilities are as follows:

1. The grade wall may be designed as a continuous beam, distributing the loads to a constant width footing.
2. A separate square column footing may be designed to carry the column plus only the wall directly over the column footing. The remainder of the wall length would be directly carried by a narrow wall footing.
3. The footing under the 10 ft solid wall portion may be designed for the column plus the wall plus the header post loads, and a minimal footing provided under the remainder of the grade wall.

All three options can be adequately designed. Option 1 is the simplest in detail and easiest to build, but requires a reasonably deep grade wall for the beam action. We will design the system for Option 3 with a wide footing 12 ft long under the solid wall. The total load on this footing will be:

Header post load:	308 plf (dead load)	
	$\times$ 16 ft $=$	4,928 lb
Roof dead load on wall:	27 psf $\times$ 4 ft $\times$ 10 ft $=$	1,080
Wall dead load:	20 psf $\times$ 17 ft $\times$ 10 ft $=$	3,400
Grade wall:	300 plf (estimate)	
	$\times$ 10 ft $=$	3,000
Girder dead load:	775 plf $\times$ 30 ft $=$	23,250
Total dead load	$=$	35,658 lb $+$ footing

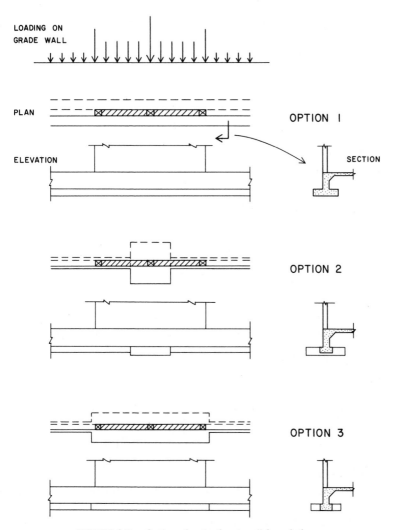

FIGURE 2.5. Options for the front wall foundation.

Using the dead load pressure determined for the end wall:

$$\text{area required} = \frac{35,658}{950} = 37.5 \text{ ft}^2$$

If 12 ft long,

$$\text{width required} = \frac{37.5}{12} = 3.13 \text{ ft}$$

We will use a 3 ft wide footing, for which the actual dead load pressure will be:

Assume a 10 in. thick footing:
Weight of footing: $3.0 \times 12 \times 0.83 \times 150$ pcf $= 4482$ lb.
Total dead load: $35,658 + 4482 \times 40,140$ lb.

$$\text{Dead load pressure: } \frac{40,140}{3 \times 12} = 1115 \text{ psf.}$$

The continuous grade wall will distribute some of this pressure to the narrow footing under the windows, which will otherwise be quite lightly loaded.

Adding the roof live load at 12 psf, the total pressure will be as follows:

$$\text{roof live load} = 30 \times 25 \times 12 \text{ psf} \times 9000 \text{ lb}$$

$$\text{total pressure} = \frac{49,140}{36} = 1365 \text{ psf}$$

This is well below the allowable of 2000 psf.

The reinforcing in the short direction should be designed for the total pressure less the weight of the footing, or approximately 1240 psf. Referring to Figure 2.6:

$$M = \frac{1240(14/12)(7)}{12} = 844 \text{ lb/ft}$$

$$\text{required } A_s = \frac{844(12)}{16,000(0.9)(6.75)} = 0.104 \text{ in.}^2/\text{ft}$$

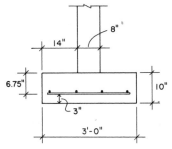
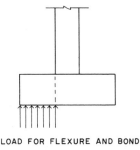

LOAD FOR FLEXURE AND BOND

FIGURE 2.6.   Details of the front wall foundation.

Or, for the entire 12 ft long footing:

$$A_s = 0.104(12) = 1.25 \text{ in.}^2$$

This may be provided by seven No. 4 bars in the short direction.

In the long direction a minimum shrinkage reinforcement of 0.02 % of the cross-section will be used:

$$A_s = 0.002(10 \times 36) = 0.72 \text{ in.}^2$$

This may be provided by using four No. 4 bars, two of which can be made continuous with the reinforcing in the narrow footing.

2.6   Design for Seismic Load

Design for the seismic forces on the building includes the following considerations:

1. Design of the roof diaphragm for forces in both directions.
2. Design of the vertical shear walls.
3. Development of the various construction details for transfer of the forces from the horizontal to the vertical diaphragms and for transfer of the forces from the shear walls to the foundations.

A critical preliminary decision is the identification of the walls to be used as shear walls. Some of the considerations in this decision are:

1. The actual magnitude of force that the walls in each direction must resist. A quick estimate of the load should be made to determine this.

2. Which walls lend themselves to being used. This has to do
    with their plan location, their length, and the type of bracing
    used. The code establishes maximum height-to-length ratios
    for various bracing: up to $3\frac{1}{2}$:1 for plywood, $1\frac{1}{2}$:1 for plaster
    or drywall.
3. What materials are planned for the wall surfaces that may be
    used for their shear resistance, and what materials or bracing
    can be added where the surfacing materials are not adequate.

We assume that the ordinary construction to be used is drywall on
the interior and cement plaster (stucco) on the exterior of the walls.
This means that only one of these surfacings can be used for the
exterior walls, since the code does not permit addition of dissimilar
materials [UBC Section 4713(a)]. Where the stucco is not sufficient,
we add plywood to the wall, ignoring the surfacing materials. Where
plywood is not required for the full length of a wall it sometimes
simplifies the detailing if it is added to the interior, rather than to the
exterior, of the wall.

Figure 2.7 shows the proposed layout of the shear wall system.
For load in the short direction the roof will span from end to end of
the building, transferring the shear to the two 45 ft long end walls.
For the load in the long direction the five 10 ft long walls will be used
on the front and the entire wall will be used on the rear, consisting of
a net wall length of 130 ft. The latter will result in some eccentricity
between the load and the centroid of the walls in the long direction,
requiring an investigation of the torsional effect.

The shear loads to the roof diaphragm are as shown in Table 2.1.
The wall loads are taken as the weight of the upper half of the walls,
ignoring openings that are generally in the bottom half. In each
direction the wall loads considered are only those of walls perpendicular to the load direction. The canopy load is assumed to be taken
by the roof in both directions. A nominal load is included for rooftop
HVAC units.

The total load in both directions is reasonably symmetrically
placed. The canopy load on the front is offset by the toilet walls and
the heavier rear wall in the long direction. The seismic design load is
calculated as follows (see UBC 2312):

$$V = ZKCISW$$

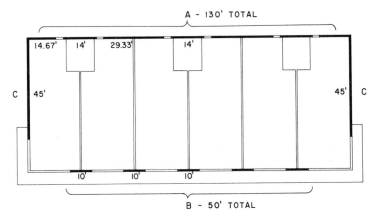

A - 130' TOTAL

14.67' 14' 29.33' 14'

C 45' 45' C

10' 10' 10'

B - 50' TOTAL

THE SHEAR WALL SYSTEM

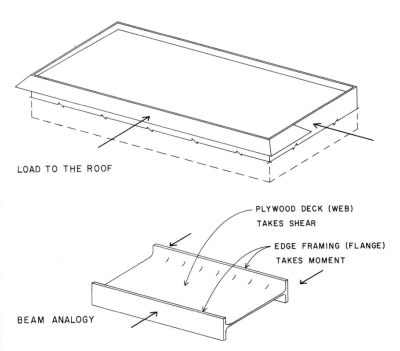

LOAD TO THE ROOF

PLYWOOD DECK (WEB) TAKES SHEAR

EDGE FRAMING (FLANGE) TAKES MOMENT

BEAM ANALOGY

FIGURE 2.7.   The wind resistive system.

TABLE 2.1. Loads to the Roof Diaphragm

	Loads (kips)	
Load Source and Calculation	N–S	E–W
Roof dead load		
$150 \times 60 \times 27$ psf	243	243
North–south exterior walls		
$\frac{1}{2} \times 60 \times 17 \times 20$ psf $\times 2$	0	20.4
East–west exterior walls		
$\frac{1}{2} \times 150 \times 17 \times 20$ psf $\times 2$	51	0
Interior dividing walls		
$\frac{1}{2} \times 60 \times 15 \times 8$ psf $\times 5$	0	18
Toilet walls		
$\frac{1}{2} \times 190 \times 15 \times 8$ psf	11.4	11.4
Canopy		
190 ft $\times$ 100 lb/ft	19	19
Rooftop HVAC units (estimate)	5	5
Total load		
(W for seismic calculation)	329.4	316.8

where Z = 1.0 for UBC zone 4 (the assumed condition)

K = 1.33 for the box system (diaphragm braced) building

I = 1.0 for this building occupancy

CS = 0.14 as a product, if S is not established by a geological analysis of the site

Thus: $V = (1.0)(1.33)(1.0)(0.14)W = 0.1862W$

$= 0.1862(329.4) = 61.3$ kips in the N–S direction

$= 0.1862(316.8) = 59.0$ kips in the E–W direction

In the north–south direction the maximum shear in the roof is

$$v = \left(\frac{1}{2}\right)\left(\frac{61,300}{60}\right) = 511 \text{ lb/ft at the end wall}$$

With $\frac{1}{2}$ in. Structural II plywood and 10d nails this requires $2\frac{1}{2}$ in. boundary and 4 in. edge nail spacing. (UBC Table 25-J; see the Appendix.) It may be desirable to reduce this spacing for areas of lower stress, as shown in Figure 2.8.

$$\text{chord force} = \frac{WL}{8d} = \frac{61,300(150)}{8(60)} = 19,156 \text{ lb}$$

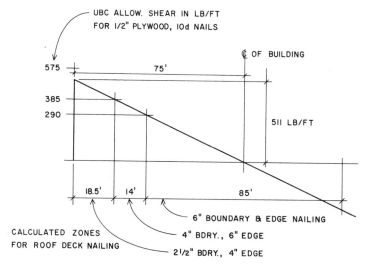

FIGURE 2.8.   Zoned nailing for the roof.

Analysis will show this to be too large for the normal double 2 × 6 top plates. Alternatives are to raise the stress grade of the plates or increase their size. Assuming No. 2 Douglas fir–larch 3 × 6 plates with $\frac{7}{8}$ in. bolts in a single row at the splices, the net tension force allowable on the plates at the splice is as follows:

$\frac{7}{8}$ in. bolts require 1 in. holes.

Deduct from cross-section an area of 5 × 1 in.

Net A: 2(13.75) − (5 × 1) = 22.5 in.²

From UBC Table 25-A-1 (see the Appendix) F_t = 825 psi and

allowable T = (22.5)(825)(1.33) = 24,688 lb

Since the plate splices will be lapped so that only one of the members is spliced at a time, the bolts will carry only one half of the total chord force at each splice. Thus the number of bolts required is

$$N = \frac{\text{total chord force}}{1.33(\text{load/bolt})} = \frac{19,156 \times \frac{1}{2}}{1.33(1990)} = 3.62$$

Use four bolts on each side of the splice.

If the studs run full height to the top of the parapet, the edge of the roof deck would be supported by a ledger fastened to the face of the studs. (See construction details that follow for these two alternatives.) If this ledger also serves as the chord, it would need to be a minimum of a 3 × 10. At splice points the full chord force would be transmitted.

The advisability of one of these alternates over the other would have to include other considerations of the wall construction. The details of the canopy and its supports would be one additional consideration. The location of the shear wall plywood on the inside or the outside would be another.

The load in the long direction is generally not critical for the roof deck, except for consideration of the transfer of force from the roof edge to the walls. Assuming a continuous transfer, this load is

$$\frac{\frac{1}{2} \times 59,000}{150} = 197 \text{ lb/ft}$$

Since this is less than the minimum capacity of the roof deck nailing (see Figure 2.8) it is not critical for the deck-to-edge transfer. If the ledger is used, this force must be passed through the wall blocking to the plywood. Using 16d nails, this would require a spacing as follows:

$$\text{maximum spacing} = \frac{\text{edge load/ft}}{1.33(\text{load/nail})}(12) = \frac{197(12)}{1.33(107)} = 16.6 \text{ in.}$$

Use: minimum of 16d at 16 in. centers.

The two end shear walls have stresses as follows:

$$v = \frac{30,650}{45} = 681 \text{ plf}$$

This requires a wall with $\frac{1}{2}$ in. plywood with 10d nails spaced at $2\frac{1}{2}$ in. at all edges. Edges must be blocked and boundary nailing must be to a minimum of 3 × members.

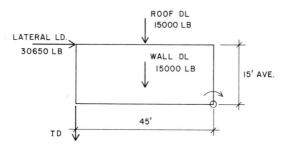

FIGURE 2.9.   Stability of wall C.

Overturn and sliding of the wall are considered as shown in the diagrams in Figure 2.9. The overturn analysis is as follows:

$$\text{overturn } M = 30.65(15) = 460 \text{ k/ft}$$

$$\text{dead load } M = 30(22.5) = 675 \text{ k/ft}$$

$$\text{safety factor} = \frac{675}{460} = 1.47$$

This is just short of the required safety factor of 1.5, but the necessary additional resistance is easily supplied by the ordinary sill bolting of the wall.

The horizontal force of 30,650 lb on the end wall must be transferred as a sliding resistance between the sill and the foundation. Using the ordinary $\frac{1}{2}$ in. bolts this requires the following: from UBC Table 26-G,

$$\text{capacity of one } \tfrac{1}{2} \text{ in. bolt} = 1000(1.333) = 1333 \text{ lb}$$

$$\text{required number} = \frac{30,650}{1333} = 23 \text{ bolts}$$

This would require bolts on 2 ft centers. If the bolt size is increased to $\frac{3}{4}$ in.:

$$\text{capacity of one bolt} = 1780(1.333) = 2373 \text{ lb}$$

$$\text{required number} = 30,650/2373 = 12.9$$

This would require the $\frac{3}{4}$ in. bolts to be on 3 ft 6 in. centers.

In the east–west direction there is a total of 180 ft of wall. If torsion is ignored, the average shear stress is

$$v = \frac{59,000}{180} = 328 \text{ lb/ft}$$

This value is used for the rear shear walls, requiring $\frac{3}{8}$ in. plywood with 4 in. nail spacing at all edges. As shown in Figure 2.10, there are two options for this wall. The first is to consider it as a series of independent piers linked together. For overturn these piers would be considered to have a height from the sill to the roof deck level. The other option is to consider the wall as a continuous diaphragm with the piers having a height equal to the door opening height. The latter option considerably reduces the overturn, but requires some additional framing and tying to reinforce the wall at the edges of the openings.

Referring to Figure 2.10, the overturn analysis for the shortest pier in the first option is as follows:

Lateral load:	(328 lb/ft)(14 ft)	= 4,592 lb
Overturn M:	4592(14 ft)(1.5 SF)	= 96,432 lb/ft
Dead load moment:	6300(7)	= 44,100
Net moment for hold-down		= 52,332 lb/ft
Required hold-down force:	$\frac{52,332}{14}$	= 3,738 lb

This option would therefore require a fairly large hold-down device at the ends of the short piers. For the other option, the analysis is as follows:

Overturn M:	4592(7)(1.5)	= 48,216 lb/ft
Dead load M:	(as before)	= 44,100
Net moment for hold-down:		4,116
Required hold-down force:	$\frac{4116}{14}$	= 294 lb

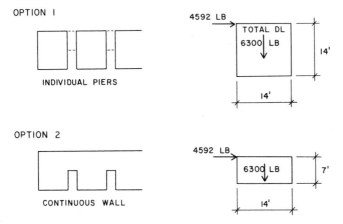

FIGURE 2.10.   Options for wall A.

This is a negligible force, easily developed by the sill bolts. However, the second option requires the addition of blocking and strapping at the level of the door headers. The cost and difficulty of this would have to be compared to that for the hold-downs for the first option.

The shear walls on the front of the building will have some added shear due to the torsional effect. This is caused by the fact that the center of gravity of the loading is eccentric from the center of stiffness of the shear walls, as shown in Figure 2.11. The analysis for this effect is as follows.

The center of stiffness is centered in the east–west direction, but is slightly north, due to the larger amount of shear wall on the north side. This distance is found as follows:

$$\bar{y} = \frac{(50)(60)}{180} = 16.67 \text{ ft from rear wall}$$

The torsional moment of inertia of the shear walls is determined as shown in Table 2.2. The added shear on the front wall is thus

$$v = \frac{Tc}{J} = \frac{(786,470)(43.33)}{636,250} = 54 \text{ lb/ft}$$

total v on wall $= 328 + 54 = 382$ lb/ft

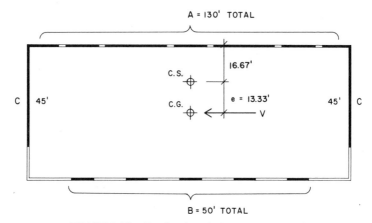

FIGURE 2.11. Torsional analysis: east-west loads.

From UBC Table 25-K (see the Appendix) this requires $\frac{1}{2}$ in. plywood with 4 in. nail spacing at all edges.

We may consider the same options for these walls as for the rear wall with regard to overturn. If we elect to strap the window headers into the solid walls, we may consider the pier height to be approximately 11.5 ft. Referring to Figure 2.12, the analysis is as follows:

$$\text{overturn } M = 3820(11.5)(1.5) = 65,895 \text{ lb/ft}$$

$$\text{dead load } M = 27,000(5) = 135,000 \text{ lb/ft}$$

If the girder dead load is considered part of the load on the wall, this is obviously a well stabilized wall. If a steel column is used, and is

TABLE 2.2. Torsional Moment of Inertia of the Shear Walls

Wall	Length (ft)	Distance from Center of Stiffness (ft)	$J = L(d)^2$
A	130	16.67	36,126
B	50	43.33	93,874
C	2(45)	75	506,250
	Total J for the shear walls		636,250

$T = V(e) = 59,000(13.33) = 786,470$ lb-ft

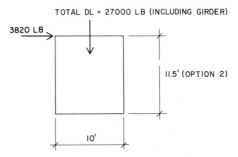

FIGURE 2.12.   Stability of wall A.

not essentially secured to the wood framed wall, tiedowns will be required at the ends of the walls.

Sliding of both the front and rear walls will be adequately resisted by minimum code-required sill bolting with $\frac{1}{2}$ in. bolts.

The overturn forces on these walls must be transmitted to, and resisted by, the foundations. This requires that there be sufficient dead weight in the grade wall and footings and some bending and shear resistance by the grade wall. Assuming the depth of grade wall as shown in the construction drawings, this resistance can be developed with minimal top and bottom continuous reinforcing. If the grade wall is quite shallow, this problem should be carefully investigated.

Obviously, some reconsideration of the building details could reduce the requirements for lateral load resistance. Use of a lighter roofing and a lighter ceiling material would considerably reduce the roof dead load and consequently the lateral force. Use of one or more permanent cross walls in the interior would reduce the stresses in the roof deck and the end shear walls and eliminate some of the large girders.

2.7 Construction Drawings—Wood Structure

The drawings that follow show the basic construction details for the wood structure. The drawings are essentially intended to show the structural details and are not all fully complete as architectural details. In many instances there are equivalent alternatives for

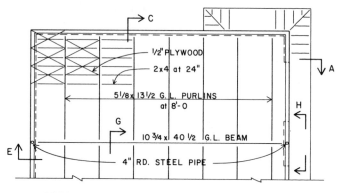

ROOF FRAMING PLAN

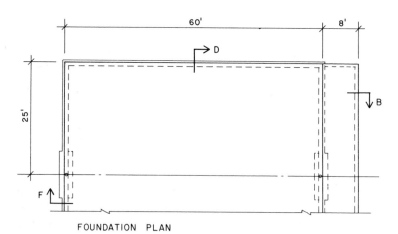

FOUNDATION PLAN

FIGURE 2.13.   Structural plans for the wood structure.

achieving the basic structural tasks, which could be more intelligently evaluated if all information about finish materials and architectural details were known. Some details may also be effected by considerations of the design of the lighting, electrical power, HVAC and plumbing systems or by problems of security, acoustics, fire ratings, and so on.

Note that the roof framing system used is System 2 as shown in

Figure 2.4. If System 1 with only the rafters and girders is used, some of the wall details would change.

Foundation and roof framing layouts are shown in the partial plans in Figure 2.13. Detail sections shown on the plans are illustrated in Figures 2.14 through 2.18. The following is a discussion of some of the considerations made in developing these details.

Detail A.   (Figure 2.14.) Detail A shows the canopy, parapet, shear wall, and roof at the front of the building. Depending on the height of the parapet and the location of the top of the canopy, it may be advisable to run the wall studs continuously to the top of the parapet. This would permit the top of the canopy to be higher than the roof deck. In any event, if the top of the canopy is not exactly at the level of the roof deck, as shown in Figure 2.14, additional framing would be required for the anchoring of the tie straps.

In the detail shown both the roof deck and wall sheathing are nailed directly to the top plate of the wall. This achieves a direct transfer of load from the horizontal to the vertical diaphragm. If the wall studs were continuous to the top of the parapet, a ledger would be provided at the face of the studs to support the rafters and provide for the edge nailing of the plywood. Transfer of the roof seismic load to the wall would then require the addition of blocking in the wall. This condition is illustrated in Detail C, Figure 2.15, in which the load transfer is from the roof plywood, through boundary nailing to the ledger, then from the ledger to the blocking, and finally from the blocking to the wall plywood.

At the point where the bottom of the canopy kicks into the wall the strut shown may be required to brace the studs. This may not be required at the solid portion of the wall, but is most likely required at openings, unless the header is designed for the combined vertical and horizontal loads.

If the parapet is simply built on top of the roof deck, as shown, the diagonal struts may be used to brace the canopy and form the cant at the roof edge.

Detail B.   (Figure 2.14.) Depending on the level of the exterior grade, the drainage situation and the wall finish materials, the sill plate may be simply put directly on the floor slab, as shown, or may be placed on top of a short curb to raise it above the floor level.

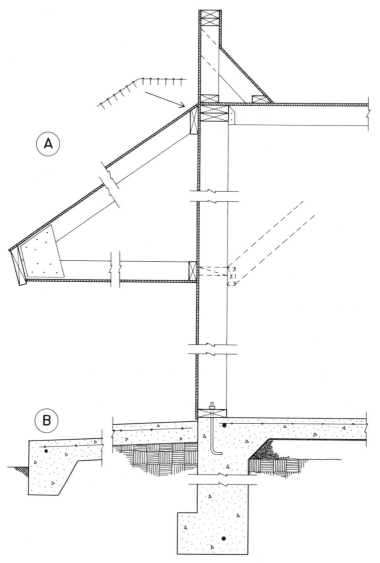

FIGURE 2.14. Details A and B.

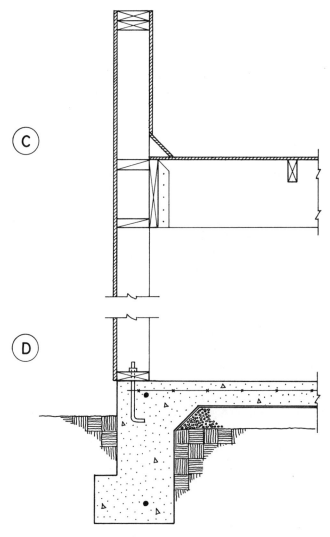

FIGURE 2.15.   Details C and D.

The details of the wall footing, grade wall and floor slab are subject to considerable variation. Some considerations are:

1. *Depth of the footing below grade.* For frost protection or simply to reach adequate bearing soil it may be necessary to have a deep grade wall. At some point this requires that it be treated as a true vertical wall with vertical reinforcement, a separate footing with dowels, and so on. In this case there would likely be three concrete pours with a cold joint between the footing, wall, and slab.

2. *Need for thermal insulation for the floor.* In cold climates it is desirable to provide a thermal break between the slab and the cold ground at the building edge. This would be done by placing insulation on the inside of the grade wall and/or by placing it under the slab along the wall.

3. *Cohesive nature of the soil.* If the soil at grade level is reasonably cohesive (just about anything but clean sand), and a shallow grade wall is possible, the footing, wall, and slab can be poured in a single pour. In this case the wall and footing are formed by simply trenching and providing a form for the outside wall surface and slab edge.

4. *Beam action of the grade wall.* Because of expansive soil, highly varying soil bearing conditions, or the use of the grade wall for distribution of concentrated forces from posts, tie-downs, and so on, it may be necessary to provide top and bottom reinforcing. In any event, a minimum of one bar should be used at each point for shrinkage and thermal stresses.

Detail C. (Figure 2.15.) Detail C shows the end wall condition where the roof purlins are supported by the wall. In this detail the wall studs are continuous to the top of the parapet and a ledger is provided to which the joist hangers for the purlins are attached. Because of the roof slope, the elevation of the purlins varies. This is simply accommodated by sloping the ledger, whereas if the wall were as in Detail A, all the studs would be different in length and the top plate of the wall would have to be sloped. Then the parapet studs would also be all different in length to achieve the level parapet top.

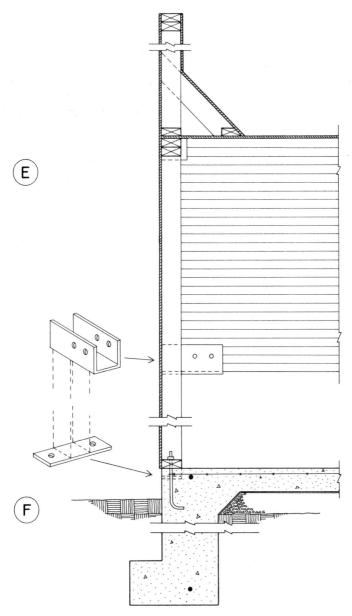

FIGURE 2.16. Details E and F.

As discussed for Detail A, the seismic load must be transferred from the roof to the wall by the circuitous route through the ledger and blocking. The vertical roof loading must also be transferred from the ledger to the studs. For a more positive tie it is recommended that the ledger be attached to the studs with lag screws. Two lag screws in each stud and one in each block would probably provide all the load transfers necessary.

Detail D. (Figure 2.15.) This is essentially the same condition as Detail B except for the absence of the exterior paving slab and the posts. Depending on the level of the exterior grade and the exterior

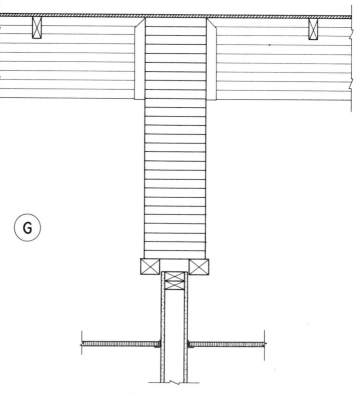

FIGURE 2.17. Detail G.

wall finish, it may be necessary to raise the sill on a curb, as previously discussed.

Detail E.   (Figure 2.16.) This shows the rear wall with the glue laminated girder framed into the wall. Note that the upper corner of the girder is notched to permit the wall plate to be continuous. The U-shaped bent plate would be welded to the steel column that is encased in the wall. If a wood column is used, the U-shaped plate would be welded to other plates which would be bolted to the wood column.

Detail F.   (Figure 2.16.) Most of the comments made for Details B and D are applicable here. The column footing would likely be poured separately with the grade wall and slab poured later. Depending on the construction sequence, as well as the height of the grade wall, it may be possible to set the base of the steel column as shown, directly on the footing, or on top of the floor slab. The detail as shown permits the wall sill to run all the way to the column, providing a maximum nailing edge for the plywood.

Detail G.   (Figure 2.17.) This detail shows the purlins framed in metal joist hangers on the sides of the girder. It also shows a detail for the top of an interior partition that allows for some live load deflection of the girder.

Detail H.   (Figure 2.18.) Detail H is a partial elevation of the framing of the front wall with the plywood removed. Shown are the following:

1.   Framing at the end of the girder, with the steel post and the bent plate.
2.   Support of the window header by a connection attached to the face of the wall end post, which permits the post to be continuous to the top of the parapet.
3.   Strapping of the end of the header to blocking in the wall, which reinforces the opening corner and allows the shear wall action as shown in Option 2 in Figure 2.10.
4.   Splicing of the top plate with bolts as described in the calculations. For ease of construction it would probably be desirable to oversize the top plate member and recess the bolt heads to clear the roof plywood.

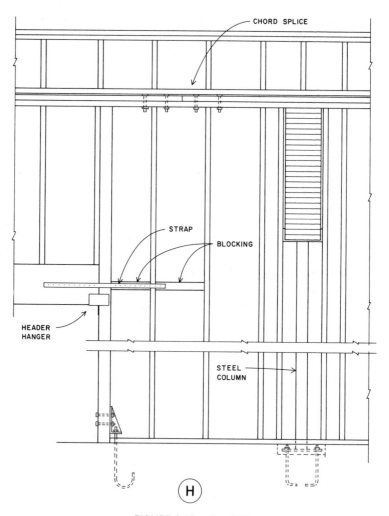

FIGURE 2.18.   Detail H.

2.8   Design of an Alternate Wood Roof

Figure 2.19 shows a solution for the wood roof structure that consists of prefabricated trusses and a plywood deck. The trusses are fabricated with wood top and bottom chords and steel web members. A number of manufacturers produce these predesigned trusses and the details vary. They are generally competitive with steel open web joists in the short to medium span range. The actual truss design is usually done by the staff or hired consultants retained by the manufacturer or distributor.

The depth of the trusses can usually be varied to facilitate the sloping roof surface, while maintaining a level bottom chord for the direct attachment of the ceiling. Direct attachment of the ceiling is usually possible, since the open webs of the trusses permit the passage of ducts and wiring. Although the trusses may be deeper than an all beam system, the resulting total distance from ceiling to roof is usually less with the trusses.

Another potential advantage of the truss system is a freeing of the structural module from the architectural planning. Location of doors, windows, and interior partitions need have no relation to the truss spacing.

Distribution of the roof gravity loads to the walls changes with this system and the walls and headers would be slightly different. The foundations for the end and rear walls would consist of continuous, constant width footings. The front wall loads will be collected into the solid wall sections, so the foundation may be the same here as in the steel column design.

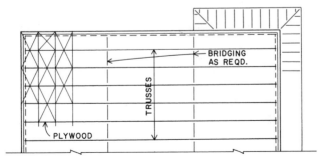

FIGURE 2.19.   Structural plan: wood truss system.

The plywood roof diaphragm and the shear wall designs would be essentially the same. Overturn of the front wall piers is less critical, since the header columns will be more heavily loaded in this scheme.

Some investigation of alternatives for the truss spacing would be done to determine the most economical system. There is a trade-off between the size of the trusses on one hand and the roof plywood thickness and ceiling framing on the other hand. Using standard 8 ft plywood sheets, the usual modules would be 24, 32, or 48 in. In

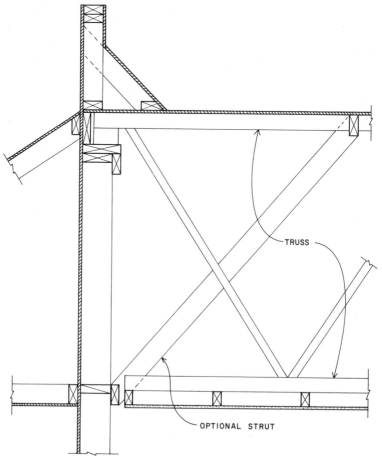

FIGURE 2.20.   Front wall detail: wood truss system.

some areas longer sheets of plywood are available and would make possible the consideration of 10 or 12 ft module increments. The use of plywood with tongue-and-groove edges may eliminate the necessity for blocking perpendicular to the trusses.

Figure 2.20 shows a modification of Detail A from the previous system. The precise detailing of the truss supports and the details for transfer of the roof diaphragm load to the walls would depend somewhat on the specific manufacturer's products.

2.9 The Steel and Masonry Structure

Figure 2.21 shows the layout for a structure for Building Two consisting of a steel framed roof and exterior masonry walls. In order to

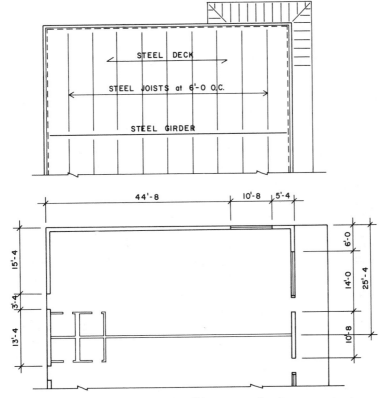

FIGURE 2.21.   Roof framing and wall layouts: steel and masonry structure.

relate to the usual 16 in. horizontal block dimension, the plan dimensions of the walls have been modified slightly, as shown on the partial plans. The roof system is similar in layout to the first wood scheme, with rolled steel sections replacing the glue laminated girders and wood joists and a light gauge steel deck replacing the plywood. Because of the seismic load condition, reinforced concrete block is used for the exterior walls.

The following materials will be used:

Structural steel: A36, $F_y = 36$ ksi.

Concrete: sand and gravel aggregate, $f_c' = 3000$ psi.

Masonry: reinforced hollow unit masonry; units: concrete block, Grade N, ASTM C90, sand and gravel, $f_m' = 1500$ psi; mortar: type S.

Reinforcing (concrete and masonry): $f_y = 40$ ksi.

2.10   Design of the Steel Roof Structure

Dead loads:

Roofing: tar and gravel, 6.5 psf.

Insulation: rigid type on top of deck, assume 2 psf.

Suspended ceiling: gypsum plaster, assume 10 psf total.

Lights, wiring, ducts, registers: assume 3 psf average.

Total dead load: 21.5 psf + the structure.

Roof deck.   A number of roof deck systems may be considered, including those with lightweight concrete or gypsum concrete fill. We will use an ordinary single sheet, ribbed steel deck, type A or B, . which can span the 6 ft between joists with a fairly light steel gauge. As the seismic design will show later, the deck gauge must be quite heavy if the roof diaphragm is made to span the entire 150 ft between the end shear walls. Design for the gravity loads is thus less critical.

We will assume the deck gauge to be approximately 18, which gives a dead load of approximately 2 psf. The relative cost of specific products in a given area and the interrelation of the deck span, the joist spacing, the seismic stresses, and so on, must be studied for each design situation.

Joists.   Several options are possible for the joists. These may be light rolled I-shaped sections, open web steel joists, or cold-formed sections of light gauge sheet metal. With the joists at 6 ft centers the loading will be:

Dead load plus live load: 23.5 + 20 = 43.5 psf.

Load/joist: 43.5 × 6 = 261 plf + the joist weight/ft.

For design use: total load = 275 plf.

Using a total load deflection limit of $L/180$, the allowable deflection will be

$$\frac{25 \times 12}{180} = 1.67 \text{ in.}$$

Using the beam load/span tables from the AISC Manual, we first determine the total load to be (see the Appendix)

$$W = 25 \times 0.275 = 6.875 \text{ kips}$$

For this load some possible selections are $W12 \times 14$ or $M12 \times 11.8$.

For the ligher M section the actual total load deflection may be interpolated from the table listed deflection as follows:

$$\text{actual deflection} = \frac{\text{actual load}}{\text{table load}} \text{ (table deflection)}$$

$$= \frac{6.875}{7.7} (1.29) = 1.15 \text{ in.}$$

Choice for a rolled section: $M12 \times 11.8$

Girder.   With the joists at 6 ft centers the actual load on the girder consists of nine joist loads plus the weight of the girder. Because of the large area supported by the girder, the live load may be reduced to 12 psf. The design load will thus be

$DL + LL$:	25.5 + 12 = 37.5 psf (including average joist weight)
Joist load:	9 × 6 × 25 × 37.5 = 50,625 lb
Assumed girder weight:	75 × 60 = 4,500
Total $DL + LL$:	= 55,125 lb

The lateral unsupported length is 6 ft, which should not be critical for this large member. Selection can be made from the load/span tables as for the joist or the maximum moment can be found and used with the S-listing tables or the graphs that incorporate the lateral unsupported length consideration (see the Appendix):

$$\text{maximum } M = \frac{WL}{8} = \frac{(55.1)(60)}{8} = 413.25 \text{ k/ft}$$

From the S listings the lightest section is a $W27 \times 84$ and the next lightest is a $W24 \times 94$. If headroom is considered critical, the 24 in. deep member may be more desirable, although its deflection should be checked as follows:

Table listed total allowable load: 59 kips (half that for a 30 ft span, since the table goes only to 50 ft).

Table deflection: 3.72 in. (four times that for 30 ft).

Actual deflection: $\dfrac{55.1}{59} (3.72) = 3.47$ in.

Allowable deflection: $60(12)/180 = 4.0$ in.

While this deflection is technically permitted, the girder should be cambered approximately 2.5 in. so that it will be flat under the dead load.

Alternate choices: $W27 \times 84$ or $W24 \times 94$.

Column for the Girder.   Options for the girder support are to use a steel column or a reinforced pilaster on the masonry wall. Since the total end load for the steel girder is close to that for the wood girder, the steel column would be similar to that previously designed. In order to allow the wall to be continuous for seismic shear resistance, it would probably be placed just inside the wall surface with some ties to the wall for lateral support.

The design of the pilaster is included in the masonry wall design which follows. Both options are shown in the construction details at the end of this section.

2.11   Design of the Masonry Walls

It is assumed that the walls will consist of reinforced, hollow concrete blocks with finishes of stucco on the exterior and gypsum drywall on furring strips on the interior. The following design is done in accordance with the UBC requirements and with the procedures illustrated in the *Concrete Masonry Design Manual* prepared by the Concrete Masonry Design Association of California (reference 10).

The exterior walls must be designed for the combined effects of gravity and lateral forces, as follows (see Figure 2.22):

1. Design for vertical gravity dead load + live load.
2. Design for vertical gravity dead load plus live load plus bending in a vertical plane due to direct lateral force.
3. Design for horizontal shear and possible overturn due to dead load only plus the transferred lateral forces caused by the walls acting as shear walls for the building.

At the front of the building the total unsupported height of the walls will be approximately 15.5 ft. This assumes the girders to be sloped to the rear of the building for roof drainage. The height of the wall is then considered to be from the floor slab to the roof deck.

UBC Table 24-I permits a maximum unsupported height-to-thickness ratio of 25 for reinforced hollow unit masonry walls. The minimum required thickness is therefore

$$\frac{15.5(12)}{25} = 7.44 \text{ in.}$$

This permits the use of a nominal 8 in. thick block, which would probably also be used for the other, shorter walls.

For vertical axial compression the UBC allows a stress of

$$f_m = 0.20 f'_m \left[1 - \left(\frac{h}{40t} \right)^3 \right] \text{[Section 2418(j)2]}$$

$$= 0.20(1500) \left[1 - \left(\frac{186}{40(7.625)} \right)^3 \right] = 232 \text{ psi}$$

UBC Table 24-H (see the Appendix) states that this value must be reduced by one half if code required inspection is not provided. UBC

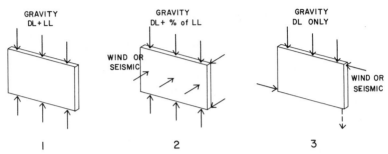

FIGURE 2.22.   Load cases for the walls.

Table 24-H also indicates that the allowable stress in hollow masonry construction is based on the net wall section. Assuming both these reductions, and an average block density of 45% solid, the allowable load per foot of wall is thus

$$w = (0.45)(7.625 \times 12)\left(\frac{232}{2}\right) = 4766 \text{ lb/ft of wall}$$

This is adequate for all of the gravity load conditions, except at the points of concentrated loads from the girders and headers. If a pilaster is used at the girder, the support becomes a solid grouted, 16 in. square column with the girder load placed approximately 4 in. eccentric from the column center. At the header supports the end of the wall becomes a solid grouted 8 in. square column. Both of these may be adequately designed for the gravity loads.

The direct lateral load on the wall is either the direct wind pressure or the effect of the seismic force due to the weight of the wall applied perpendicular to its surface. Assuming the 8 in. block wall with grouted cells at 32 in. and the applied finishes of stucco and drywall, the wall weighs approximately 80 lb/ft². UBC Table 23-J requires a C_p of 0.20, which makes the lateral design load:

$$F_p = 0.20(W) = 0.20(80) = 16 \text{ psf}$$

Since this is less than the wind pressure of 20 psf, we will check this condition for gravity plus wind. The stress condition consists of adding the axial compression due to gravity to the bending due to wind with the wall spanning vertically. The gravity load used is the dead load plus half the roof live load. (See UBC 2311j.)

The rear wall is least critical due to its shorter height, the low roof load, and the absence of the canopy. We assume its height to be 13.75 ft from the floor to the bottom of the steel ledger that supports the deck.

Axial load:	Roof $(23.5 + 10)(3)$	$= 100.5$ plf
	Wall $(80$ psf$)(18$ ft$)$	$= 1440$ plf
Axial compression:	$1540.5/(7.625 \times 12 \times 0.45) =$	37.4 psi
	(This is conservative, since it ignores the concrete filled cavities in the wall.)	
Bending:	$M = wL^2/8 = 20(13.75)^2/8 =$	472.7 lb/ft

For the initial reinforcing design we ignore the axial compression and design for wind only. From UBC 2418(b) the allowable f_s is 20 ksi, increased for wind to 26.7 ksi. From UBC Table 24-H the modulus of the block wall is $500(f'_m)$ or 750,000 psi. Thus,

$$n = \frac{E_s}{E_c} = \frac{30}{0.75} = 40$$

Assuming the reinforcing in the center of the wall,

$$\text{effective } d = \frac{7.625}{2} = 3.812 \text{ in.}$$

From UBC Table 24-H

$$f_m = 1.33(0.166 f'_m) = 331 \text{ psi}$$

To find an approximate area of steel we assume a j of 0.85. Then

$$A_s = \frac{M}{f_s(jd)} = \frac{0.473(12)}{26.7(0.85)(3.812)}$$

$$= 0.0656 \text{ in.}^2/\text{ft of wall length}$$

Try: No. 5 at 48, $A_s = 0.31/4 = 0.0775$ in.^{2}/ft.

With a steel area determined we can now find the actual values for k and j and check the stresses in the steel and the masonry. Any tables, graphs, or equations could be used for this. We have used the tables from page III-70 of the *Concrete Masonry Design Manual* (reference 10).

$$p = \frac{A_s}{bd} = \frac{0.0775}{12 \times 3.812} = 0.00169$$

$$np = 40(0.00169) = 0.0676$$

Then

$$k = 0.3063, \qquad j = 0.8979$$

$$f_s = \frac{M}{A_s(jd)} = \frac{0.473(12)}{0.0775(0.8979)(3.812)}$$

$$= 21.40 \text{ ksi (less than the allowable of 26.7)}$$

$$f_m = \frac{M}{bd^2}\left(\frac{2}{kj}\right) = \frac{473(12)(2)}{(12)(3.812)^2(0.3063)(0.8979)}$$

$$= 236.7 \text{ psi (less than the allowable of 331)}$$

For the combined stress condition:

$$\frac{f_a}{F_a} + \frac{f_b}{F_b} = \frac{37.4}{1.33(116)} + \frac{236.7}{331} = 0.242 + 0.715 = 0.957 < 1$$

For the end walls the height increases from the rear to the front of the building. At the window openings the ends of the walls will be designed as columns to take the vertical and horizontal loads from the headers. The long solid wall is similar to the rear wall, except for the increased height and a higher roof load. We will assume a maximum height of 14.5 ft and check it as follows:

Axial load:	Roof $(25.5 + 10)(12.5 \text{ ft})$	=	444 plf
	Wall $(80 \text{ psf})(18 \text{ ft})$	=	1440 plf
Axial f_m:	$1884/(7.625 \times 12)(0.45)$	=	45.8 psi
Bending:	$M = wL^2/8 = 20(14.5)^2/8$ =		526 lb/ft

With the same reinforcing of No. 5 at 48 (by proportion from the previous calculations):

$$f_s = 21.40\left(\frac{526}{473}\right) = 23.8 \text{ ksi}$$

$$f_m = 236.7\left(\frac{526}{473}\right) = 263.2 \text{ psi}$$

With these stresses the combined stress condition will slightly exceed one, so that it will be necessary to increase the bar size or reduce the spacing of the bars. No. 5 bars at 32 in. spacing will be found as one solution.

At the large wall openings the headers will transfer both vertical and horizontal loads to the ends of the supporting walls. The ends of these walls will be designed as reinforced masonry columns for this condition. Figure 2.23 shows the details and the loading condition for the header columns. In addition to this loading the columns are

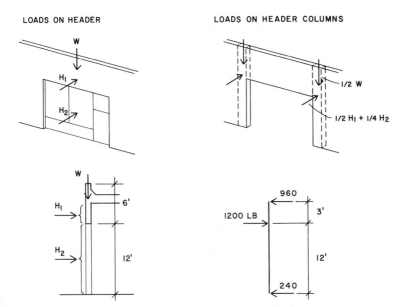

LOADS ON HEADER

LOADS ON HEADER COLUMNS

FIGURE 2.23. Loads on the header and columns.

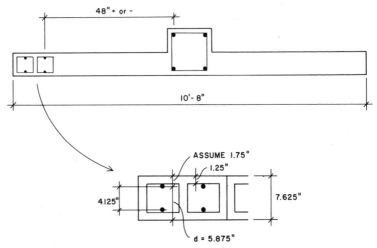

FIGURE 2.24.   Details of the front wall.

part of the wall and must carry some of the axial load and bending as previously determined for the typical wall.

Figure 2.24 shows a plan layout for the entire solid front wall section, which includes the pilaster for the support of the girder. Because of its relative stiffness, the pilaster column will tend to take a large share of the direct wind load, so we will assume only a 2 ft strip of wall loading on the end column. As shown in Figure 2.24, the end column is a doubly reinforced beam for the direct wind loading.

Gravity load
on the header: Roof   = 100 plf (same as rear wall)

Wall   = (80) psf)(6 ft) = 480 plf

Canopy   = 100 plf (assumed)

Total load = 680 plf

Wind load   (see Figure 2.23)

Assuming the window mullions span vertically and a 2 ft high strip of loading for H_1:

$$H_1 = (20 \text{ psf})(2 \times 15) = 600 \text{ lb}$$

$$H_2 = (20 \text{ psf})(12 \times 15) = 3600 \text{ lb}$$

Thus the column loads from the header are:

vertical load $= (680 \text{ plf})(15/2) = 5100 \text{ lb}$

horizontal load $= (\frac{1}{2}H_1 + \frac{1}{4}H_2) = 300 + 900 = 1200 \text{ lb}$

moment $= 960(3) = 2880 \text{ lb/ft}$ (see Figure 2.23)

For the direct wind load on the wall we assume a 15 ft vertical span and a 2 ft wide strip of wall loading. Thus

$$M = \frac{wL^2}{8} = \frac{(20 \text{ psf})(2)(15)^2}{8} = 1125 \text{ lb/ft}$$

These two moments do not peak at the same point, so without doing a more exact analysis we will assume a maximum combined moment of 3800 lb/ft. Then, for the moment alone, assuming a j of 0.85:

$$\text{required } A_s : \frac{M}{f_s(jd)} = \frac{3.8(12)}{26.7(0.85)(5.9)} = 0.34 \text{ in.}^2$$

$$\text{approximate } f_m : \frac{M}{bd^2}\left(\frac{2}{kj}\right) = \frac{3800(12)(2)}{(16)(5.9)^2(0.4)(0.85)} = 482 \text{ psi}$$

Here f_m is high but we have ignored the effect of the compressive reinforcing. The following is an approximate analysis based on the two moment theory with 2 No. 5 bars on each side of the column.

Assuming the axial load to be almost negligible compared to the moment, we analyze for the full moment effect only. With a maximum stress of 331 psi we first determine the moment capacity with tension reinforcing only as follows:

$$M_1 = \frac{f_m(bd^2)(k)(j)}{2}\left(\frac{1}{12}\right) = \frac{331(16)(5.9)^2(0.4)(0.85)}{2(12)} = 2612 \text{ lb/ft}$$

This leaves a moment for the compressive reinforcing of

$$M_2 = 3800 - 2600 = 1200 \text{ lb/ft}$$

If the compressive reinforcing is two #5 bars, then

$$f_s' = \frac{M_2}{A_s'(d - d')} = \frac{1200(12)}{(0.62)(4.125)} = 5630 \text{ psi}$$

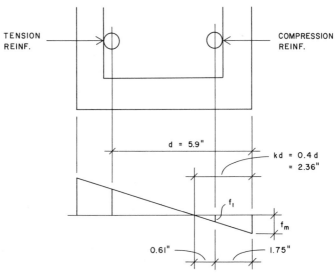

FIGURE 2.25.   Stress in the header column.

This is a reasonable stress, even with the assumed low k value of 0.4. As shown in Figure 2.25, if k is 0.4 and f_m is 331, the compatible strain value for f_s' will be

$$f_s' = 2n(f_c) = 2(40)(3.31)\left(\frac{0.61}{2.36}\right) = 6844 \text{ psi}$$

As shown by the preceding calculation, the stress in the tension reinforcing will not be critical. This approximate analysis indicates that the column is reasonably adequate for the moment. The axial load capacity should also be checked, using the procedure shown later for the pilaster design.

Window Header.   As shown later in Figure 2.26, the header consists of a 6 ft deep section of wall. This section will have continuous reinforcing at the top of the wall and at the bottom of the header. In addition there will be a continuous reinforced bond beam in the wall at the location of the steel ledger that supports the edge of the roof deck.

Using the loading previously determined, and an approximate design moment of $wL^2/10$, the steel area required for gravity alone will be as follows:

$$A_s = \frac{M}{f_s(jd)}$$

where $M = wL^2/10 = 680(15)^2/10 = 15,300$ lb/ft

d = approximately 68 in.

Then

$$A_s = \frac{15.3(12)}{(20)(0.85)(68)} = 0.159 \text{ in.}^2$$

This indicates that the minimum reinforcing at the top of the wall may be two #3 bars or one #4 bar. This should be compared with the code requirement for minimum wall reinforcing. UBC 2418(j)3 calls for a minimum of 0.0007 times the gross cross-sectional area of the wall in either direction and a sum of 0.002 times the gross cross-sectional area of the wall in both directions. Thus:

minimum $A_s = 0.0007(7.625)(12) = 0.064 \text{ in.}^2$/ft of width or height
with two #3 bars $A_s = 0.22 \text{ in.}^2$

$$\text{required spacing} = \frac{0.22}{0.064} = 3.44 \text{ ft or } 41.3 \text{ in.}$$

The minimum horizontal reinforcing would then be two #3 bars at 40 in., or every fifth block course.

At the bottom of the header there is also a horizontal force consisting of the previously calculated wind load plus some force from the cantilevered canopy. Estimating this total horizontal force to be 250 lb/ft, we add a horizontal moment as follows:

$$M = \frac{wL^2}{10} = \frac{0.25(15)^2}{10} = 5.625 \text{ k/ft}$$

For which we require:

$$A_s = \frac{M}{f_s(jd)} = \frac{5.625(12)}{(26.7)(0.85)(5.9)} = 0.504 \text{ in.}^2$$

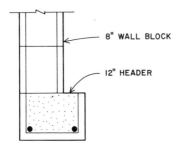

8" WALL BLOCK

12" HEADER

FIGURE 2.26. Alternate header detail.

This must be added to the previous area required for the vertical gravity loads:

$$\text{total } A_s = 0.504 + \frac{(\frac{1}{2})(0.159)}{1.33} = 0.504 + 0.060 = 0.564 \text{ in.}^2$$

The requirement for vertical load is divided by 2, since it is shared by both bottom bars. It is divided by 1.33, since the previous calculation did not include the increase of allowable stresses for wind loading. If this total area is satisfied, the bottom bars in the header would have to be two #7s. An alternative would be to increase the width of the header at the bottom by using a 12 in. wide block for the bottom course, as shown in Figure 2.26. This widened course would be made continuous in the wall.

The Pilaster/Column.   In order to permit the wall construction to be continuous, the girder stops short of the inside of the wall and rests on the widened portion of the wall, called a pilaster. As shown in Figure 2.27, the pilaster and wall together form a 16 in. square column. The principal gravity loading on the column is due to the end reaction of the girder. Since this load is eccentrically placed, it produces both axial force and bending on the column. The parapet, canopy, and column weight add to the axial compression.

Because of its increased stiffness, the column tends to take a considerable portion of the wind pressure on the solid portion of the wall. We will assume it to take a 6 ft wide strip of this load. As shown in Figure 2.28, the direct wind pressure on the wall (pushing inward on the outer surface) causes a bending moment of opposite sign from

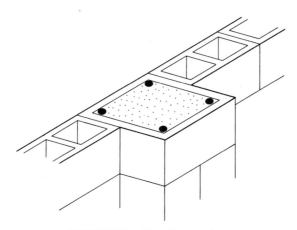

FIGURE 2.27.   The pilaster column.

that due to the eccentric girder load. The critical wind load is therefore due to the outward wind pressure (suction force) on the wall. For a conservative design we will take this to be equal to the inward pressure of 20 psf. The combined moments are thus

$$\text{wind moment} = \frac{wL^2}{8} = \frac{(20)(6)(13.33)^2}{8} = 2665 \text{ lb/ft}$$

Assuming an e of 4 in. for the girder (see Figure 2.36):

$$\text{girder moment} = \frac{23.5(4)}{12} = 7.833 \text{ k/ft, or } 7833 \text{ lb/ft}$$

For the combined wind plus gravity loading we have used only half the live load [see UBC 2312(j)]. With the allowable stress increase, it should be apparent that this loading condition is not critical, so we will design for the gravity loads only. For this we will redetermine the girder-induced moment with full live load:

$$\text{girder } M = \frac{27.6(4)}{12} = 9.2 \text{ k/ft}$$

The gravity loads of the canopy, parapet, roof edge, and column must be added. We will therefore assume a total vertical design load

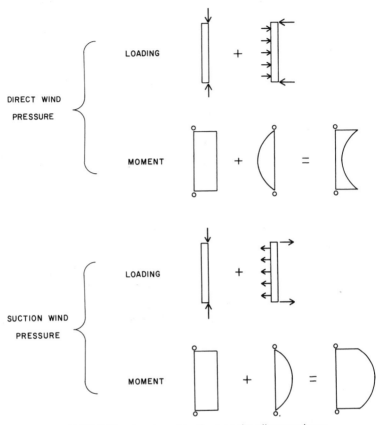

FIGURE 2.28. Load combinations on the pilaster column.

of approximately 35 kips. With this total load the equivalent eccentricity for design will be

$$e = \frac{M}{N} = \frac{9.2(12)}{35} = 3.15 \text{ in.}$$

UBC 2418(k)1 requires a minimum percentage of reinforcing of 0.005 of the gross column area. Thus

$$\text{minimum } A_s = 0.005(16)^2 = 1.28 \text{ in.}^2$$

with 4 No. 6 bars $A_s = 1.76 \text{ in.}^2$, actual $p_g = 0.0069$

Then from UBC 2418(k)2 the allowable axial load is

$$P = A_g(0.18f'_m + 0.65p_gf_s)\left[1 - \left(\frac{h}{40t}\right)^3\right]$$

for which

$$A_g = 256 \text{ in.}^2, \qquad f_s = 0.40f_y = 16 \text{ ksi}$$
$$h = 13.3 \text{ ft} = 160 \text{ in.}$$

$$P = 256[(0.18)(1.5) + 0.65(0.0069)(16)]\left[1 - \left(\frac{160}{40(16)}\right)^3\right]$$

$$= 86.1 \text{ kips}$$

Ignoring the compression steel, the approximate moment capacity is

$$M = A_s f_s(jd) = \frac{0.88(20)(0.85)(13.5)}{12} = 16.83 \text{ k/ft}$$

Although a more exact analysis should be performed, this indicates generally that the column is reasonably adequate for the axial load and moment previously determined.

2.12   Design of the Foundations

The foundations for this structure will be essentially similar to those for the wood structure. Continuous wall footings will be provided under all the exterior walls, except at the columns. The same options described for the previous structure are possible for the column footing.

For the end walls the load is:

Roof:	45.5(12.5) =	569 plf
Wall:	80(18)	= 1440
Grade wall and footing		= 300 (estimate)
Total load		= 2309 plf
Width required:	2309/2000 =	1.15 ft or 14 in. minimum

At the front wall the column load and header loads are carried by the solid wall portion. If the same scheme used in the previous structure is desired, we would provide a 12 ft long footing for this total load.

Girder end reaction: 27.6 kips.

Roof edge load: 3(25)(37.5 psf) = 2.8 kips.

Header dead load: 80(6)(14) = 6.7 kips.

Wall dead load: 80(18)(10.67) = 15.4 kips.

Pilaster: 1.8 kips.

Grade wall and footing: 700 plf(12) = 8.4 kips (estimate).

Total footing load: 62.7 kips.

Width required: 62.7/(2)(12) = 2.61 ft.

This is actually less than the width used for the other, lighter structure, because the design in that case was done for equalized dead load. With the higher proportion of dead to live load in this structure, this equalization is more questionable. If done, however, it would probably result in approximately the same footing as for the wood structure.

A consideration for the detailing of the foundations for this structure is the need for placing of the dowels for the wall reinforcing. The construction details shown later illustrate this problem.

2.13 Design for Seismic Load

The lateral load resistive system for this structure is basically the same as that for the wood structure, consisting of the horizontal roof diaphragm and the vertical shear walls. The only significant difference is the increased load due to the heavier construction; most notably due to the exterior walls which are approximately four times as heavy. Reference may be made to the general discussion and illustrations for the previous design.

The calculation of the loads applied to the roof diaphragm is shown in Table 2.3. In the north–south direction the load is symmetrically placed, the shear walls are symmetrical in plan, and the long diaphragm is reasonably flexible, all of which results in very

TABLE 2.3.   Loads to the Roof Diaphragm (Kips)

Load Source and Calculation	North–South Load (in the Short Direction)	East–West Load (in the Long Direction)
Roof dead load		
150 × 60 × 28.5 psf	257	257
North–south exterior walls		
50 × 11 × 80 psf × 2	0	88
10 × 6 × 80 × 2	0	10
10 × 6 × 10 psf × 2	0	1
North wall		
150 × 12 × 80 psf	144	0
South wall		
65.3 × 10 × 80 psf	52	0
84 × 6 × 80	40	0
84 × 6 × 10	5	0
Interior north–south partitions		
60 × 7 × 10 psf × 5	0	21
Toilet walls		
Estimated 150 × 7 × 10 psf	10	10
Canopy		
South: 150 × 100	15	15
East and West: 40 × 100	4	4
Rooftop HVAC units (estimate)	5	5
Total load	532	411

little potential torsion. Although the code requires that a minimum torsion be considered by placing the load off center by 5% of the building long dimension, the effect will be very little on the shear walls.

At the ends of the building the shear stress in the edge of the diaphragm will be

$$\text{north–south total } V = 0.1862(532) = 99 \text{ kips}$$

$$\text{maximum } v = \frac{49{,}500}{60} = 825 \text{ plf}$$

This is a very high shear for the metal deck. It would require a heavy gauge deck and considerable welding at the diaphragm edge. While it would probably be wise to reconsider the general design and possibly use at least one permanent interior partition, we will assume the deck to span the building length for the shear wall design.

In the other direction the shear in the roof deck will be considerably less.

$$\text{east--west total } V = 0.1862(411) = 76.5 \text{ kips}$$

$$\text{maximum } v = \frac{38,250}{150} = 255 \text{ plf}$$

This is very low for the deck, so if any interior shear walls are added, the deck gauge could probably be reduced to that required for the gravity loads only.

In the north–south direction, with no added shear walls, the end shear force will be taken almost entirely by the long block walls because of their relative stiffness. Ignoring any stress in the shorter walls, the load on the long walls will be

$$v = \frac{49,500}{44.67} = 1108 \text{ plf of wall}$$

And the stress on the net block area will be

$$v = \frac{1108}{(7.625)(12)(0.45)} = 26.9 \text{ psi}$$

From UBC Table 24-H, with reinforcing taking all shear and no special inspection, the allowable shear is dependent on the value of M/Vd for the wall. This is determined as follows:

$$\frac{M}{Vd} = \frac{49,500(15 \text{ ft})}{49,500(44.67)} = 0.336$$

Interpolating between the table values for M/Vd of 1 and 0:

$$\text{allowable } v = 51.6 \text{ psi}$$

A footnote to the table requires that the shear load be increased by a factor of 1.5 for shear stress calculations. Thus

$$\text{critical design shear stress} = 1.5(26.9) = 40.35 \text{ psi}$$

This indicates that the masonry stress is adequate, but we must check the wall reinforcing for its capacity as shear reinforcement. With the previously determined minimum horizontal reinforcing of two No. 3 bars at 40 in., the critical shear load on the bars would be

$$\text{total } V = 1108 \text{ plf}\left(\frac{40}{12}\right)(1.5) = 5540 \text{ lb}$$

$$\text{required } A_s = \frac{5540}{26,667} = 0.21 \text{ in.}^2$$

actual A_s with 2 No. 3 bars $= 0.22$ in.^{2}

Additional shear will be placed on these walls because of the effect of torsion, requiring an increase in the reinforcing. As the following analysis will show, the critical torsion is due to the eccentricity of the east–west lateral force.

In the east–west direction the shear walls are not symmetrical in plan, which requires that a calculation be made to determine the location of the center of rigidity so that the torsional moment may be determined. The total loading is reasonably centered in this direction, so we will assume the center of gravity to be in the center of the plan.

The following analysis is based on the examples in the *Concrete Masonry Design Manual* (reference 10.) The individual piers are assumed to be fixed at top and bottom and their stiffnesses are found from the table on p. III-98 of the reference (see the Appendix.) The stiffness of the piers and the total wall stiffnesses are determined in Figure 2.29. For the location of the center of stiffness we use the values determined for the north and south walls:

$$\bar{y} = \frac{(R \text{ for the S wall})(60 \text{ ft})}{(\text{sum of the } R \text{ values for the N and S walls})} = \frac{2.96(60)}{17.57}$$

$$= 10.11 \text{ ft}$$

The torsional resistance of the entire shear wall system is found as the sum of the products of the individual wall rigidities times the square of their distances from the center of stiffness. This summation

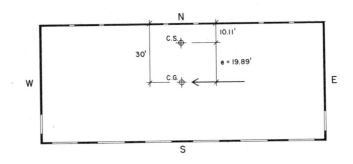

EAST & WEST WALLS

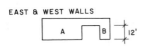

PIER	H ft.	D ft.	H/D	R*	No.	ΣR
A	12	44.67	0.269	3.03	1	3.03
B	12	5.33	2.251	0.14	1	0.14

TOTAL WALL R = 3.17

NORTH WALL

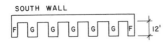

C	7	15.33	0.457	1.71	2	3.42
D	7	13.33	0.525	1.45	3	4.35
E	7	29.33	0.239	3.42	2	6.84

14.61

SOUTH WALL

| F | 12 | 6 | 2 | 0.18 | 2 | 0.36 |
| G | 12 | 10.67 | 1.125 | 0.52 | 5 | 2.60 |

2.96

* FROM REF. NO. 10 - SEE APPENDIX

FIGURE 2.29.   Stiffness analysis of the masonry walls.

120

TABLE 2.4   Torsional Resistance of the Masonry Shear Walls

Wall	Total Wall R	Distance from Center of Stiffness (ft)	$R(d)^2$
South	2.96	49.89	7,367
North	14.61	10.11	1,495
East	3.17	75	17,831
West	3.17	75	17,831
Total torsional moment of inertia (J)			44,524

is shown in Table 2.4. The torsional shear load for each wall is then found as follows:

$$V_w = \frac{Tc}{J} = \frac{(V)(e)(c)(\text{the } R \text{ for the wall})}{(\text{the sum of the } Rd^2 \text{ for all walls})}$$

In the north–south direction UBC 2312(e)5 requires that the load be applied with a minimum eccentricity of 5 % of the building length, or 7.5 ft. While this produces less torsional moment than the east–west load, it is additive to the direct north–south shear, and therefore critical for the end walls. The torsional load for the end walls is thus

$$V_w = \frac{(99)(7.5)(75)(3.17)}{44,524} = 3.96 \text{ kips}$$

As mentioned previously, this should be added to the direct shear of 49,500 lb for the design of these walls.

For the north wall:

$$V_w = \frac{(76.5)(19.89)(10.11)(14.61)}{44,524} = 5.05 \text{ kips}$$

This is actually opposite in direction to the direct shear, but the code does not allow the reduction, so the direct shear only is used. For the south wall:

$$V_w = \frac{(76.5)(19.89)(49.89)(2.96)}{44,524} = 5.05 \text{ kips}$$

The total direct east–west shear will be distributed between the north and south walls in proportion to the wall stiffnesses:

$$\text{for the north wall:}\ V_w = \frac{76.5(14.61)}{17.57} = 63.6\ \text{kips}$$

$$\text{for the south wall:}\ V_w = \frac{76.5(2.96)}{17.57} = 12.9\ \text{kips}$$

The total shear loads on the walls are therefore

$$\text{north:}\ V = 63.6\ \text{kips}$$

$$\text{south:}\ V = 5.05 + 12.9 = 17.95\ \text{kips}$$

The loads on the individual piers are then distributed in proportion to the pier stiffnesses (R) as determined in Figure 2.29. The calculation for this distribution and the determination of the unit shear stresses per foot of wall are shown in Table 2.5. A comparison with the previous calculations for the end walls will show that these stresses are not critical for the 8 in. block walls.

TABLE 2.5   Shear Stresses in the Masonry Walls

Wall	Shear Force on Wall (kips)	Wall R	Pier	Pier R	Shear Force on Pier (kips)	Pier Length (ft)	Shear Stress in Pier (lb/ft)
North	63.6	14.61	C	1.71	7.44	15.33	485
			D	1.45	6.31	13.33	473
			E	3.42	14.89	29.33	508
South	17.95	2.96	F	0.18	1.09	6	182
			G	0.52	3.15	10.67	296

In most cases the stabilizing dead loads plus the doweling of the end reinforcing into the foundations will be sufficient to resist overturn effects. The heavy loading on the header columns and the pilasters will provide considerable resistance for most walls. The

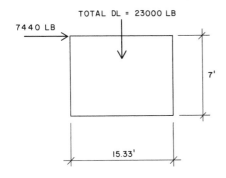

FIGURE 2.30.   Stability of wall C.

only wall not so loaded is wall C, for which the loading condition is shown in Figure 2.30. The overturn analysis for this wall is as follows:

$$\text{overturn } M = (7400)(7.0)(1.5) = 78,120 \text{ lb/ft}$$

$$\text{stabilizing } M = 23,000\left(\frac{15.33}{2}\right) = 176,295 \text{ lb/ft}$$

This indicates that the wall is stable without any requirement for anchorage.

2.14   Design of an Alternate Steel Roof Structure

Figure 2.31 shows a layout for a roof system utilizing open web steel joists. This system is essentially similar to the alternate system for the wood structure, although the spacing is free of the constraints of the plywood span and module limits.

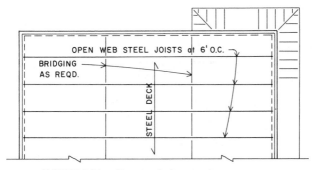

FIGURE 2.31.   Structural plan: steel truss system.

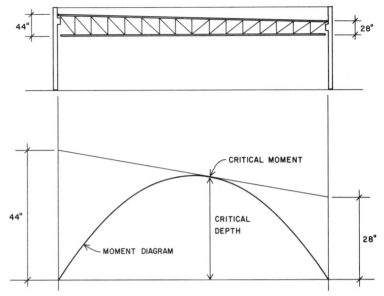

FIGURE 2.32.   Depth variation of the steel truss.

With the joists on 6 ft centers the joist depth would be from 30 to 36 in., depending on the type of joist used. Assuming a design depth of 32 in., Figure 2.32 shows how the depth could be varied to facilitate roof drainage.

Figure 2.33 shows a modification of the front wall for this system. (For comparison see Figure 2.14.) The parapet wall is reduced in thickness to 6 in. and the wall below the joist seat and down to the bottom of the header is thickened to 12 in. This provides a 6 in. shelf to accommodate the steel ledger for the deck and the seat for the joist. The thickened portion produces a heavier header for the larger loading.

Below the header the wall could be maintained as a 12 in. wall or could consist of a series of 12 by 16 in. columns at the wall ends with an 8 in. wall between. These possibilities are shown in the sketches in Figure 2.34. At the north wall, without the header condition, the thickened portion could be reduced to two courses. If the wall is capable of the eccentric loading, it could be 8 in. below this point.

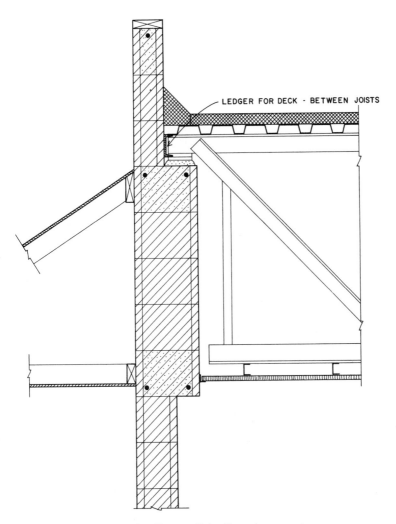

LEDGER FOR DECK - BETWEEN JOISTS

FIGURE 2.33. Front wall detail: steel truss system.

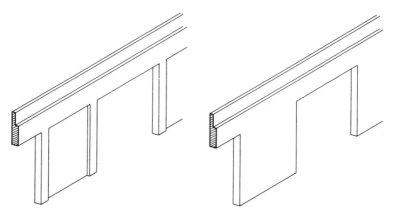

FIGURE 2.34. Options for the front wall.

If not, it could be increased to 12 in. or also use a series of pilaster columns.

2.15 Construction Drawings—Steel and Masonry Structure

Figures 2.35 through 2.38 show the layout and details for the steel and masonry structure. The roof framing and foundations plans show two options for the support of the roof purlins. The first of these is the clear span girder with the pilaster columns and the widened wall footing, which was the system as discussed in the design calculations. Also shown is an option for a bearing wall that would replace the girder. If the bearing wall is used, the pilaster and widened footing would be omitted, as shown in the drawings.

Detail A. (Figure 2.36.) This shows the typical front wall condition at the solid wall. The girder, pilaster, pilaster pier, and widened footing are seen in the background. A steel channel is bolted to the masonry wall to receive the end of the steel deck, which in this view is seen at right angle to the corrugations. The deck would be welded to the channel and the channel bolted to the wall to transfer the shear load from the roof diaphragm to the wall.

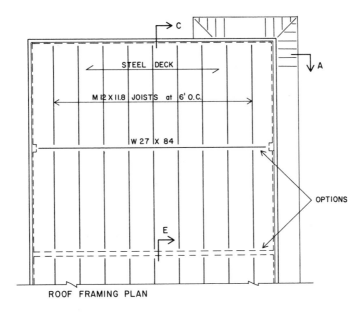

ROOF FRAMING PLAN

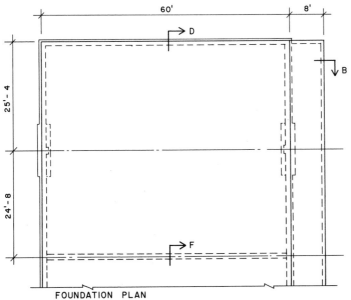

FOUNDATION PLAN

FIGURE 2.35. Structural plans: steel and masonry structure.

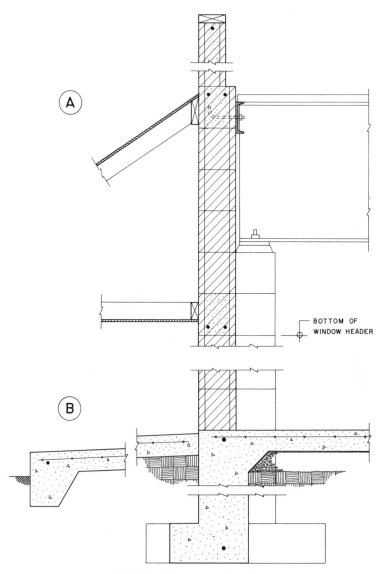

A

B

BOTTOM OF
WINDOW HEADER

FIGURE 2.36.   Details A and B.

128

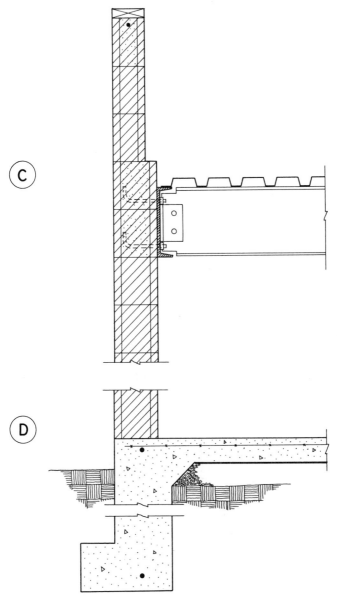

FIGURE 2.37.   Details C and D.

For the reinforced masonry wall the code requires a minimum vertical spacing of solid horizontal reinforced bond courses. In addition to the minimum spacing, these would be used at the top of the wall, the bottom of the header, and the location of the canopy and roof edge bolting to the wall.

Detail B. (Figure 2.36.) This shows the foundation edge at the front, which is essentially similar to that for the wood structure. The sill bolts would be replaced by dowels for the masonry wall. The pier would be added below the pilaster to carry the load down to the widened footing.

Detail C. (Figure 2.37.) This shows the roof edge condition at the building ends. The steel angle performs the dual task of providing vertical support for the ends of the purlins and transfers the lateral loads from the steel deck to the masonry wall. Because of the roof slope, the top of the steel angle varies 15 in. from front to rear of the building. The horizontal filled block courses and the cutoff to the narrower parapet would be staggered to accommodate this slope. A somewhat larger than usual cant would be used to cover the jog in the wall to the narrower parapet block.

Detail D. (Figure 2.37.) This detail is also essentially similar to that for the wood structure. If a footing of increased width is required, care should be taken to ensure that the centroid of the vertical loads is close to the center of the width of the footing.

Detail E. (Figure 2.38.) This shows the detail at the top of the interior bearing wall. The continuous steel beam on top of the wall is one means for providing the necessary support for the ends of the purlins and the transfer of lateral load from the steel deck to the wall. It is also possible to simply rest the ends of the purlins on a bearing plate and to provide some sort of blocking between the purlins, so that the lateral loads are transferred through the welds between the deck and the purlins. The purlins would then be welded to the plate and the plate bolted to the wall to complete the transfer.

Detail F. (Figure 2.38.) This shows the base of the interior wall with a typical trenched wall footing. Depending on the slab thickness

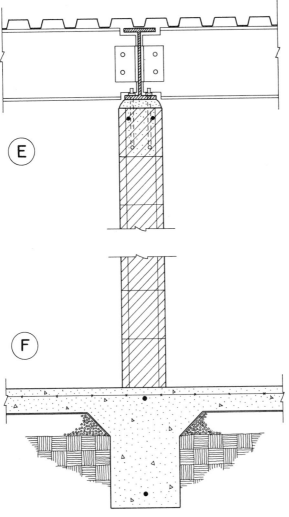

FIGURE 2.38. Details E and F.

and reinforcing and the nature of the subsoil, it may be advisable to provide this type of footing for all major interior walls. In the event that the slab is to be poured after the masonry walls are built, an optional footing would be as shown for the interior basement wall in Building One.

3

Building Three

||||||||||||||||||||||||||||||||||||||||||||||||||||||||||

Building Three is a multistory office building. Complete structural
calculations for this building would be quite voluminous. We will
therefore show only the design of some of the typical elements of the
structural system. The building will be designed first as a steel frame
and then as a reinforced concrete frame, with some options shown
for each material.

3.1   The Building

The basic form of the building is shown in Figures 3.1 through 3.6.
As with Building Two, the intent is to have minimum permanent
construction to allow for rearrangement of interior partitioning.
This will be achieved by using a basic planning module, in this case
4 ft, within which the partitioning, modular ceiling system and
exterior wall mullions and columns will be coordinated. Partitioning
may then be accomplished with various patented demountable wall
systems, although masonry or plastered walls could also be used.
  The building must be conceived as a vertical, superimposed stack
of four separate plans: the basement, ground floor, typical office
floor, and roof-penthouse. Location of columns, elevator shafts,

133

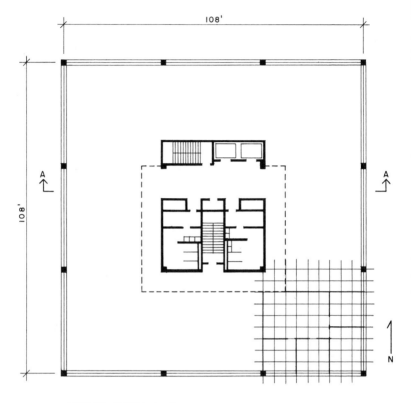

TYPICAL FLOOR 2-6

FIGURE 3.1.   Building Three: plan of the typical office floor.

stairs, duct shafts, and risers for the plumbing, power, and communications systems must be coordinated from level to level. The key plan is that of the typical office floor, since its functioning is the reason for the building existing.

To avoid the problems of developing complex architectural detailing, we will be somewhat vague about the exterior skin wall, assuming it to have the general form shown and to consist of metal framing with an exterior skin of metal and glass and interior surfaces of plaster. Power and communication distribution will generally be

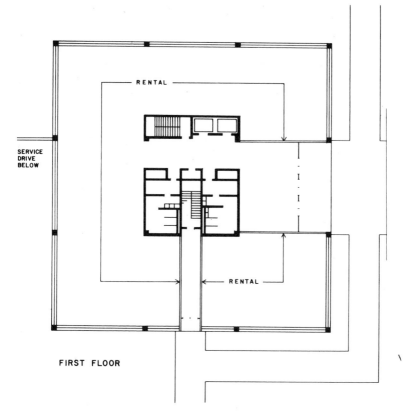

FIGURE 3.2. First floor plan.

accomplished through typical underfloor modular systems incorporated in a concrete fill on top of the structural deck.

A peripheral hot water heating system will be incorporated in the exterior wall, as shown in the drawings. Ventilation, cooling, and supplementary heating will be achieved through a system incorporated in the ceiling space, using supply ducts from the major vertical risers in the core.

Major equipment elements for the HVAC, power, communication and elevator systems will be housed in the roof penthouse and in the

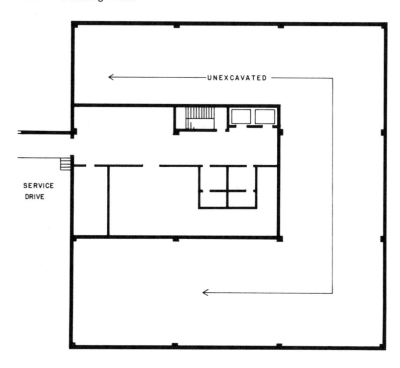

BASEMENT

FIGURE 3.3.   Basement plan.

basement. The building management offices and equipment and facilities for the maintenance staff will be in the basement. The service entrance is also in the basement.

Some of the design criteria are:

Roof live load: 20 psf.

Floor loads: 50 psf or concentrated load per code for the office areas. 20 psf partition load per code.

Lateral loads: 30 psf wind (code base pressure). Seismic zone 1 (not critical for design).

Soil capacity: 8000 psf maximum.

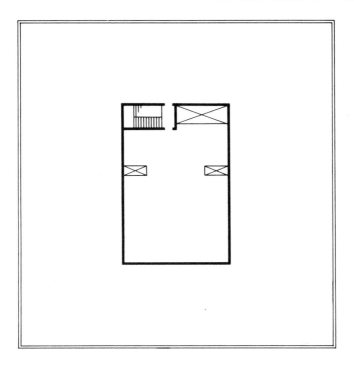

ROOF & PENTHOUSE

FIGURE 3.4.   Roof and penthouse plan.

3.2   The Steel Structure

Figure 3.7 shows the framing system for the typical floor, using steel H-shaped columns and steel beams and girders. The basic floor system consists of the 9 ft on center beams supporting a one-way spanning deck. Every fourth beam frames directly to the columns; the remaining beams are supported by the girders. Four vertical bents are described in each direction and constitute the lateral load resisting system, together with the floor diaphragms.

Within this basic system scheme there are some variables to be considered. The spacing of the beam system is one. The type of deck used and the depth restriction for the beams would influence this

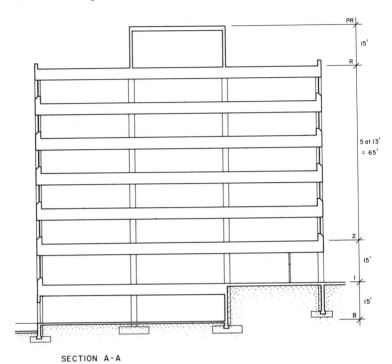

SECTION A-A

FIGURE 3.5. Section A-A: building cross-section.

choice. Within the 36 ft column module logical possibilities are 6, 9, 12, and 18 ft spacings. The 9 ft spacing chosen seems reasonable with the steel formed deck we are using.

Orientation of the steel columns is another consideration. Since we are using the frame for lateral load resistance, the system shown was chosen so that there are eight columns in each direction turned to present their major stiffness. Although not exactly geometrically symmetrical, this does give reasonable biaxial stiffness to the frame.

As shown, location of major openings for duct shafts, elevators and stairs should be developed so as not to interfere with any of the girders or beams on the column lines. The major plumbing and power risers should also not be on the column lines.

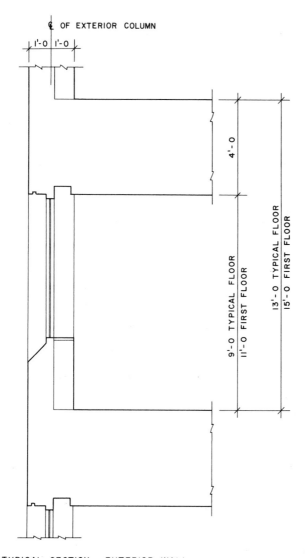

TYPICAL SECTION - EXTERIOR WALL

FIGURE 3.6.   Typical section: exterior wall.

139

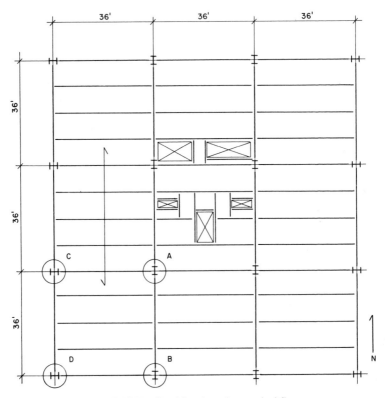

FIGURE 3.7.   Steel framing plan: typical floor.

Similar framing systems would likely be used for the roof and the portion of the first floor over the basement. A concrete slab or a concrete framing system poured on fill would be used over the unexcavated areas of the ground floor.

Two options exist for the steel column bases. These may occur at the ground floor level, with concrete piers or columns extending down to the footings. The other option is to extend the steel columns down to the footings and simply encase them in concrete up to the ground floor level. For a building of this height either option is feasible.

Some consideration must be given to the fireproofing of the steel frame and deck. We will assume this to be accomplished as follows:

1. Top of the steel deck and exposed faces of the spandrel beams and beams at openings: poured concrete (probably of light-weight aggregate).
2. Exterior columns, interior sides of beams and girders, and the underside of the steel deck: sprayed-on fireproofing.
3. Interior columns; metal lath and plaster.

A36 steel will be used for all steel frame members. Elastic analysis will generally be used in the design.

3.3   Design of the Steel Floor System

Loads:

Live loads:	50 psf for the office areas	
	100 psf for lobbies, corridors, stairs	
	2000 lb concentrated load per UBC 2304(c).	
Dead loads:	Deck (steel plus concrete fill)	= 35 psf
	Ceiling, lights, ducts	= 15
	Partitions (UBC 2304d)	= 20
	Total dead load	= 70 psf + steel framing

Several options are possible for the steel deck. Since a two-way distribution system for the power and communication systems is to be incorporated in the deck and fill, the choice must obviously be done in cooperation with the design of these systems and with the office layout design. Figure 3.8 shows some details and options for this type of system. We will assume a system using a $1\frac{1}{2}$ in. deep corrugation and $2\frac{1}{2}$ in. minimum fill over the deck for a total depth of 4 in.

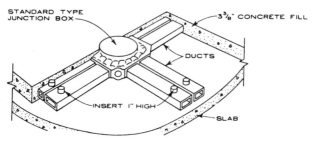

STANDARD TYPE JUNCTION BOX

3⅜" CONCRETE FILL

DUCTS

INSERT 1" HIGH

SLAB

STANDARD TYPE DUCT

Placed on top of structural slab. Duct supports are required if the duct is not placed on top of slab.

Junction boxes are available in the following sizes: 3", 2½", flush box and standard heights.

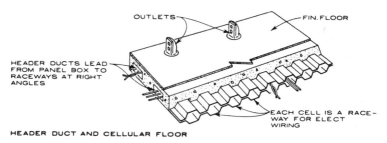

OUTLETS

FIN. FLOOR

HEADER DUCTS LEAD FROM PANEL BOX TO RACEWAYS AT RIGHT ANGLES

EACH CELL IS A RACE-WAY FOR ELECT WIRING

HEADER DUCT AND CELLULAR FLOOR

FIGURE 3.8. Details of wiring systems incorporated in floors. (From *Architectural Graphic Standards*, reference 6.)

The typical beam is a 36 ft span, simple beam carrying the following load:

Dead load: $9 \times 36 \times 70$ psf $= 22,680$ lb

Beam, at 50 pfl $= \underline{1,800}$

Total $= 24,480$ lb

Live load: $9 \times 36 \times 50(0.75) = 12,150$ lb (based on live load reduction of 0.25 per UBC 2306)

Total load $= 36,630$ lb

Since the deck provides continuous lateral support, we may select directly from the load tables in the AISC Manual, from which we find the following options:

$$W18 \times 50, \qquad W21 \times 49$$

Since these two choices are approximately the same weight, the selection is arbitrary and would involve other considerations, some of which are:

1. *Deflection.* The deeper beam will have less deflection, although both are within design limits.
2. *Depth.* The shallower beam will allow more headroom within the ceiling space for ducts and lights. The floor-to-floor height may thus be reduced; a savings of a few inches per floor adds up quickly in the multistory building.
3. *Flange width.* The 21 in. beam is 1 in. narrower. Not a major difference, but it relates to clearance at floor openings.
4. *Bent members.* If deeper members are required for the beams and girders in the bents, the depth savings previously mentioned may become less meaningful.

In view of the last comment, the selection of the typical floor beam would probably be delayed until some analysis of the bents has been done.

The seven story high, three bay wide bents are considerably indeterminate. In addition, loading conditions are numerous. The three basic loading conditions are:

1. Gravity dead load plus live load. This includes the consideration of skip loading for the live load.
2. Wind load plus gravity load for maximum combinations. This condition, using the allowable one third increase for stresses, would be compared with case 1 for critical design.
3. Wind load plus dead load only for possible reversal effects, tiedown requirements, and so on.

There are essentially four different column/beam bents: the interior and exterior bents in each direction. The lack of symmetry of the core, the basement and the penthouse causes some minor variations on these as well. In present professional practice it is hard to conceive of the final analysis of these bents being done without a computer program, in view of the relative availability of such programs and the facilities for their use. The approximate analysis shown here should be used only for preliminary sizing of members and connections to be used for cost estimates, feasibility studies, and development of architectural details.

The East–West, Exterior Bent.   This consists of the four exterior columns and the spandrel beams. Loading on the beam consists of approximately one half of the floor load on the typical beam plus the wall load:

1/2 beam dead load:	$4\frac{1}{2} \times 36 \times 70 =$	11,340 lb
1/2 beam live load:	$4\frac{1}{2} \times 36 \times 50 =$	8,100
Wall (estimate at 30 psf):	$13 \times 36 \times 30 =$	14,040
Beam + fireproofing (estimate at 200 plf $\times$ 36):	$=$	7,200
Total load	$=$	40,680 lb

For a first guess we assume a critical moment of 85% of the simple beam moment. We thus use 85% of this total load to select a beam from the AISC beam load tables. Thus

$$\text{design } W = 0.85(40,680) = 34,578 \text{ lb}$$

From the AISC tables the possible choices are

$W21 \times 44,$ carries 36 kips on the 36 ft span
$W18 \times 45,$ carries 35 kips

At the roof the design load will be lower because of less wall load, no partitions, and the lower live load. For preliminary purposes we may reduce the beam by a few sizes.

The East–West, Interior Bent.   The loading on these beams is the same as for the typical beam. The total load, previously determined, is close to that for the spandrel, so that we could use the same preliminary sizes. The loading of the middle span at the core should be determined once the exact core layout and the materials of the core walls are known.

The North–South, Interior Bent.   This consists of the interior girders, the two interior columns, and the two exterior columns

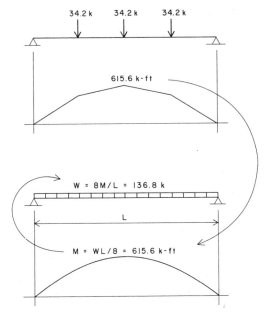

FIGURE 3.9.   Equivalent uniform load for the girder.

labeled "B." The principal loading on the girders consists of the end reactions of the beams. Added to this is a uniform load consisting of the weight of the girder and a strip of the floor directly over the girder. For simplification we will consider a concentrated load equal to the full 36 ft span load on the beam and will ignore the uniform load. This produces the quarter point loading shown in Figure 3.9. Note that this is slightly less than the beam load because of the higher reduction factor for live load, since the girder carries more floor area.

The quarter point loading produces a moment diagram sufficiently similar to the parabolic diagram for uniform load, so that we may use an equivalent uniform load, as shown in the figure. Assuming, as before, that the rigid frame continuity reduces the actual critical moment to approximately 85% of the simple beam effect, we use a design load of

$$W = 0.85(136.8) = 116 \text{ kips}$$

From the AISC load tables we find

$$W24 \times 110, \quad \text{carries 123 kips}$$
$$W27 \times 102, \quad \text{carries 119 kips}$$
$$W30 \times 99, \quad \text{carries 120 kips}$$

The North–South, Exterior Bent.   For the spandrel girders the floor loading is approximately one half of that for the interior girders and the wall load is the same as for the east–west spandrel beams.

1/2 of the EUL:	136.8/2	= 68.4 kips
Wall load		= 14.0
Total load		= 82.4 kips
Design W:	0.85(82.4)	= 70 kips

From the AISC load tables:

$$W24 \times 76, \quad \text{carries 78 kips}$$
$$W21 \times 82, \quad \text{carries 75 kips}$$

On the basis of this first approximation a preliminary sizing of the beams and girders is made. These initial assumptions are shown in Table 3.1.

TABLE 3.1.   First Approximation—Bent Beams and Girders

Level	North–South Interior Girders	North–South Exterior Girders	East–West Interior Beams	East–West Exterior Beams
Roof	$W24 \times 94$	$W21 \times 62$	$W18 \times 35$	$W18 \times 35$
2–6	$W24 \times 110$	$W24 \times 76$	$W21 \times 44$	$W21 \times 44$

3.4   Design of the Steel Columns and Bents

The next step is to determine approximate column sizes. This will be done using the gravity loads only as a first trial. To do this we will make some assumptions for the moments induced in the columns

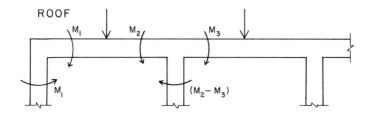

ROOF

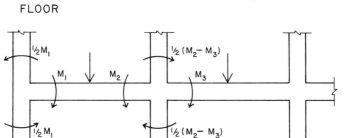

FLOOR

FIGURE 3.10. Assumed moment distribution in the bents: gravity loads.

TABLE 3.2. First Approximation—Column Moments Due to Gravity

| Moments (k-ft) | Direction | | | | | | | |
| | North–South Columns | | | | East–West Columns | | | |
	A	B	C	D	A	B	C	D
At roof								
Simple beam M	493	493	297	297	132	146	132	146
Percentage of M assumed for column	$\frac{1}{10}$	$\frac{1}{3}$	$\frac{1}{10}$	$\frac{1}{3}$	$\frac{1}{10}$	$\frac{1}{10}$	$\frac{1}{3}$	$\frac{1}{3}$
Column M	49	164	30	99	13	15	44	49
At floor								
Simple beam M	616	616	371	371	165	183	165	183
Percentage of M assumed for column	$\frac{1}{10}$	$\frac{1}{4}$	$\frac{1}{10}$	$\frac{1}{6}$	$\frac{1}{10}$	$\frac{1}{10}$	$\frac{1}{3}$	$\frac{1}{3}$
Column M	62	154	37	61	16	18	55	61

TABLE 3.3. Column Axial Loads Due to Gravity

Level		Column A, 1296 ft²			Columns B and C, 648 ft²			Column D, 324 ft²		
		DL	LL	Total						
PR	Roof	15	10							
	Wall	20								
	Column	—								
	Total/level	35	10							
	LL reduction		—							
	Design load			45						
R	Roof	78	80		39	13		20	7	
	Wall	—			4			4		
	Column	2			2			2		
	Total/level	115	90		45	13		26	7	
	LL reduction		—			—			—	
	Design load			205			58			33
6	Floor	104	65		52	33		26	17	
	Wall	—			13			13		
	Column	2			2			2		
	Total/level	221	155		112	46		67	24	
	LL reduction	(60%)	62		(60%)	18		(50%)	12	
	Design load			283			130			79
5	Floor	104	65		52	33		26	17	
	Wall	—			13			13		
	Column	3			3			2		
	Total/level	328	220		180	79		108	41	
	LL reduction	(60%)	88		(60%)	32		(60%)	16	
	Design load			416			212			124
4	Floor	104	65		52	33		26	17	
	Wall	—			13			13		
	Column	3			3			3		
	Total/level	435	285		248	112		150	58	
	LL reduction	(60%)	114		(60%)	45		(60%)	23	
	Design load			549			293			173
3	Floor	104	65		52	33		26	17	
	Wall	—			13			13		
	Column	3			3			3		
	Total/level	542	350		316	145		192	75	
	LL reduction	(60%)	140		(60%)	58		(60%)	30	
	Design load			682			374			222
2	Floor	104	65		52	33		26	17	
	Wall	—			13			16		
	Column	4			3			3		
	Total/level	650	415		384	178		237	92	
	LL reduction	(60%)	166		(60%)	71		(60%)	37	
	Design load			816			455			274
1	Floor	104	65		52	33		26	17	
	Wall	60			20			20		
	Column	6			5			5		
	Total/level	820	580		461	211		288	109	
	LL reduction	(60%)	192		(60%)	85		(60%)	44	
	Design load			1012			546			332

by the rigid frame continuity. Then the axial loads will be tabulated so that a design can be made for the axial load plus moment conditions.

Figure 3.10 shows the assumptions for the relations of moment between the horizontal and vertical members of the bents. On the basis of these assumptions and the previous load calculations, we make the first approximation of the column moments as shown in Table 3.2.

The gravity load calculation for the axial column loads is shown in Table 3.3. We assume the loads on columns B and C to be essentially the same. The live loads and dead loads are tabulated separately so that they may be combined for various purposes in the foundation design as well as the column design.

With the moment assumptions and axial loads we may proceed to pick approximate column sizes. Before doing so we must make some assumptions about the location of column splices. These are usually made a short distance above the beam level and are commonly not made at every floor, since the connections are quite

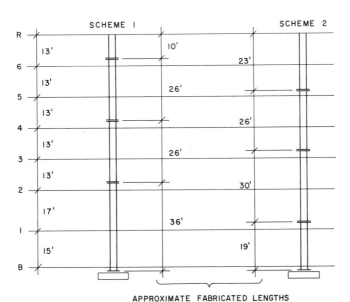

FIGURE 3.11.   Options for the column splices.

expensive and time consuming in the field erection process. Figure
3.11 shows two possible schemes for the location of the splices. We
will select Scheme One and omit the sixth floor splice for the purpose
of column size selection.

The column selection is thus reduced to determining three sizes
for each column in the plan. The floor load moments will thus be
added to the axial loads at the basement, the second story, and the
sixth story. For this approximation we will assume a K factor for
slenderness of 1.5 for the unbraced rigid frame. Column interaction
is considered by using the B_x and B_y factors to convert the moments
to additional axial load. With a final design load and the appropriate
KL we then pick a column size from the AISC column load tables;
14 in. wide flange members will be used throughout.

The following is an example of this process, using the data for
column A. Table 3.4 summarizes the design loads, KL assumptions,
and column choices for the four types of columns.

TABLE 3.4.   First Approximation of Column Sizes

Level	Assumed Critical KL	Column A Design Load[a]	Choice	Column B Design Load	Choice	Column C Design Load	Choice	Column D Design Load	Choice
R									
6	19 ft	416	$W14$	212	$W14$	212	$W14$	124	$W14$
		138	$\times$ 136	342	$\times$ 136	122	$\times$ 111	135	$\times$ 127
5		96		108		222		366	
		$\overline{650}$		$\overline{662}$		$\overline{556}$		$\overline{625}$	
4	19 ft	682	$W14$	374	$W14$	374	$W14$	222	$W14$
		138	$\times$ 176	342	$\times$ 158	122	$\times$ 142	135	$\times$ 142
3		96		108		222		366	
		$\overline{916}$		$\overline{824}$		$\overline{718}$		$\overline{723}$	
2	22 ft	1012	$W14$	455	$W14$	546	$W14$	274	$W14$
		138	$\times$ 246	342	$\times$ 184	122	$\times$ 184	135	$\times$ 158
1		96		108		222		366	
B		$\overline{1246}$		$\overline{905}$		$\overline{890}$		$\overline{775}$	

[a] Design load = $P + P'_x \times P'_y$.

Column A—First Approximation

At the fourth story:

Axial loads = 416 kips, $KL = 1.5(13) = 19.5$, use 19 ft. (We guess at B_x and B_y for a try; then verify them.)

Try $B_x = 0.185$, $B_y = 0.50$.

$M_x = 62$ k-ft, $M_y = 16$ k-ft.

$$P + P'_x + P'_y = 416 + 0.185(62 \times 12) + 0.50(16 \times 12)$$
$$= 416 + 138 + 96 = 650 \text{ kips.}$$

Pick: $W14 \times 136$ (see the Appendix).

Check: $B_x = 0.186$, $B_y = 0.520$.

At the second-story:

Axial load = 682 kips, $KL = 19$ ft, $M_x = 62$ k-ft, $M_y = 16$ k-ft.

Try $B_x = 0.185$, $B_y = 0.50$.

$$P + P'_x + P'_y = 682 + 138 + 96 = 916 \text{ kips.}$$

Pick: $W14 \times 176$, $B_x = 0.184$, $B_y = 0.484$.

At the basement:

Axial load = 1012 kips, $KL = 22$ ft, $M_x = 62$ k-ft, $M_y = 16$ k-ft.

Try $B_x = 0.185$, $B_y = 0.50$.

$$P + P'_x + P'_y = 1012 + 138 + 96 = 1246 \text{ kips.}$$

Pick: $W14 \times 246$, $B_x = 0.183$, $B_y = 0.481$.

Inspection of the basement plan in Figure 3.3 will show that the majority of the first floor structure consists of construction over unexcavated ground. We will assume this to be of reinforced concrete poured directly onto backfill. The load from this portion of the floor will be transmitted directly to the basement and grade walls and the foundations. Thus the only first floor loadings transmitted to the steel columns will be from the first floor construction over the basement area. An illustration of this construction is shown in the construction drawings in Section 3.8.

With this assumption, the majority of the steel columns would be designed for the first story loading. Only the four interior columns and the two exterior columns on the west side would be designed

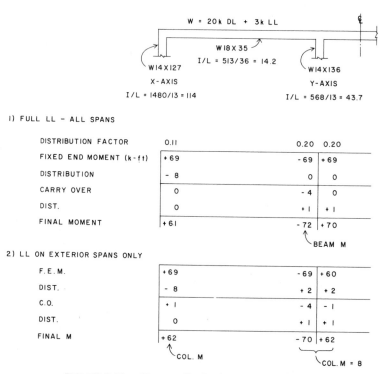

FIGURE 3.12.   Moment distribution: roof gravity load.

for the basement load condition. In a final, more exact analysis, however, it may be found that the first story condition is actually more critical for these columns as well, because of a higher *K* factor, greater story height, and so on. Thus, while the basement loads tabulated in Table 3.3 may be useful for sizing the column base plates and the foundations, the column design would probably be for the first story loads.

With approximate sizes for the columns established, we may now do a slightly more accurate analysis for the gravity moments on the bents. This will consist of an analysis of the three-span beams, assuming the columns to be fixed at the levels above and below. The two loading conditions considered are that of full live load on all spans and live load on the exterior spans only. The first will produce

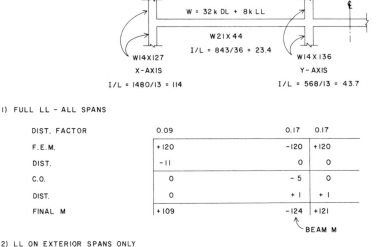

FIGURE 3.13.   Moment distribution: 6th floor gravity load.

the maximum beam moment and the second the maximum column moments. We will do the analysis for the beams at the roof, sixth floor and second floor and interpolate for values between these levels.

Figures 3.12 through 3.14 show the analysis of the east–west, exterior bent using the method of moment distribution. Results of this analysis and similar ones for the other bents, not shown for sake of space, are summarized in Table 3.5. These slightly more accurate values could now be used to select a second set of approximate member sizes. However, we have not so far considered the effects of wind on the bents. It is therefore probably a better procedure to do an approximate analysis for wind effects and then to combine the results with the gravity analysis for the next approximation of sizes.

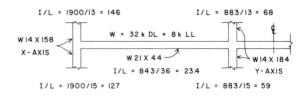

I) FULL LL – ALL SPANS

DIST. FACTOR	0.08		0.13	0.13
F.E.M.	+120		–120	+120
DIST.	–10		0	0
C.O.	0		–5	0
DIST.	0		+1	+1
FINAL M	+110		–124	+121

↑ BEAM M

2) LL ON EXTERIOR SPANS ONLY

F.E.M.	+120		–120	+96
DIST.	–10		+3	+3
C.O.	+1		–5	–1
DIST.	0		+1	+1
FINAL M	+111		–121	+99

↑ COL. M = 111/2 = 56   COL. M = 22/2 = 11

FIGURE 3.14.   Moment distribution: 2nd floor gravity load.

TABLE 3.5.   Second Approximation—Bent Moments Due to Gravity

Bent	East–West Exterior			East–West Interior			North–South Exterior			North–South Interior		
	Column D	Column B		Column C	Column A		Column D	Column C		Column B	Column A	
Level	x-Axis	y-Axis	Beam	x-Axis	y-Axis	Beam	y-Axis	y-Axis	Girder	x-Axis	x-Axis	Girder
R	62	8	72	84	7	98	110	16	225	219	36	385
6	56	11	124	51	15	115	66	19	241	158	63	451
5	56	11	124	51	15	115	66	19	241	158	63	451
4	56	11	124	52	16	114	69	21	241	161	67	449
3	56	11	124	52	16	114	69	21	241	161	67	449
2	56	11	124	52	16	113	72	22	240	164	71	446

154

3.5   Design for Wind

Complete design for wind effects on this building would include the following:

Inward and outward pressure on the exterior walls, involving the sizing of window glazing, structural mullions, attachment of wall elements to the structure, and so on.

Inward pressure and uplift on the roof.

Diaphragm action of the roof and floor decks.

Lateral rigid frame action of the column/beam bents.

Overturn, sliding, and lateral earth pressures at the building-to-ground interface.

Since we are not detailing the window wall, we will not consider its wind resistance, other than to assume that it acts to transfer the wind

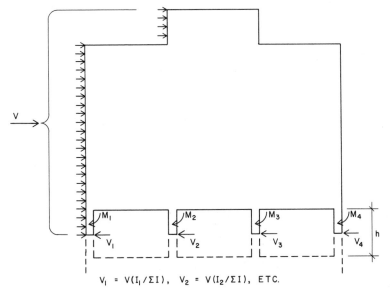

$$V_1 = V(I_1/\Sigma I), \quad V_2 = V(I_2/\Sigma I), \quad ETC.$$

$$M_1 = V_1(h/2), \quad M_2 = V_2(h/2), \quad ETC.$$

FIGURE 3.15.   Assumed wind shear and moments in the columns.

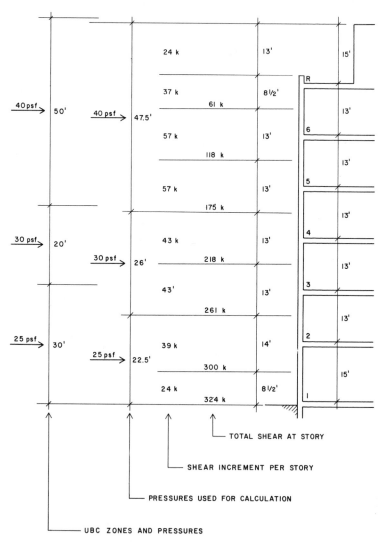

FIGURE 3.16.   Wind shear analysis.

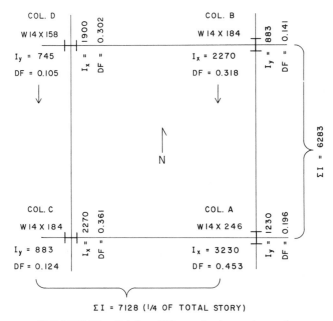

FIGURE 3.17.   Relative stiffness of columns: lower tier.

load to the edges of the horizontal structure at all levels. The metal deck and concrete fill will be considered to be adequate to transfer these forces at all levels to the rigid bents. Our main concern will be with the wind effects on the steel column/beam bents and the foundations.

We will assume that the horizontal diaphragms are sufficiently stiff so that the force in shear at each story is distributed to the columns in proportion to their individual stiffnesses. Thus in each direction the shear on an individual column will be calculated as the total story shear times the ratio of the individual column stiffness to the sum of all column stiffness values at that story. For the first approximate analysis we ignore the effect of rotation at the joints and assume the column stiffness to be simply the I/L value.

Figure 3.15 shows the method for approximation of the shear and moment in the columns due to wind load. The total shear force at each story is taken as the wind load on the portion of the building

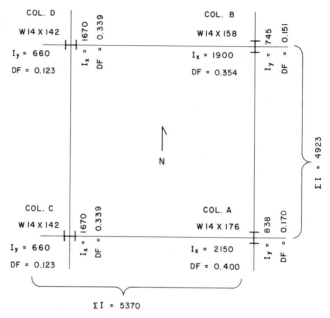

FIGURE 3.18.   Relative stiffness of columns: middle tier.

above the midheight of the story. This total shear force is distributed between the columns at each story as previously discussed.

Figure 3.16 shows the basis for determination of the total wind shears at each story. The variation of wind pressure with height is taken from UBC Table 23-F.

Note that with the scheme used for column splices there are only three column sizes in the seven story columns. The critical column design locations are thus at the basement or first story, at the upper portion of the second story, and at the upper portion of the fourth story. In addition, assuming the structure to be reasonably biaxially symmetrical in plan, we may reduce the design at each story to the four typical columns: A, B, C, and D. The result of these simplifications means that we must design only 12 columns, while there are actually a total of 16 in plan which, when multiplied by seven stories, equals 112 columns.

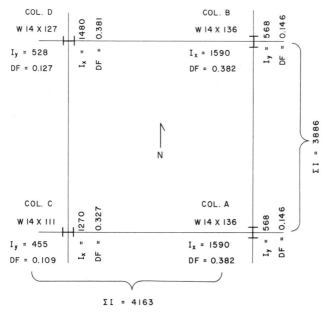

FIGURE 3.19.   Relative stiffness of columns: upper tier.

Figures 3.17 through 3.19 show the basis for determination of the distribution of shears at the three critical stories. The column sizes assumed for this distribution are those approximated from the gravity load analysis, as summarized in Table 3.4. A summary of the shears and moments in the columns and the moments in the bent beams and girders are shown in Table 3.6. Figure 3.20 illustrates the basis for determination of the moments in the horizontal members of the bents.

In addition to the horizontal shear effect on the building, the wind produces a bending effect on the whole building, resulting in axial loads on the columns: tension on the windward side, compression on the leeward side. In a very tall, relatively slender building these may be of considerable magnitude. With this building—which is quite squat in profile, being wider than it is tall—the axial loads thus produced are relatively small.

160   Building Three

TABLE 3.6. Wind Moments in the Bent Members

Level	Total Story Shear (kips)	Column: Axis:	A x	A y	B x	B y	C x	C y	D x	D y
R		Beam M	19	7	38	7	33	6	38	12
		Column DF	0.382	0.146	0.382	0.146	0.327	0.109	0.381	0.127
	61	Column V^a	5.8	2.2	5.8	2.2	5.0	1.7	5.8	1.9
		Column M	38	14	38	14	33	11	38	12
6		Beam M	56	24	111	21	95	16	111	36
		Column DF	0.382	0.146	0.382	0.146	0.327	0.109	0.381	0.127
	118	Column V	11.3	4.3	11.3	4.3	9.6	3.2	11.2	3.7
		Column M	73	28	73	28	62	21	73	24
5		Beam M	91	35	182	35	155	26	182	60
		Column DF	0.382	0.146	0.382	0.146	0.327	0.109	0.381	0.127
	175	Column V	16.7	6.4	16.7	6.4	14.3	4.8	16.7	5.6
		Column M	109	42	109	42	93	31	109	36
4		Beam M	126	51	234	48	213	38	229	80
		Column DF	0.400	0.170	0.354	0.151	0.339	0.123	0.339	0.123
	218	Column V	22	9.3	19.3	8.2	18.5	6.7	18.5	6.7
		Column M	143	60	125	53	120	44	120	44
3		Beam M	156	66	275	59	264	48	264	48
		Column DF	0.400	0.170	0.354	0.151	0.339	0.123	0.339	0.123
	261	Column V	26	11.1	23.1	9.9	22.1	8.0	22.1	8.0
		Column M	169	72	150	64	144	52	144	52
2		Beam M	212	91	329	72	347	61	314	111
		Column DF	0.453	0.196	0.318	0.141	0.361	0.124	0.302	0.105
	300	Column V	34	14.7	23.9	10.6	27.1	9.3	22.7	7.9
		Column M	255	110	179	80	203	70	170	59
1										

^{a} Column $V = (DF)$(total story shear/4).

The basis for determination of these axial loads is shown in Figure 3.21. The structure is assumed to flex about its axis of symmetry, and a moment of inertia is determined on the basis of the column areas. For calculation the areas are assumed as relative values; one for the smallest column (D) and proportionate numbers for the others. Table 3.7 shows the calculation of this I value, consisting of a summation of the products of the column areas times the square of their distance from the axis of bending.

The axial load on an individual column is thus

$$P = \frac{(\text{relative } A)(\text{total story } M)(\text{ distance of column from axis})}{(\text{total } I \text{ for the story})}$$

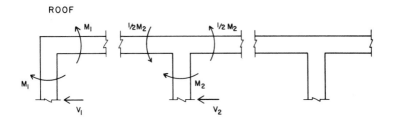

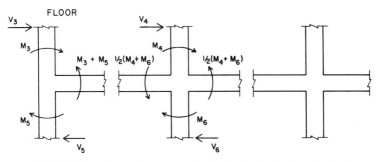

FIGURE 3.20.   Assumed moment distribution in the bents: wind load.

For the first story columns:

$$\text{column D}: P = \frac{(1.0)(15,833)(54)}{28,719} = 29.8 \text{ kips}$$

$$\text{column C}: P = \frac{(1.16)(15,833)(54)}{28,719} = 34.5 \text{ kips}$$

$$\text{column B}: P = \frac{(1.16)(15,833)(18)}{28,719} = 11.5 \text{ kips}$$

$$\text{column A}: P = \frac{(1.56)(15,833)(18)}{28,719} = 15.5 \text{ kips}$$

Since these are small values in comparison to the axial loads and moments due to gravity and the moments due to wind, we will not use them for the approximate design.

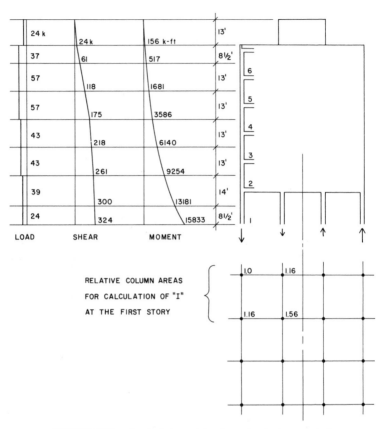

FIGURE 3.21. Analysis for axial column loads due to wind.

TABLE 3.7. Calculation of *I* for Axial Loads Due to Wind

Column	Relative *A*	Total *A*	Distance to Axis	$I = A(D)^2$
A	1.56	6.24	18	2,022
B	1.16	4.64	18	1,503
C	1.16	4.64	54	13,500
D	1.00	4.00	54	11,664
Total *I*				28,719

3.6   Second Approximation of the Columns and Bents

We will now consider the effects of wind plus gravity on the columns and beams of the bents. Our procedure is to determine the critical load for gravity only and compare it with three fourths of the load for wind plus gravity. We then use the higher of the two for design.

For the beam designs we will use the maximum gravity moment plus the maximum wind moment. This may be slightly conservative in some cases, since these two may not occur at the same place. Figure 3.22 illustrates this problem, using the east–west exterior bent at the second floor. The gravity moments are taken from the analysis in Figure 3.14 and the wind moments from Table 3.6. Since the error is small, we will simply use the tabulated maximums and add them for our approximate design.

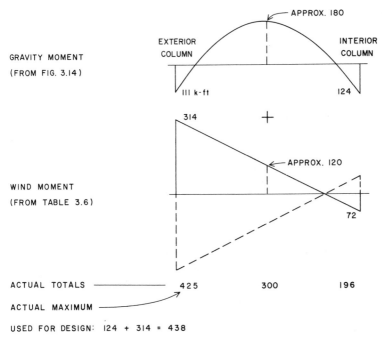

FIGURE 3.22.   Addition of beam moments due to gravity and wind.

The north–south interior girder:

At the second floor: $M_g = 446$ k/ft (from Table 3.5)

Or $M_g + M_w = (\tfrac{3}{4})(446 + 329) = 581$ k/ft

Since the combination is higher, we use it to pick $W24 \times 120$ (from AISC S_x tables).

At the third floor: $M = 449$ k/ft

Or $M = (\tfrac{3}{4})(449 + 275) = 543$ k/ft

Use $W24 \times 110$

At the fourth floor: $M = 449$ k/ft

Or $M = (\tfrac{3}{4})(449 + 234) = 512$ k/ft

Use $W24 \times 110$

At the fifth floor: $M = 451$ k/ft

Or $M = (\tfrac{3}{4})(451 + 182) = 475$ k/ft

Use $W24 \times 100$

At the sixth floor: $M = 451$ k/ft (wind not critical)

Use $W24 \times 100$

At the roof: $M = 385$ k/ft (wind not critical)

Use $W24 \times 84$

The north–south exterior girder:

At the second floor: $M = 240$ k/ft

Or $M = (\tfrac{3}{4})(240 + 111) = 263$ k/ft

Wind is not critical, use $W24 \times 61$ for all floor levels.

At the roof: $M = 225$ k/ft

Use $W24 \times 55$

The east–west interior beam:

At the second floor: $M = 113$ k/ft

Or $M = (\tfrac{3}{4})(113 + 347) = 345$ k/ft

Use $W24 \times 76$

At the third floor: $M = 114$ k/ft

Or $M = (\tfrac{3}{4})(114 + 264) = 284$ k/ft

Use $W24 \times 68$

At the fourth floor: $M = 114$ k/ft

Or $M = (\frac{3}{4})(114 + 213) = 245$ k/ft

Use $W24 \times 61$

At the fifth floor: $M = 115$ k/ft

Or $M = (\frac{3}{4})(115 + 155) = 202$ k/ft

Use $W24 \times 55$

At the sixth floor: $M = 115$ k/ft

Or $M = (\frac{3}{4})(115 + 95) = 158$ k/ft

Use $W21 \times 44$

At the roof: $M = 92$ k/ft

Or $M = (\frac{3}{4})(92 + 33) = 94$ k/ft

Use $W18 \times 35$

The east–west exterior beam:

At the second floor: $M = 124$ k/ft

Or $M = (\frac{3}{4})(124 + 314) = 329$ k/ft

Use $W24 \times 76$

At the third floor: $M = (\frac{3}{4})(124 + 264) = 291$ k/ft

Use $W24 \times 68$

At the fourth floor: $M = (\frac{3}{4})(124 + 229) = 265$ k/ft

Use $W24 \times 68$

At the fifth floor: $M = (\frac{3}{4})(124 + 182) = 230$ k/ft

Use $W24 \times 61$

At the sixth floor: $M = (\frac{3}{4})(124 + 111) = 176$ k/ft

Use $W21 \times 49$

At the roof: $M = 72$ k/ft

Or $M = (\frac{3}{4})(72 + 38) = 83$ k/ft

Use $W18 \times 35$

The second estimate of beams and girder sizes is summarized in Table 3.8. In column A we assume the first story to be critical for the lower column.

TABLE 3.8. Second Approximation—Bent Beams and Girders

Level	North–South Interior	North–South Exterior	East–West Interior	East–West Exterior
R	$W24 \times 84$	$W24 \times 55$	$W18 \times 35$	$W18 \times 35$
6	$W24 \times 100$	$W24 \times 61$	$W24 \times 44$	$W21 \times 49$
5	$W24 \times 100$	$W24 \times 61$	$W24 \times 55$	$W24 \times 61$
4	$W24 \times 110$	$W24 \times 61$	$W24 \times 61$	$W24 \times 68$
3	$W24 \times 110$	$W24 \times 61$	$W24 \times 68$	$W24 \times 68$
2	$W24 \times 120$	$W24 \times 61$	$W24 \times 76$	$W24 \times 76$

Case 1: Gravity only, $P = 816$ kips, $M_x = 71$ k/ft, $M_y = 16$ k/ft
Assume $B_x = 0.180$, $B_y = 0.470$
$$P + P'_x + P'_y = 816 + (0.180)(71 \times 12)$$
$$+ (0.470)(16 \times 12)$$
$$= 816 + 154 + 90 = 1060 \text{ kips}$$

Case 2: Gravity plus wind on x-axis of column
$$M_x = 71 + 255 = 326 \text{ k/ft}$$
$$P + P'_x + P'_y = 816 + (0.18)(326 \times 12) + 90$$
$$= 816 + 704 + 90 = 1610 \text{ kips}$$

Case 3: Gravity plus wind on y-axis of column
$$M_y = 16 + 110 = 126 \text{ k/ft}$$
$$P + P'_x + P'_y = 816 + 154 + (0.47)(126 \times 12)$$
$$= 816 + 154 + 711 = 1681 \text{ kips}$$

Case 3 is critical; for design use $(\frac{3}{4})(1681) = 1261$ kips.

Assuming a K of 1.5 and using the load tables from the AISC Manual (reference 8, see the Appendix):

$$KL = 1.5(15) = 22.5, \text{ say } 22 \text{ ft}$$

$$\text{use: } W14 \times 264$$

With the splice above the second floor, the critical consideration for the second tier of the column is the second story axial load and column moment due to wind plus the gravity moment from the third floor beams.

Case 1:   Gravity only, $P = 682$ kips, $M_x = 67$ k/ft, $M_y = 16$ k/ft

Assume $B_x = 0.185$, $B_y = 0.480$

$$P + P'_x + P'_y = 682 + (0.185)(67 \times 12)$$
$$+ (0.48)(16 \times 12)$$
$$= 682 + 149 + 92 = 923 \text{ kips}$$

Case 2:   Gravity plus wind on *x*-axis of column

$$M_x = 67 + 169 = 236 \text{ k/ft}$$
$$P + P'_x + P'_y = 682 + (0.185)(236 \times 12) + 92$$
$$= 682 + 524 + 92 = 1298 \text{ kips}$$

Case 3:   Gravity plus wind on *y*-axis of column

$$M_y = 16 + 72 = 88 \text{ k/ft}$$
$$P + P'_x + P'_y = 682 + 149 + (0.48)(88 \times 12)$$
$$= 682 + 149 + 507 = 1338 \text{ kips}$$

Case 3 is critical; for design use $(\frac{3}{4})(1338) = 1004$ kips.

Assuming $KL = 1.5(13) = 19.5$, say 19 ft, use $W14 \times 193$.

With the second splice above the fourth floor, the critical loads for the top tier will be the axial load and wind moment at the fourth story and the gravity beam moments from the fifth floor.

Case 1:   Gravity only, $P = 416$ kips, $M_x = 63$ k/ft, $M_y = 15$ k/ft

Assume $B_x = 0.185$, $B_y = 0.50$

$$P + P'_x + P'_y = 416 + (0.185)(63 \times 12)$$
$$+ (0.50)(15 \times 12)$$
$$= 416 + 140 + 90 = 646 \text{ kips}$$

Case 2:   Gravity plus wind on *x*-axis of column

$$M_x = 63 + 109 = 172 \text{ k/ft}$$
$$P + P'_x + P'_y = 416 + (0.185)(172 \times 12) + 90$$
$$= 416 + 382 + 90 = 888 \text{ kips}$$

Case 3:   Gravity plus wind on *y*-axis of column

$$M_y = 16 + 42 = 58 \text{ k/ft}$$
$$P + P'_x + P'_y = 416 + 140 + (0.50)(58 \times 12)$$
$$= 416 + 140 + 348 = 904 \text{ kips}$$

Case 3 is critical; for design use $(\frac{3}{4})(904) = 678$ kips.

Assuming $KL = 19$ ft, use $W14 \times 136$.

TABLE 3.9. Column Sizes—Second Approximation

Level	Assumed Critical KL	Column A Design Load[a]	Choice	Column B Design Load	Choice	Column C Design Load	Choice	Column D Design Load	Choice
R									
6	19 ft	678	$W14 \times 136$	661	$W14 \times 136$	485	$W14 \times 95$	831	$W14 \times 158$
5									
4									
	19 ft	1004	$W14 \times 193$	886	$W14 \times 176$	701	$W14 \times 136$	810	$W14 \times 158$
3									
2									
1	22 ft	1261	$W14 \times 264$	1024	$W14 \times 202$	865	$W14 \times 176$	890	$W14 \times 184$
B									

[a] Design load $= P + P'_x + P'_y$.

From these calculations, and similar ones for the other columns, we summarize a new set of column sizes as shown in Table 3.9.

Having obtained a reasonable approximation of column and beam sizes, the next step would be to perform a more rigorous analysis for the gravity and wind loads on the frames. Assuming that the approximate analysis and design has been carefully performed, this should not result in any startling changes in member sizes. Since an "exact" analysis and design of the bents is beyond the scope of this book, we will proceed with the design using the approximate answers so far obtained. In any event, these sizes are reasonably adequate for use in cost estimates, development of architectural details, and preliminary design of structural connections.

As was mentioned previously, the complete structural design and detailing of this building would be a task involving an amount of work several times the total size of this book. We will, however, briefly discuss some of the additional considerations to be made in the design of the steel frame.

Connections for the steel frame could be all of a relatively routine form. Most members not involved in the bents would use the "standard" framed connections; probably double angles, either bolted or welded. The beam-to-column connections in the bents must be of a moment-resistive form. The variety of possibilities for these is considerable; the commonest types being well illustrated in the AISC Manual. Actually, it is usually desirable to involve the steel fabricator in the final development of these details, since the variables of field conditions and fabricating shop facilities are important considerations. In theory, just about any of the ordinary types of connection could be used for this structure.

The column splices may also be done with a variety of techniques, as shown in the steel manual. The situation is simplified here by the fact that all the columns are of the same nominal size. Because of the rigid frame action, the splices must develop some significant moment resistance in both directions, as well as transmit the axial compression.

The column base connection consists essentially of a rectangular steel bearing plate that functions to transmit the highly concentrated bearing stress from the column into a much lower, distributed bearing stress on the top of the concrete foundation. This involves considerable bending in the plate if it cantilevers significantly from the face of the column. The three basic determinants for the plate size and thickness are therefore the size of the column, the value of the total axial compression load, and the allowable bearing on the concrete.

TABLE 3.10. Base Plates for the Steel Columns

Column	Design Load (kips)	Size Selected and Actual Dimensions (Width × Depth)	Size for which Plate is Designed (AISC Table)[a]	Plate Size (in.)
A	1012	$W14 \times 264$ $16\frac{1}{2} \times 16$	$W14 \times 167$ $15\frac{1}{8} \times 15\frac{5}{8}$	$29 \times 32 \times 3\frac{1}{8}$
B	546	$W14 \times 202$ $15\frac{5}{8} \times 15\frac{3}{4}$	$W14 \times 95$ $14\frac{1}{8} \times 14\frac{1}{2}$	$22 \times 24 \times 1\frac{7}{8}$
C	546	$W14 \times 176$ $15\frac{1}{4} \times 15\frac{3}{4}$	$W14 \times 95$ $14\frac{1}{8} \times 14\frac{1}{2}$	$22 \times 24 \times 1\frac{7}{8}$
D	332	$W14 \times 184$ $15\frac{3}{8} \times 15\frac{5}{8}$	$W14 \times 61$ $13\frac{7}{8} \times 10$	$16 \times 20 \times 1\frac{1}{2}$

[a] See the Appendix. Based on $f_y = 36$ ksi, $f'_c = 3000$ psi.

Approximate sizes for the plates can be obtained from the tables in the steel manual. Individual plate sizes are tabulated for each of the wide flange column sizes. However, the axial load used assumes a full development of maximum compressive stress in the column. Since our column sizes are considerably increased by the bending moments, this means that the size of plate shown for the columns is larger than necessary. The approximate plate size should therefore be selected by using the tabulated "maximum load" rather than the column size. This will result in a plate of reasonably correct total bearing area size, but may result in a conservative thickness, since the bending may be less if the column size is larger. A set of bearing plates selected on this basis is shown in Table 3.10.

The steel frame and metal deck must be protected to obtain the fire ratings required by the code. The means for this, as assumed in the determination of dead loads and shown later in the construction drawings, are as follows:

Top surface of the metal deck and beams is protected by the concrete fill. At openings and at the spandrel this is sometimes carried around the exposed face of the beam to the level of the bottom flange.

Bottom of the metal deck and bottom and sides of the beams are protected by sprayed-on fireproofing.

Depending on the architectural details, the columns may be protected by cast concrete jackets, by sprayed-on fireproofing, or by lath and plaster encasement.

The exterior curtain wall design involves a number of structural detailing considerations. The wall itself must be designed for the gravity and wind forces and the attachments to the structural frame must transmit these forces to the frame. The variety of possibilities is virtually endless, with the variables of the materials and details of the wall, the location of the wall relative to the columns and spandrel beams, the incorporation of HVAC elements and the facilitation of interior partitioning. The construction details shown later present a fairly common solution, involving an exterior wall of metal and glass and the facilitation of a modular interior partitioning system.

Another detail consideration is that of the support necessary for the various items that must be hung from the underside of the roof and floor structure. This includes the ceiling systems, HVAC ducts and components, lights, electrical conduits, and so on. Support will usually be provided by brackets from the beams or by wires from the deck. With the use of a modular ceiling system most of this support will be achieved by hanging a basic framing system that accommodates elements of the modular ceiling. Lights and HVAC registers will usually be a part of the ceiling system and will be supported by this frame. Large ducts and wiring for the lights may be separately hung within the ceiling void space. Individual support is usually provided for any heavy fans, reheat units, and similar features that are incorporated in this space. The needs for this equipment and the means for supporting it must be considered in establishing the floor-to-floor dimension and the details of the floor framing.

As shown in Figure 3.5, we have provided a total of 48 in. for the distance from the bottom of the ceiling to the top of the floor fill. Some preliminary sizing and coordination of the structure, the HVAC and lighting systems, and the architectural details would have to be done to establish this dimension. A major consideration is often the size of the large supply ducts for the air handling system, which must pass under the beams. If cooling is achieved with the air system, the ducts will be insulated and of larger size, which further increases the clearance required.

A final consideration for the steel frame is that of the tolerable vertical deflection of the floor and roof systems. This is a complex issue involving considerable judgment and not much factual criteria. Some of the specific considerations are:

The bounciness of the floors. This is essentially a matter of the stiffness and fundamental period of vibration of the deck. Use of static deflection limits generally recommended will usually assure reasonable lack of bounce.

Transfer of bearing to the curtain wall and partitions. The deformations of the frame caused by live gravity loads and wind must be considered in developing the joints between the structure and the nonstructural walls. Flexible gaskets, sliding connections, and so on, must be used to permit the movements caused by these loads as well as those due to thermal expansion and contraction.

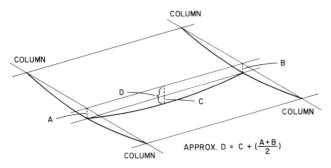

FIGURE 3.23. Deflection of the floor.

Dead load deflection of the floor structure. As shown in Figure 3.23, there is a cumulative deflection at the center of a column bay because of the deflection of the girders plus the deflection of the beams. Within the normally permitted deflections, this could add up to a considerable amount for the 36 ft spans. If permitted to occur, the result would be that the top of the metal deck would be several inches below that at the columns. Since the top of the concrete fill must be as flat as possible, this could produce a much thicker fill in the center of the bays. The usual means for compensating for this is to specify a camber for the beams approximately equal to the calculated dead load deflection.

Where heavy permanent walls and openings for stairs, elevators, and duct shafts occur, special framing must be provided, as shown in the framing plans in Figure 3.7 and in the construction drawings. Light partitions may be supported directly by the deck, but heavy masonry walls should be placed over framing members.

3.7 Design of the First Floor, Basement, and Foundations

The basement plan, shown in Figure 3.3, shows that part of the first floor will be framed as a spanning structure over the basement area and part will be placed over unexcavated (actually backfilled) earth. Several options are possible for each of these conditions. We will assume that the portion over the basement will consist of the same basic system as the typical floor: steel beams with metal deck and concrete fill. The beams would frame directly to the steel columns or would be seated on the concrete basement walls.

Because of the considerable amount of backfill that would be required, it is probably not advisable to use a simple slab on fill for the remainder of the floor, since considerable settlement would occur. The other options are to use a framed floor over a crawl space or a concrete framed system poured directly on fill. The plan and some details for the latter option are shown in the construction drawings. The system consists of a two-way concrete slab on edge supports with a beam system providing support on 18 ft centers in each direction. The beams are supported by the steel columns, the basement walls, and a series of small piers in the center of the 36 ft spans.

Since the building plans indicate that the first floor will also be used for rental office space, it is assumed that the distribution of power and communication in the floor is required. In the floor area over the basement this would be accomplished as for the typical floor, using the metal deck voids and the concrete fill. In the remainder of the floor it would be necessary to deal with this as for a concrete framed floor, with the distribution done in a lightweight concrete fill on top of the structural concrete. Details of this system are shown in Figure 3.8 as utilized for the concrete floor system in the next example.

The partial basement also produces two different conditions for the steel columns and the footings. Those in the area of the basement must be dropped below the level of the basement floor. Those in the remainder of the plan could theoretically be quite higher; only a short distance below the first floor structure. However, for a number of reasons they would probably be fairly deep. Some of the considerations are:

To obtain the relatively high allowable soil bearing and to assure equalized settlement of the foundations.

To avoid influence of the pressure of the higher footings on the deeper adjacent ones.

To allow for tying or strutting of the isolated footings, as would be required if seismic loads were critical.

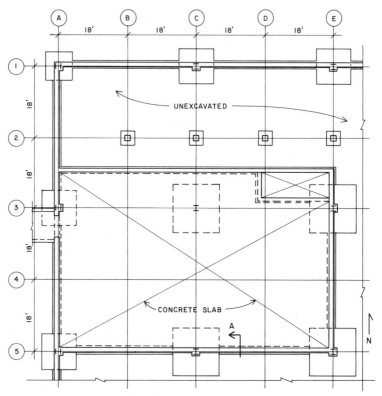

FIGURE 3.24.   Partial basement and foundation plan.

Because of the elevator pit and the driveway on the west side of the basement, some of the footings would be dropped an additional distance. The result is that the bottoms of the footings for this building will occur at several different elevations. The foundation plan shown in Figure 3.24 in the construction drawings indicates this condition.

The "typical" footings are designed as shown in Table 3.11. Sizes are shown for the three basic column load conditions and for the first floor intermediate piers. The design loads include the previously tabulated steel column loads plus the loads from the first floor and the basement walls. The footing sizes and reinforcement are derived

TABLE 3.11.   Typical Footings

Footing For	Load on Footing (kips)	Footing Size	Reinforcing Each Way
Column A	1100	12 ft. 3 in. × 12 ft. 3 in. × 43 in.	20 No. 10
Column B	600	9 ft. × 9 ft × 32 in.	14 No. 9
Column D	400	7 ft. 3 in. × 7 ft. 3 in. × 27 in.	12 No. 8
First floor pier	100	3 ft. 9 in. × 3 ft. 9 in. × 14 in.	7 No. 5

from the tables in the ACI *Reinforced Concrete Design Handbook* (SP-3) using f_c' of 3000 psi and soil pressure of 8000 psf.

The basement walls and the grade walls between columns in the unexcavated area will be placed on wall footings. However, they will also tend to span between columns because of their high relative stiffness as deep beams. It is probably advisable to consider them as spanning and to provide adequate reinforcing for this as well as some additional size for the column footings.

3.8   Construction Drawings—Steel Structure

The illustrations that follow show some of the construction details for the building with the steel frame. Since we did not discuss the design of the roof and penthouse, we have shown the structural plans for the typical floor the first floor and the basement and foundations only.

There are obviously many details that need coordination between the structure and the various architectural elements. We have shown some possibilities for some of the architectural elements of the ceilings, walls, floors, and the exterior curtain wall in order to illustrate the relations that need consideration. Since our principal concern is for the structure, however, we have not shown the complete building construction details.

Basement and Foundation Plan.   (Figure 3.24.) The partial plan in Figure 3.24 shows most of the typical situations for the basement and foundation construction. The foundations consist of bearing footings for the walls and the concentrated pier and column loads. Particular characteristics of the soil strata, the ground water condition, site grading, and so on, may influence the detailing of these subgrade elements. We have assumed a relatively high soil capacity of 8000 psf and have developed the construction details in response to various structural and building planning considerations. Some of these considesations are as follows:

1. Depth of column footings. Where the basement occurs the column footings must be dropped a distance sufficient to permit the steel base plate and anchor bolts to fit above the footing without protruding above the floor slab. Although the basement slab itself could be used to provide part of the cover, we have shown the footing dropped to allow for a separate encasement of the base plate and the anchor bolts. By having the floor slab float freely above this encasement, it is possible for the granular subbase and a waterproofing membrane to be placed continuously under the floor slab. If a serious water condition exists, more details would be required to prevent water from entering the basement.

   Where there is no basement, the column footings could be raised. The height of these footings would depend on:

   The level at which the desirable soil bearings can be found.

   The need for frost protection (depth of the footing below the adjacent finished grade).

   Depth of adjacent excavation or construction: other column footings, walls, elevator pit, utility trenches, tunnels, and so on.

2. Depth of wall footings. There are two basic types of walls: the basement walls and walls that serve as grade walls at the edges of the ground floor. The basement walls must be carried below the level of the basement floor slab as a minimum. Since they will rest directly on the column footings at some points, the minimum location of the bottom of the walls would probably be at the tops of the column footings, as shown in Detail A (Figure 3.27). If the wall footing is placed at this depth, it would be considerably higher than the adjacent deep column footings. Its effectiveness would therefore be limited in the vicinity of the column footings. To allow for this the wall footing can be stepped down to the level of the bottom of the

column footing, or the walls can be designed to span across this short distance.

Where there is no basement the walls would probably be reduced in height. They may be designed for bearing on their own footings, or may be designed as beams spanning between the column footings. In either case, a wall footing would probably be used as a construction platform for the wall forms.

3. Use of walls as ties. In addition to their functions as walls or grade beams, the concrete walls serve as ties, holding the whole subgrade construction together as a structural entity. This is considered as a critical requirement when seismic forces are the major lateral load condition. In this case there would probably be some additional tie walls or struts provided between the interior column footings to supplement the basement and grade walls shown in the plan. Where wind is the major lateral load consideration, the basement floor slab and the first floor concrete construction as shown would probably be sufficient.

First Floor Framing Plan.   (Figure 3.25.) The first floor area over the basement is shown with a structure similar to that for the typical upper level floors. At the unexcavated portions the first floor structure consists of a concrete slab and beam system poured directly over fill. The typical beam is formed as shown in Detail C (Figure 3.29). This network of beams on 18 ft centers is supported by the basement and grade walls and by a series of intermediate piers. The typical slab is a two-way slab on edge supports, with a few one-way slabs at the north side of the basement. Since this same system is used for the concrete structure, its design is discussed in that section.

These two systems interface at the interior basement walls, as shown in Detail E (Figure 3.31). The concrete fill is continuous over both systems. A special detail required is the support for the steel beams at the concrete walls, as shown in Details D and E (Figures 3.30 and 3.31). This consists of a pocket in the wall with some erection bolts and a bearing plate for the end of the beam.

Typical Floor Framing Plan—Upper Levels.   (Figure 3.26.) The typical floor consists of the steel deck placed over the network of beams that provide supports at 9 ft centers as well as at the

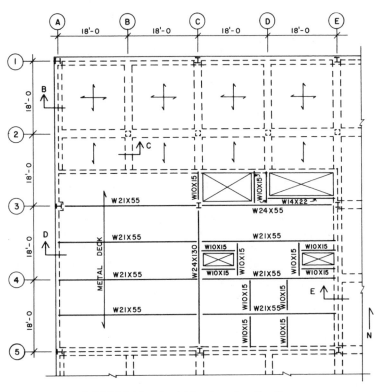

FIGURE 3.25. Partial framing plan: first floor.

building edges and at the edges of large openings. Some of the considerations in the detailing of this system are as follows:

1. Attachment of the steel deck. The deck units are normally welded to the steel beams in the valleys of the deck corrugations. These connections must transfer the lateral loads from the floor, acting as a diaphragm, to the steel beams, which in turn transfer the loads to the column/beam bents. Details for this attachment and load ratings for the connections and deck are usually provided by the deck manufacturers.

2. Support for the hung ceiling, lights, ducts, and so on. The usual method of support for the ceiling is by wires that are installed

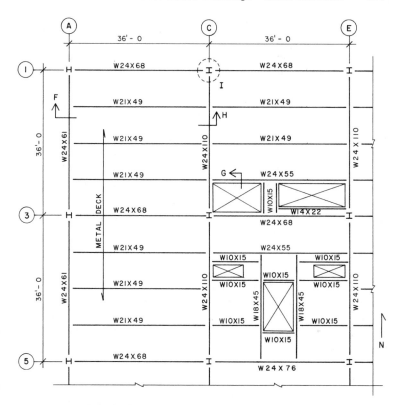

FIGURE 3.26.   Partial framing plan: typical floor.

through holes in the steel deck. Wire sizes and spacing and details for instalation will depend on the type of ceiling and the specific type of deck used. Lighting units, ceiling registers, and small ducts may be supported as part of the ceiling construction, using the same wire hangers. Heavy ducts and equipment elements of the HVAC system will usually be supported by brackets or hangers attached directly to the beams.

3. Fireproofing of the floor construction. As discussed previously, the system used here consists of utilizing the concrete fill on top of the deck to protect the upper surface of the deck as well

as the faces of beams at the building edge and the edges of openings. The underside of the deck and the remaining exposed surfaces of beams are protected by sprayed-on fireproofing.

4.   Support for interior walls. Planning of this building envisions two basic types of interior walls: permanent and demountable. Permanent walls are limited to those in the core and would consist of masonry or metal framed plastered partitions. The weight of these plus their permanency would dictate that the floor structure provide both vertical and lateral support as part of the permanent structural system. Construction and finish of these walls would be influenced by desired architectural details, as well as by considerations of structural design, required code fire rating, acoustic separation, and similar factors.

Demountable walls may consist of a variety of constructions. Some of them may consist of masonry or plastered partitions, although the design of the floor deck should consider this if such is the case. It is expected, however, that most walls will consist of some relatively light construction, including possibly the use of some patented, modular system of relocatable units. The choice of the ceiling system and its detailing would need to consider the necessity for providing attachment and lateral support for whatever walls are anticipated.

The framing plans shown are abbreviated for clarity. Complete construction drawings would include sufficient information to establish the exact location of all beams, to establish the elevations of beam tops, to indicate required camber of beams, and to identify the type of connection for each beam. Some of this information may also be provided in details or schedules and be referred to by notes or symbols on the plans.

Detail A.   (Figure 3.27.) This section shows the relations between the basement floor, the basement wall and the steel column and its footing. The basement floor is a paving slab over compacted fill. Necessity for a moisture barrier under the slab and moisture penetration resistant treatment at the slab-to-wall intersection would depend on the ground water conditions at the site.

The basement wall at this point is a retaining wall, spanning vertically from the basement floor to the first floor construction.

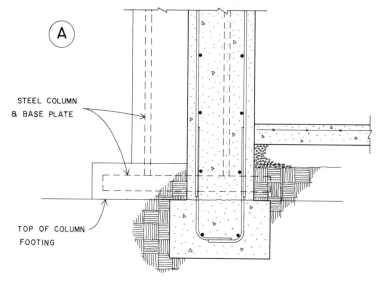

FIGURE 3.27.   Detail A.

Location of the wall footing was discussed previously in regard to the foundation plan. As shown in the detail, and also discussed previously, the top of the column footing is shown dropped so that the base plate and anchor bolts can be encased below the floor slab.

Detail B.   (Figure 3.28.) This shows the general condition at the building edge adjacent to the unexcavated lower level. To accommodate the rental areas on the first floor the first story wall is assumed to be similar in detail to that for the typical floor, as shown in Detail F (Figure 3.32).

The first floor structural slab, although poured over fill, is a spanning slab and is supported vertically by the grade wall. In cold climates there should be some insulation for the floor at the building edge and a thermal break between the floor slab and the exterior wall.

Detail C.   (Figure 3.29.) This shows the typical beam for the unexcavated portion of the first floor. If the fill material is reasonably cohesive, the lower stem of this beam may be excavated by trenching,

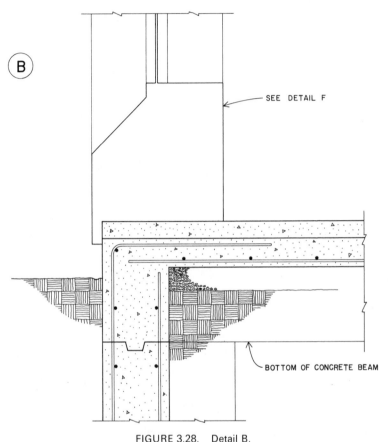

SEE DETAIL F

BOTTOM OF CONCRETE BEAM

FIGURE 3.28. Detail B.

as shown. The reinforcing in the beam requires the usual 3 in. cover as for footings.

The piers for these beams (midway between columns) would probably be poured with column forms before the fill is placed, with the pour stopped at the level of the bottom of the beams and the pier vertical reinforcing extending into the beam.

Detail D. (Figure 3.30.) This shows the edge condition adjacent to the steel framed floor. The first story wall is assumed to be similar

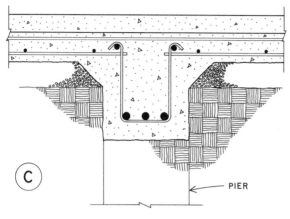

FIGURE 3.29.   Detail C.

to that for Detail B (Figure 3.28). The steel beams are shown as supported by the wall, with a pocket, bearing plate and erection anchor bolts.

Some consideration should be given to the transfer of horizontal force between the top of the wall and the floor construction, if the basement wall is a retaining wall. At the section cut this is not the case because of the truck dock area.

Detail E.   (Figure 3.31.) This shows the intersection between the two types of floor construction at the top of the basement wall. Since the concrete fill is continuous over both structures, the tops of the steel deck and the structural concrete slab are at the same level.

The key at the top of the wall pour should be adequate to provide for the lateral force due to the retained fill. The top of the wall pour is dropped to the level of the bottom of the concrete beams in order to allow the bottom reinforcing in the beams to extend over the supporting wall.

Detail F.   (Figure 3.32.) This shows the typical spandrel condition at the upper floors. The metal framed window wall is shown centered on the column line with the finished face of the spandrel brought out flush with the finished face of the column. Although not shown in

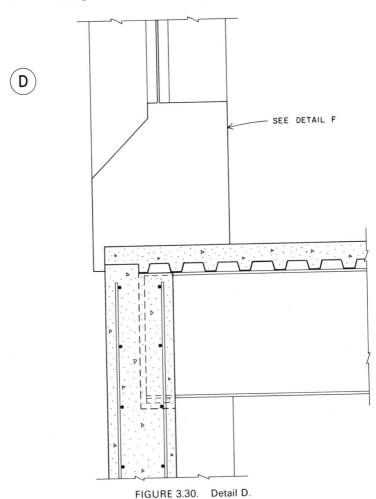

SEE DETAIL F

FIGURE 3.30.   Detail D.

detail, it is assumed that the building skin at the spandrels and columns consists of insulated units with an exterior metal facing. These units are shown supported by brackets from the floor and the spandrel beam. The window wall units rest on a short steel stud wall with a wide sill brought out to the finished face of the column. The space under these sills may house HVAC units, if such a system is

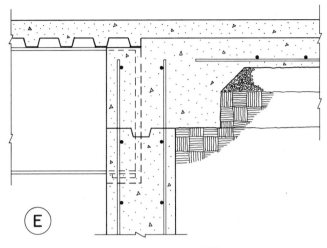

FIGURE 3.31. Detail E.

used. Lateral support must also be provided for the top of the window units. One way to achieve this would be to add some additional elements to the bracket that is attached to the bottom of the spandrel beam.

These details are of major concern in the architectural design and are subject to considerable variation without significant change in the basic structural system for the building.

Detail G. (Figure 3.33.) This shows one possibility for the floor edge condition at the large openings for the stair, elevators, and duct shafts. Although the section has concrete block for the wall, other materials may be used if a thinner wall is desired. One variation would be to stop the concrete closer to the steel beam and to run the wall past the face of the concrete.

Detail H. (Figure 3.34.) This illustrates a typical beam connection using standard double angle connectn the angles are typically welded to the beams in connected to the girders with bolts.

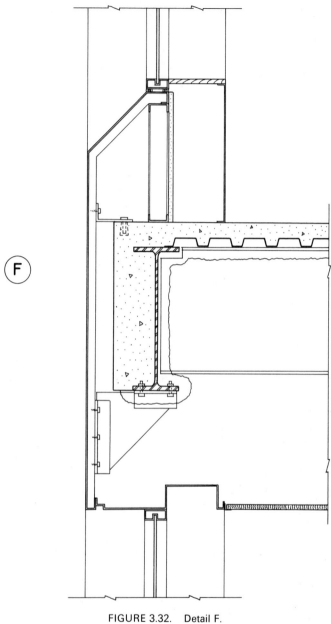

FIGURE 3.32. Detail F.

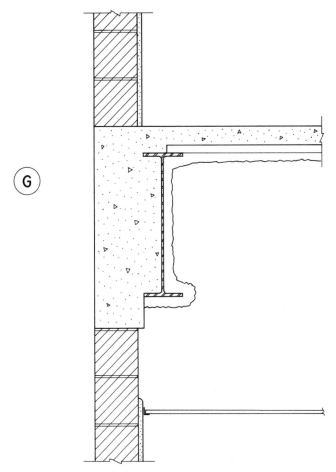

FIGURE 3.33.   Detail G.

Detail I.   (Figure 3.35.) This shows one possibility for the beam-to-column and girder-to-column connections to achieve the column/beam bents. For erection and shear transfer vertical plates would be added to connect the beam webs to the columns. The moment connections are achieved by butt welding the beam and girder flanges to the face of the column or to the stiffener plates that are coped and welded to the column web and inside face of the flanges.

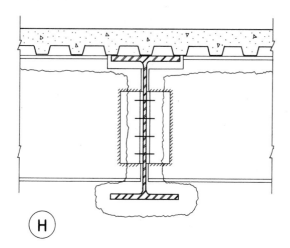

FIGURE 3.34.   Detail H.

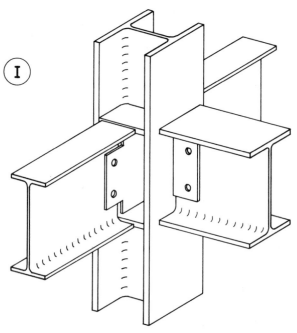

FIGURE 3.35.   Detail I.

188

Since shop fabrication and field erection practices vary somewhat locally, as well as between different steel fabricators, the final details and specifications for these connections should be worked out cooperatively between the building designer and the steel fabricator.

3.9 The Concrete Structure

Figure 3.36 shows a framing plan for the typical floor using a reinforced concrete slab and beam system and reinforced concrete columns. The basic system consists of a series of beams on 12 ft centers supporting a multiple span, one-way slab. The orientation of the beams was elected to preserve the continuity of the majority

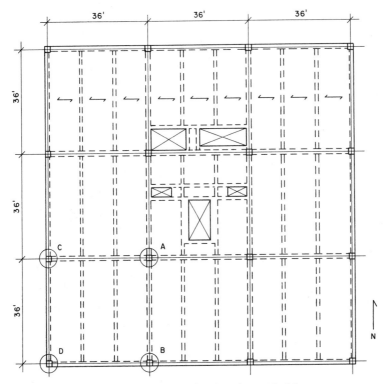

FIGURE 3.36. Concrete framing plan: typical floor.

of the beams; the only interrupted beams being at the opening for the elevators. As with the steel system, the beams and girders on the column lines form a series of rigid bents for the resistance of lateral loads.

The beam spacing is related to the slab thickness, which must be a minimum of $4\frac{1}{2}$ in. for the required two hour fire rating. Since the girders will be quite large, there is not much gain to be made by forcing the beams to a minimum depth. Other options for the beam spacing would be 9 ft or 18 ft. For various reasons, the 12 ft spacing seems to be best.

As with the steel structure, the exterior curtain wall could be a skin system completely covering the structure. In order to show some different detailing situations, however, we will use an exposed exterior structure, with the exterior columns and the spandrel beams forming part of the exterior building surface. On the interior of the building the structure will be covered by the floor fill, by the ceiling, and by plaster finish on the interior sides of columns.

A similar framing system would be used for the roof structure and for the portion of the first floor over the basement area. The penthouse, however, would probably be a light steel frame structure. The basement and foundations and the portion of the first floor on fill would be similar to that for the steel structure.

The basic concrete strength used will be an f_c' of 4000 psi. This is a matter of some variation regionally, being effected by economics as well as practical considerations of available materials and construction practices. It is advisable to use a slightly higher than average value for the concrete quality if the structure is to be exposed to the weather. It is sometimes possible to use a higher strength for the concrete in the lower story columns, in order to keep their sizes down.

For the beams and slabs we will use steel with f_y of 50,000 psi. For the columns we will use two grades of steel: f_y of 60,000 psi in the upper stories and f_y of 75,000 psi in the lower stories. The various ramifications of these choices will be discussed during the design illustration that follows.

3.10   Design of the Concrete Floor System

Since the majority of the beams are multiple span and/or part of the indeterminate column bents, exact analysis would most likely be done with computer programs. For a reasonably approximate design we will use the coefficients given in Chapter 8 of the ACI Code (reference number 9). For simplification we will also use the working stress method for most of the design, which will produce somewhat conservative results in most cases when compared to those that would be obtained using the ultimate load method.

Design of the Floor Slab

Live loads: 50 psf for the office areas
100 psf for lobbies, corridors, stairs
2000 lb concentrated load per UBC 2304(c)

Dead loads:
Slab (estimate 5 in.)	=	63 psf
3 in. lightweight fill	=	30
Ceiling, lights, ducts	=	15
Partitions [UBC 2304(d)]	=	20
Total dead load:	=	128 psf + beam stems

The total design load for the slab is thus 178 psf for the typical office areas. With a beam width of 15 in. the clear span for the interior spans will be 10 ft 9 in. Because of the exposed spandrels, the end spans will be slightly larger. We will assume them to be 11 ft 3 in. Referring to Figure 3.38, the maximum moment in the slab will be $(\frac{1}{10})wL^2$ on the end span. We may thus check the slab for this condition as follows:

$$\text{maximum } M = (\tfrac{1}{10})(178)(11.25)^2 = 2253 \text{ lb/ft}$$

Using $f_c' = 4000$ psi and $f_s = 20,000$ psi, for a 1 ft strip:

$$\text{required } bd^2 = \frac{M}{K} = \frac{2253(12)}{324} = 83.44 \text{ in.}^3$$

$$\text{required } d = \frac{\sqrt{83.44}}{12} = 2.64 \text{ in.}$$

As shown in Figure 3.37, with a 1 in. cover and maximum bar size of #5, the actual d will be 3.94 in. This means that the concrete stress

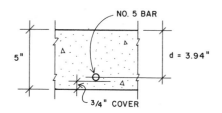

FIGURE 3.37.   Detail of the concrete slab.

in flexure will not be critical and all sections will be in the classifica-
tion of underreinforced. This makes the true j values all higher than
that for the balanced section.

Except for very short, highly loaded spans, shear stress will not be
critical for a one-way spanning slab. Limiting deflection may be
checked against the requirements in Chapter 9 of the ACI Code.
These call for a minimum thickness of $\frac{1}{24}$th of the span with one end
discontinuous and $\frac{1}{28}$th of the span with both ends continuous. Thus:

$$\frac{11.24(12)}{24} = 5.625 \text{ in. for the end spans}$$

$$\frac{10.75(12)}{28} = 4.607 \text{ in. for the interior spans}$$

Since the large spandrel beams will actually provide considerable
restraint, it seems reasonable to use the 5 in. slab.

Using an approximate value for j, the required steel areas at the
various critical sections are determined and the bars selected as
shown in Figure 3.38. The steel areas may be derived directly from
the moment coefficients as follows:

$$M = CwL^2 = C(178)(11.25)^2 = C(22{,}528) \text{ for the end span}$$

$$A_s = \frac{M}{f_s jd} = \frac{C(22{,}528)(12)}{(20{,}000)(0.88)(3.94)}$$

$$= C(3.90) \text{ for the end span, and } C(3.56) \text{ for interior spans}$$

In order to save steel tonnage an alternating system of long and
short bars may be used, as shown in the bottom part in Figure 3.38.

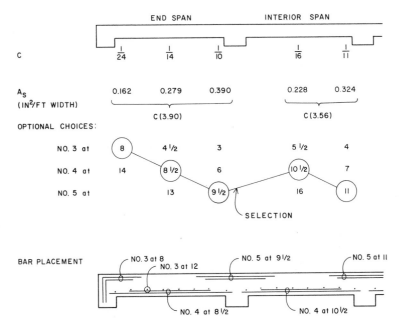

FIGURE 3.38.   Design of the slab reinforcement.

Design of the Typical Beam.

The beams not on the column lines are mostly three-span members carrying uniform load from a 12 ft wide strip of floor. We will design these for the span of 36 ft using the moment coefficients from the ACI Code. Without deflection calculations the minimum depth is limited to $L/18.5$, or approximately 24 in. For a preliminary calculation we will assume a 15 in. wide by 24 in. high section. The design load will then be:

Dead load:	Slab at 128 psf × 12	= 1536 lb/ft
	Beam stem (19 by 15)	= 297
	Total dead load	= 1833 lb/ft
Live load:	33 psf × 12	= 396 (reduced for area)
Total design load		= 2229 lb/ft

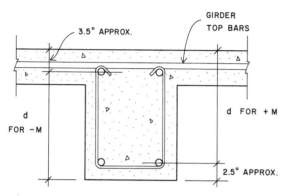

FIGURE 3.39.   Detail of the typical beam.

The maximum moment at the first interior support will be:

$$M = (\tfrac{1}{10})(wL^2) = (\tfrac{1}{10})(2.229)(36)^2 = 289 \text{ k/ft}$$

For a rough guide the section chosen should be capable of about two thirds of this moment without compressive reinforcing. We thus compare the critical moment just determined with the balanced moment capacity of the section:

$$M = Kbd^2 = \frac{(0.324)(15)(20.5)^2}{12} = 170 \text{ k/ft}$$

Since this indicates that the balanced moment capacity of the trial section is only 59 % of the critical required moment, we will reselect the section. Note that the actual value for d, as shown in Figure 3.39, is taken as approximately 3.5 in. less than the overall height for negative moment. This permits the top reinforcing in the girders to be placed above that in the intersecting beams, giving the heavier loaded girders the advantage. For positive moment, however, this problem does not exist, since the beam and girder will have different depths. Thus the d for positive moment will be approximated by deducting 2.5 in. from the height.

Based on the preliminary calculations, we will select the beam size for an approximate balanced moment capacity of 200 k/ft. If

$$M = 200 \text{ k/ft} = Kbd^2$$

Then

$$bd^2 = \frac{M}{K} = \frac{(200)(12)}{0.324} = 7407.$$

And

if $b = 12$ in., $d = \sqrt{\dfrac{7407}{12}} = \sqrt{617} = 24.8$ in.

if $b = 15$ in., $d = \sqrt{\dfrac{7407}{15}} = \sqrt{494} = 22.2$ in.

For a second trial we will select a 15 × 26 in. overall size with a d of approximately 22.5 in. for negative moment. This beam should now be checked for shear stress as follows. From the ACI Code the maximum shear is taken as $1.15(wL/2)$. Using a maximum clear span of 34.5 ft, the maximum end shear will be

$$V = 1.15\left(\frac{wL}{2}\right) = 1.15(2260)\left(\frac{34.5}{2}\right) = 44{,}833 \text{ lb}$$

For design the critical shear may be taken at a d distance from the support. We thus deduct $(22.5/12)(2260)$, or 4238 lb from the end shear and design for a shear of 40,595 lb.

The maximum design shear stress will be

$$v = \frac{V}{bd} = \frac{40{,}595}{(15)(22.5)} = 120 \text{ psi}$$

With the f_c' of 4000 psi the allowable shear stress on the concrete is 70 psi. Deducting this from the maximum shear stress leaves 50 psi to be carried by the shear reinforcing. With #3 U stirrups and an allowable stress of 20 ksi, the required spacing at the end of the beam is

$$s = \frac{(A_v)(f_v)}{(v')(b)} = \frac{2(0.11)(20{,}000)}{(50)(15)} = 5.87 \text{ in.}$$

This is quite reasonable for a beam of this size, so the section is not critical for shear. We now proceed to a preliminary selection of the beam reinforcing using the ACI Code coefficients for the critical moments. The required steel areas will be determined from the moments as follows: For positive moment the section is a T, and we will use an approximate jd equal to d minus $t/2$. Thus

$$jd = d - \frac{t}{2} = 23.5 - 2.5 = 21.0$$

$$A_s = \frac{M}{f^s jd} = \frac{M(12)}{20(21)} = 0.0286M \ (M \text{ in k/ft})$$

For negative moment, as discussed previously, $d = h - 3.5$. Thus, using the balanced section value for j, we have

$$d = 26 - 3.5 = 22.5 \text{ in.}$$

$$A_s = \frac{M}{f_s jd} = \frac{M(12)}{20(0.86)(22.5)} = 0.0310M$$

This may be used for moment up to 200 k/ft (the balanced capacity) with an additional reinforcing for the double reinforced section for moment in excess of 200 k/ft. This addition will be

$$A_s = \frac{M}{f_s(d - d')} = \frac{M(12)}{20(22.5 - 2.5)} = 0.30M$$

Actually the A_s values could be derived directly from the ACI Code coefficients. The author, however, prefers to see the values of the moments calculated for a better sense of the design forces.

Figure 3.40 shows the calculations for determination of the critical moments and steel areas for the typical beam. Before final selection of the reinforcing the bond stresses must be checked and the allowable stress for the compressive reinforcing verified. The placement of the reinforcing must also be selected with the details of the girder and its reinforcing.

With regard to the beam itself, some of the placement considerations are shown in Figure 3.40. In order to keep the reinforcing in one layer at the bottom of the beam in the exterior span, the beam width must be increased. An alternative to this would be to increase the depth, if headroom is not critical. The depth increase would slightly reduce the steel area required and would add less additional concrete to the section.

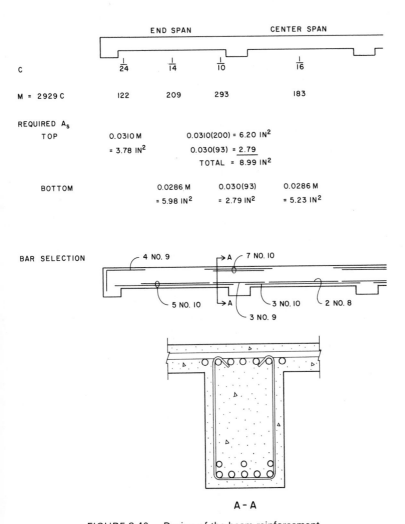

FIGURE 3.40.   Design of the beam reinforcement.

In the top of the beam it is possible to place some of the reinforcing outside the stirrups, as shown, as long as the minimum cover is maintained. For the negative moment at the interior support the added bars shown would have to be placed in a second layer, which slightly reduces the $(d - d')$ moment arm that was assumed in the calculations.

The reinforcing for the compression side of the double reinforced section may be provided by a separate set of bars as shown. If so, they would have to be placed in a second layer. An alternative would be to bend the bars from the interior span to fit over those in the end span. Doing this at both ends, however, would result in rather long bars, which may not be desirable for handling.

Design of the Column Bent Beam. The interior beam on the column line will have the same combination of wind and gravity moments as was illustrated in the design of the steel structure. We will use a process of designing the beams for the gravity moments first and then investigate the need for any changes required for the added wind moments. As will be seen, this works reasonably well for this building, but may not be as useful for buildings of greater height or shorter beam spans.

For the gravity load design the only difference for the column line beam will be an increase of the end moment at the outside column to $(\frac{1}{16})wL^2$. This is an increase of 50 % over that used for the end moment at the spandrel girder for the typical beam.

Some general design considerations for the column line beams are:

1. The beam reinforcing must pass through the columns. The size and spacing of the column reinforcing must be carefully coordinated with that for the beam to allow for this.
2. Some of the top reinforcing should be made continuous to provide for reversal moment and to add torsional strength to the bents.
3. Some of the bottom reinforcing in the end span should be extended into the exterior column and bent into the outside face of the column. This is to provide for the reversal wind moment.

4. Full loop stirrups (similar to column ties) should be provided through the length of the beam to increase its torsional strength.

With the exposed structure, as discussed previously, the design of the spandrel beams and girders must be coordinated with the general architectural design of the exterior walls. Figure 3.41 shows one possibility for the spandrel. Although it would be poured with a construction joint as shown, the section could be considered as a single structural unit with doweling of the vertical reinforcing and a series of horizontal shear keys at the pour joint. This very deep section, with an approximate d of 70 in., would result in a much higher stiffness for the exterior column/beam bents, which means that they would take a higher percentage of the total wind force on the building. This effect will be considered later in the wind design.

With the section as shown in Figure 3.41, the wall load on the spandrel will be as follows:

Spandrel: (14 by 75 approximately) = 1094 lb/ft
Window wall: 6 ft at 15 psf   =   90
Total wall load   = 1184 lb/ft

Added to this will be approximately one half of the dead and live loads for the typical beam. Because of the slightly smaller area of floor supported by the spandrel beam, the live load reduction will be less. The design loads are thus

Total dead load: 1184 + ($\frac{1}{2}$)(1536) = 1952 lb/ft
Life load: 42 psf × 6   =   252 lb/ft
Total design load   = 2204 lb/ft

Since this total is approximately the same as that for the typical beam, the design gravity moments will be similar. The spandrel has such a large d, however, that the calculated steel areas will be quite small. Because of its depth, its exposure, and the high wind moments in the exterior bents, the spandrels should be reinforced with continuous top and bottom reinforcing, with other minimal reinforcing as for a wall, and with vertical loop ties throughout their length.

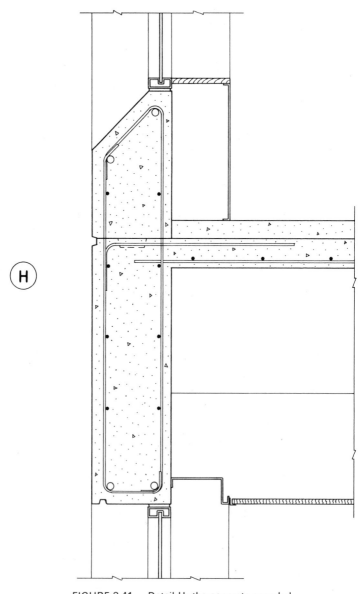

FIGURE 3.41.　Detail H: the concrete spandrel.

Design of the Girders.   As in the steel structure, the girders carry a combination of uniform and concentrated loads. The proportion of the uniform to the concentrated load is slightly higher here, because of the heavier girder and the two-way action of the slab which pulls some of the floor load to the girder at the ends of the beams. For an approximate design we will determine the total load on the girder and consider it to be carried as uniform load, using the ACI Code coefficients for design moments. The load on the interior girder is as follows:

Beams: Dead load $= 2 \times 34.5 \times 1860$ lb/ft $= 128{,}340$ lb
Live load $= 2 \times 34.5 \times 12 \times 30$ psf $= 24{,}840$ lb

Assuming an 18×30 girder:

Stem dead load $= (18 \times 25)(150/144)(34) =$ $15{,}938$ lb
Floor dead load $= 1.5 \times 34 \times 128$ psf $=$ $6{,}528$ lb
Floor live load $= 1.5 \times 34 \times 30$ $=$ $1{,}530$ lb
Total load on girder $= \overline{177{,}176}$ lb

On the spandrel girder the load will be approximately one half of that due to the beams plus the spandrel dead load as calculated for the spandrel beam. Thus

$\frac{1}{2}$ of beam load $=$ $76{,}590$ lb
spandrel $+$ wall $=$ $40{,}256$
total load $= \overline{116{,}846}$

For the spandrel girder the maximum moment and area of steel required are

$$M = (\tfrac{1}{10})WL = (\tfrac{1}{10})(117)(34) = 397.8 \text{ k/ft}$$

$$A_s = \frac{M}{f_s jd} = \frac{397.8(12)}{20(0.86)(70)} = 3.96 \text{ in.}^2$$

The selection of the reinforcing should be delayed until the wind analysis is made.

For the interior girder, assuming an 18×30 in. section with a d of 27.5 in.:

$$M = (\tfrac{1}{10})(177)(34) = 601.8 \text{ k/ft}$$

$$A_s = \frac{601.8(12)}{20(0.86)(27.5)} = 15.3 \text{ in.}^2$$

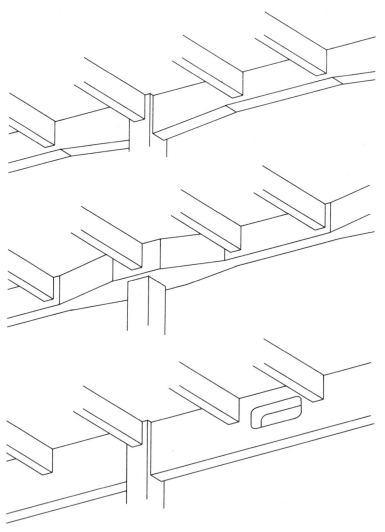

FIGURE 3.42.   Options for increasing the girder strength.

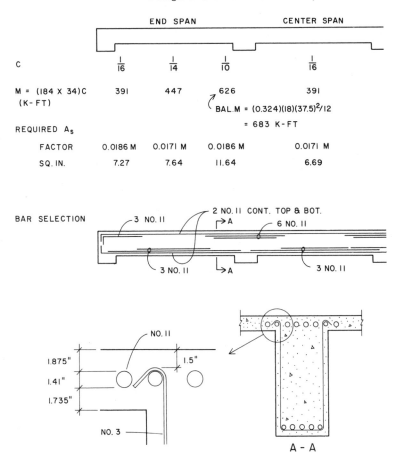

C	$\frac{1}{16}$	$\frac{1}{14}$	$\frac{1}{10}$	$\frac{1}{16}$
M = (184 X 34)C (K-FT)	391	447	626	391

BAL.M = $(0.324)(18)(37.5)^2/12$

= 683 K-FT

REQUIRED A_s

FACTOR	0.0186 M	0.0171 M	0.0186 M	0.0171 M
SQ. IN.	7.27	7.64	11.64	6.69

FIGURE 3.43.   Design of the reinforcement for the interior girder.

This is a lot of reinforcing; furthermore, the balanced moment capacity of the section is only about 60 % of the critical moment. At this point it would have to be established whether the limiting depth has been reached for the girder. Referring to Figure 3.6, it may be seen that a total of 48 in. has been allowed from the finished floor to the bottom surface of the ceiling. Subtracting for the floor fill and ceiling construction, this leaves approximately 42 in. With a 30 in. deep girder there would be a maximum clearance of 12 in. below

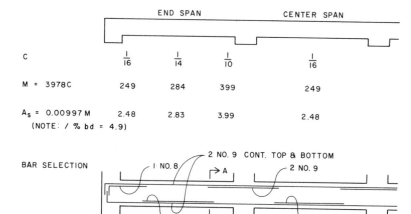

C	$\frac{1}{16}$	$\frac{1}{14}$	$\frac{1}{10}$	$\frac{1}{16}$
M = 3978C	249	284	399	249
A_s = 0.00997 M	2.48	2.83	3.99	2.48
(NOTE: / % bd = 4.9)				

END SPAN   CENTER SPAN

BAR SELECTION

2 NO. 9 CONT. TOP & BOTTOM
I NO. 8
2 NO. 9
I NO. 8
I NO. 8

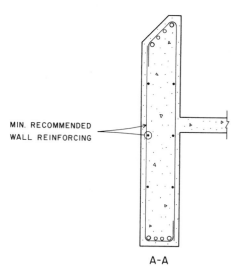

MIN. RECOMMENDED
WALL REINFORCING

A-A

FIGURE 3.44.   Design of the reinforcement for the exterior girder.

the girder for a duct. If the duct layout can be arranged so as to avoid having the largest ducts pass under the girders, this may be adequate. However, any reduction of this clearance by increase in the girder depth seems unfeasible.

The sketches in Figure 3.42 show three possible solutions to this problem. The first two consist of increasing the negative moment capacity of the girder by either widening it or increasing its depth at the ends. The other possibility shown is that of using the entire depth available and providing holes through the web of the girder. A rough rule of thumb for these holes is that they should not exceed one third of the beam depth in height.

On the basis of these considerations we will assume a 40 in. overall height girder with holes provided as required for ducts up to 12 in. deep. The weight of the girder will be slightly more, so we will use a total design load of 184 kips for the calculations. The determination of the critical moments and required steel areas for the girders is summarized in Figures 3.43 and 3.44. Selection of the final reinforcing should be delayed until the wind analysis is made.

3.11 Design of the Concrete Columns

As with the steel structure, the columns must be designed for the combination of gravity axial compression, rigid frame moments due to gravity, and the bending and axial force due to wind. Because of the higher gravity dead loads with the concrete structure, it is less likely that wind will be a critical factor in the bent design. It is even more logical, therefore, to use the procedure illustrated in the design of the steel structure: that of designing first for gravity alone to obtain approximate sizes of members.

A tabulation of the column axial loads for the concrete structure could be done using the format illustrated for the steel structure in Table 3.3. Since the basic building plan is the same, the live loads for the columns would be the same for both structures. Thus the only new tabulation necessary is for the dead loads. To save effort, we will approximate these by comparing the unit loads for the two structures.

Referring to the earlier calculations for the slab design, the unit dead load for the typical floor is 128 psf, which includes the slab, fill, the partition load, the ceiling, and the suspended equipment.

Added to this will be the weight of the beam and girder stems. For the typical 36 ft square bay these will be:

$$3 \text{ beams/bay at 15 in. by 21 in.} \times 34 \text{ ft} = 33{,}469 \text{ lb}$$
$$1 \text{ girder/bay at 18 in. by 35 in.} \times 34 \text{ ft} = 22{,}313 \text{ lb}$$
$$\text{total stem weight/bay} = \overline{55{,}782} \text{ lb}$$

Or

$$\frac{55{,}782}{(36)^2} = 43 \text{ psf average}$$

Adding this to the other dead load, the total dead load is 171 psf for the typical floor. Since the column weights and the exterior wall loads will also be higher, we will approximate the dead loads for the concrete structure by using twice the tabulated loads for the steel structure. Table 3.12 gives the column loads determined on this basis, using the design live loads plus twice the dead loads for each column as determined in Table 3.3.

TABLE 3.12.   Gravity Loads for Concrete Columns (kips)

Level	Column A $DL + \%LL =$ Design Load	Columns B and C $DL + \%LL =$ Design Load	Column D $DL + \%LL =$ Design Load
P			
R	$70 + 10 = 80$		
R			
	$230 + 90 = 320$	$90 + 13 = 103$	$52 + 7 = 59$
6			
	$442 + 62 = 504$	$224 + 18 = 242$	$134 + 12 = 146$
5			
	$656 + 88 = 744$	$360 + 32 = 392$	$216 + 16 = 232$
4			
	$870 + 114 = 984$	$496 + 45 = 541$	$300 + 23 = 323$
3			
	$1084 + 140 = 1224$	$632 + 58 = 690$	$384 + 30 = 414$
2			
	$1300 + 166 = 1466$	$768 + 71 = 839$	$474 + 37 = 511$
1			
	$1640 + 192 = 1832$	$922 + 85 = 1007$	$576 + 44 = 620$
B			

Variation of the column strength from top to bottom of the building is a different matter for the concrete structure. It was reasonable to accomplish this variation in the steel structure with no change in the finish size of the columns. This is less reasonable here, especially for the exterior columns which are exposed architecturally. For the interior columns the variation of size may cause some variation in the plan dimensions of the core layout, although there are possibilities for accommodating this. For the exterior columns the method of variation, as well as the actual dimensions, must be coordinated with the detailing of the exterior walls and the spandrel-to-column relationships.

Figure 3.45 shows some of the relationships and the scheme that will be used for effecting dimensional changes in the exterior columns.

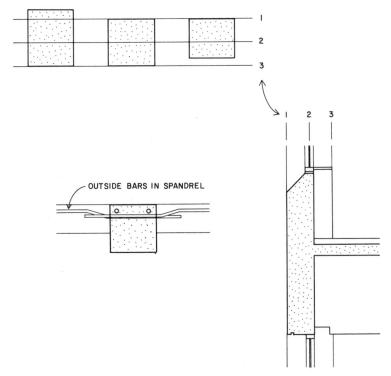

FIGURE 3.45.   Size variation: exterior columns.

For reasons of simplification of the window detailing, the external face of the columns will be kept at a constant width of 24 in., with changes occurring in the other direction. The exterior face may project beyond the spandrel and the interior face may be brought in from the window sill edge, as shown. The simplified spandrel section shows the basis for these limits. Because of its two exposed faces, the corner column will be maintained at a constant size of 24 in. square.

Since the spandrel and column have the same requirements for cover of the reinforcing, the bars closest to the exposed face would normally be the same distance from the edge if the spandrel and column are flush. This problem is eliminated if the column face is a few inches outside the spandrel. However, if the flush face condition is desired, the outside bars in the spandrel must be bent to'pass the column verticals, as shown in the sketch in Figure 3.45.

As has been mentioned previously, there is a general problem of coordination of the column reinforcing with that of the intersecting beams and girders. At every column there is a three-way intersection of reinforcing and the column verticals must be placed so that the beam and girder bars can pass through. With a high percentage of reinforcing in a column, and especially with spiral columns, this can be a severe problem. Carefully drawn layouts or mockups should be done to avoid nasty calls from the construction site.

Figure 3.46 shows a first trial design for the interior columns, using only the axial gravity loads previously tabulated. Three sizes have been used, varying from 20 in. square at the top to 28 in. square at the bottom. Some of the considerations made in the reinforcing selection are as follows:

The number of bars used in each column has been coordinated to avoid adding splice bars; that is, there are no columns with more reinforcing than in the column below.

The number of bars and the tie layouts have been selected to avoid having complex tie layouts with ties cluttering up the center space, which makes concrete placing difficult. Although the use of spiral columns, especially in the lower stories, could reduce the column size, we have avoided them principally because they make placing of the beam and girder reinforcing more difficult.

COLUMN A – FIRST TRY – AXIAL LOAD ONLY

	DESIGN LOAD	SIZE (INCHES)	REINFORCING	F_y	ACTUAL CAPACITY	LAYOUT
R						
	320	20 X 20	4 NO. 9	60	422	
6						
	504	20 X 20	8 NO. 9	60	503	
5						
	744	24 X 24	8 NO. 11	60	745	
4						
	984	24 X 24	16 NO. 11	60	999	
3						
	1224	24 X 24	20 NO. 11	75	1286	
2						
	1466	28 X 28	20 NO. 11	75	1462	
1						
	1832	28 X 28	20 NO. 14	75	1814	
B						

FIGURE 3.46.   Design of column A; axial gravity load only.

An increased f_y of 75 ksi has been used to help hold down the size of the lower columns. This increases the required embedment length in the footings, which must be considered in the foundation design.

Use of a higher strength concrete could also reduce the size of the lower columns. This creates some problems with the footings and with the continuous pouring of columns and horizontal framing, however.

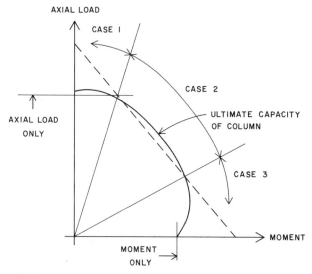

FIGURE 3.47.   Column interaction: axial load plus moment.

We must, of course, consider the combined effects of axial compression and bending on all columns. Figure 3.47 shows the general relation of these effects in the form of the typical interaction graph. Three general cases are described in the illustration. Case 1 occurs when the moment is minor compared to the axial load. This is the case for most interior columns, especially at the lower stories. In this case the moment does not cause significant change from the design for axial load only.

Case 3 occurs when the moment is major compared to the axial load. This is likely to occur with exterior columns at the upper stories and possibly with wind moments in the lower stories. In this case it is reasonable to design essentially for the moment only, with a little bonus for the axial load.

Case 2 is the general case, when both the axial load and moment are significant. There is no simple way to approach this design other than by trial and error. Use of handbooks or canned computer programs is to be recommended if more than a few sections must be designed.

Some approximation of axial loads and moments must be obtained before any judgment can be made as to the situation for a particular column. We will therefore develop approximate gravity moments and approximate wind moments for the bents before attempting to design the exterior columns.

For a first approximation of gravity moments in the bents we may use the end moments from the beam and girder designs, as determined from the ACI Code coefficients. At the roof this results in a moment of $(\frac{1}{16})wL^2$ on the sixth story column. At all other levels the moment will be $(\frac{1}{32})wL^2$, since two columns resist the beam end. For an approximate design we have assumed the total roof design load to be equal to that for the typical floor. Table 3.13 gives a tabulation of these moments for the four typical columns.

TABLE 3.13.   Approximation of Gravity Moments on Exterior Columns

	Column B		Column C		Column D	
	N–S	E–W	N–S	E–W	N–S	E–W
Moment at roof $M = (\frac{1}{16})wL^2$ (k-ft)	183	x	x	391	183	249
Moment at floor $M = (\frac{1}{32})wL^2$ (k-ft)	92	x	x	196	92	125

The two most critical bending conditions occur at the roof level at columns C and D. A quick check should be made to assure that these two conditions will be possible with the size limits established in the preliminary design. For column C the condition is that of a major moment from the interior girder combined with a small axial load and a small moment from the spandrel beam. This column can be designed quite literally as a 24 in. square doubly reinforced beam for the large moment of 391 k/ft.

With the values of 4000 psi for f_c' and 60 ksi for f_y, the balanced moment capacity of the section will be

$$M = Kbd^2 = \frac{(0.295)(24)(21)^2}{12} = 260 \text{ k/ft}$$

For this moment the area of steel required in tension will be

$$A_s = \frac{M}{f_s jd} = \frac{(260)(12)}{(24)(0.85)(21)} = 7.28 \text{ in.}^2$$

Since this moment is only about 62 % of the required moment, we must rely on the compressive reinforcing with some additional tension reinforcing to develop the additional resistance. The additional area of steel required is

$$A_s = \frac{M}{f_s(d - d')} = \frac{(131)(12)}{(24)(18)} = 3.64 \text{ in.}^2$$

The total area of tension reinforcing required is thus 10.92 in.². If provided by No. 11 bars, the number required is

$$N = \frac{10.92}{1.56} = 7$$

If placed in a single layer in the outside face of the column, this would require a column 28 in. wide. If it is necessary to keep the column width of 24 in., we must place reinforcing in two layers in the outside face or increase the dimension perpendicular to the plane of the outside wall. Choosing the second alternative, we will increase this dimension to 30 in., which makes the column face project 6 in. beyond the spandrel. The balanced moment capacity of the column now increases to

$$M = Kbd^2 = \frac{(0.295)(24)(27)^2}{12} = 430 \text{ k/ft}$$

This means that in theory the compressive reinforcing is not required and the area of tension reinforcing may be simply calculated as follows:

$$A_s = \frac{M}{f_s jd} = \frac{(391)(12)}{(24)(0.85)(27)} = 8.52 \text{ in.}^2$$

This area can be provided by six No. 11 bars, with a total of 9.36 in.². Actually the small axial compressive force slightly increases the moment capacity, as shown in the interaction graph in Figure 3.47. The design for moment alone is therefore conservative.

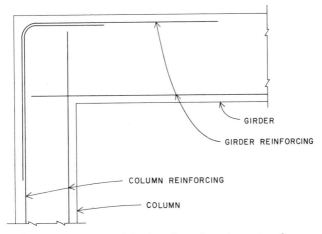

FIGURE 3.48.   Reinforcing of exterior column at roof.

As shown in Figure 3.48, part of the tension reinforcing in the outside face of the column may be provided by bending down the top bars from the girder. Thus the column is actually shown in the column design table as having only four No. 11 bars, one in each corner. The two outside corner bars plus the four bars bent down from the girder provide the necessary six bars for the tension reinforcing in the column.

At the sixth floor level the moment in the column drops to half that at the roof. Considering this moment only, the tention reinforcing requirement drops to three No. 11 bars in the outside face. The minimum reinforcing used from this point down is therefore three No. 11 bars in the outside column face.

Figure 3.49 presents a summary of the design for column C. The size of 24 by 30 in. is maintained throughout the height of the column, since it is adequate for the axial load at the bottom as well as for the moment at the top.

Column B has less moment since the beam end moments are smaller. However, for the purpose of balance in the architectural details, it would probably also be made a constant size of 24 by 30 in. throughout its height.

COLUMN C – FIRST TRY – GRAVITY LOAD ONLY

	AXIAL LOAD (KIPS)	MAJOR MOMENT (K-FT)	e	CASE FOR M/N (SEE FIG. 3.47)	SIZE (INCHES)	REINFORCING	LAYOUT
R							
	103	391	46"	3	24X30	4 NO. 11	
6							
	242	196	9.7"	2	"	6 NO. 11	
5							
	392	"	6.0"	2	"	6 NO. 11	
4							
	541	"	4.4"	2	"	6 NO. 11	
3							
	690	"	3.4"	1	"	6 NO. 11	
2							
	839	"	2.8"	1	"	8 NO. 11	
1							
	1007	"	2.3"	1	"	12 NO. 11	
B							

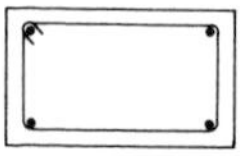

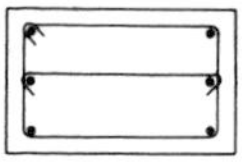

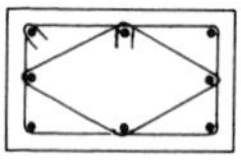

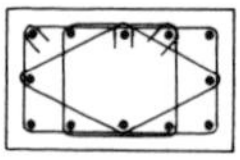

FIGURE 3.49. Design of column C: gravity load only.

Column D, the corner column, sustains considerable bending in both directions. As with columns B and C, the large gravity bending moments at the roof level are major design considerations. As has been previously discussed, the shape and size of this column are a matter of architectural detailing and construction considerations as well as structural behavior. The sketches in Figure 3.50 show some of the possibilities for this column.

In the upper sketch the exterior width of 24 in. is maintained on both column faces, matching the width of the intermediate columns on the building elevation. This limits the column size to 24 by 24 in.

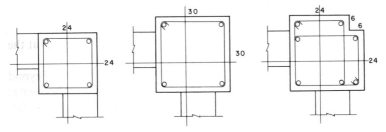

FIGURE 3.50. Options for the corner column.

COLUMN D – FIRST TRY – GRAVITY LOAD ONLY

30" SQUARE – FULL HEIGHT

	AXIAL LOAD (KIPS)	MOMENT X-AXIS/Y-AXIS (K-FT)	e (INCHES)	CASE FOR M/N (SEE FIG 3.47)	REINFORCING	LAYOUT
R						
	59	322 / 183	65 / 37	3	8 NO. 9	
6						
	146	161 / 92	13 / 7.6	3	8 NO. 10	
5						
	232	"	8.3 / 4.8	2	"	
4						
	323	"	6 / 3.4	2	"	
3						
	414	"	4.7/2.7	2	"	
2						
	511	"	3.8/2.2	2	"	
1						
	620	"	3.1 / 1.8	2	"	
B						

FIGURE 3.51. Design of column D: gravity load only.

215

and would require considerable reinforcing for the moments at the roof.

The second sketch shows the outside faces pulled out 6 in. beyond the spandrel, as was done for the intermediate columns. This creates a 30 in. square column which is fine for the moments at the roof, but a bit large for the axial loads at lower levels. It also means that the column face in the building elevation is wider than the intermediate columns.

The third sketch is a compromise, with a 6 in. square nick taken out of the corner of the 30 in. square. This leaves the 30 in. depth for bending in both directions and presents a face width to match the intermediate columns on the elevation. Reinforcing placement and tie layouts are a little more complicated for this option, but can be handled. For axial load design the section is still essentially a 30 in. square with a loss of only about 4% of its area in one corner.

As with the intermediate exterior columns, the moment at the roof level can be partly developed by bending down the top end bars from the spandrel beams and girders. The location of these bars is shown in the sketches in Figure 3.50.

Figure 3.51 presents a summary of the design of column D, based on the use of a 30 in. square section for the full height of the column. As it turns out, the reinforcing required at the top story for the gravity bending at the sixth floor is approximately the same as that required for the total load combination at the basement. It is probably practical, therefore, to use the same reinforcing for the full height to simplify bar placement, dowelling, and tie layouts.

3.12 Design for Wind

The wind load on the building was previously determined for the design of the steel structure, as shown in Figure 3.16. As for the steel structure, an approximate wind design may be done by assuming the total wind shear at each story to be distributed to the columns in proportion to their individual stiffnesses. Because of the larger dead loads in the concrete structure, it develops that there are only a few considerations that need to be made to alter the design for the gravity loads in order to have adequate resistance of the bents to wind. To demonstrate this, and avoid the work of a complete wind

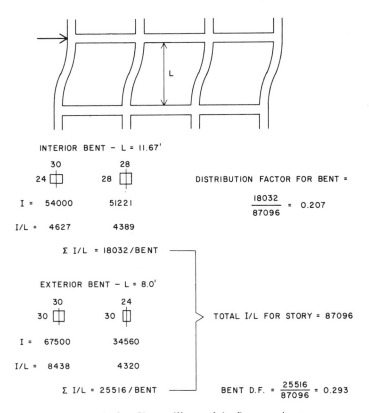

INTERIOR BENT — L = 11.67'

	30	28
	24 ⊞	28 ⊞
I =	54000	51221
I/L =	4627	4389

Σ I/L = 18032/BENT

DISTRIBUTION FACTOR FOR BENT =

$$\frac{18032}{87096} = 0.207$$

EXTERIOR BENT — L = 8.0'

	30	24
	30 ⊞	30 ⊡
I =	67500	34560
I/L =	8438	4320

Σ I/L = 25516/BENT

TOTAL I/L FOR STORY = 87096

BENT D.F. = $\dfrac{25516}{87096} = 0.293$

FIGURE 3.52.   Shear stiffness of the first story bents.

analysis, we will determine the maximum wind shears and moments at the first story and the second floor level.

Figure 3.52 illustrates the method for determination of the shear distribution to the first story columns. The column heights used are based on the interior girder depth of 40 in. and the spandrel girder depth of 7 ft. Because of the deep spandrels, the exterior bents will resist a higher proportion of the total story shear.

Figure 3.53 illustrates the basis for determination of the column shears and moments and the girder moments. Comparison of these column moments with those approximated for the gravity loads, as

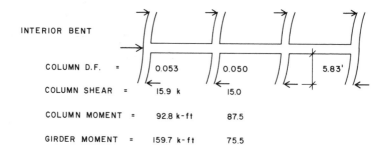

INTERIOR BENT

COLUMN D.F. =	0.053	0.050	5.83'
COLUMN SHEAR =	15.9 k	15.0	
COLUMN MOMENT =	92.8 k-ft	87.5	
GIRDER MOMENT =	159.7 k-ft	75.5	

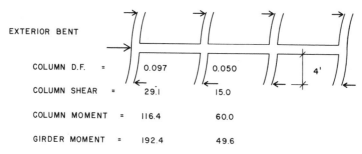

EXTERIOR BENT

COLUMN D.F. =	0.097	0.050	4'
COLUMN SHEAR =	29.1	15.0	
COLUMN MOMENT =	116.4	60.0	
GIRDER MOMENT =	192.4	49.6	

FIGURE 3.53. Wind analysis: first story columns and second floor girders.

given in Table 3.13, should indicate that the wind loads will not be a factor in the column designs.

A similar comparison of the girder moments with those used in the girder designs in Figures 3.43 and 3.44 will show that the only consideration necessary is a slight increase in the end moment at the corner column for the spandrel girder.

None of the wind moments calculated will result in reversals of the sign of the end moments in the girders. There will, however, be some redistribution of the moments throughout the length of the spans which will cause some shifts from the moment variations assumed in the development of typical details for bar cutoffs and extensions. For this reason, as well as to add a general increased toughness to the bents, some continuous top and bottom bars should be used in all the column line beams and girders. These bars

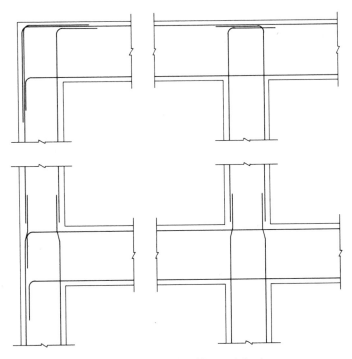

FIGURE 3.54.   Details of bent reinforcing.

will be made continuous through the interior columns and will be hooked into the exterior columns. For the same reasons the column reinforcing in the top story will be bent into the girders. The sketches in Figure 3.54 show some of these details.

The effects of the wind moments on the column line beams in the north–south direction will be somewhat more critical, since the gravity loads are less on these members. The same continous bars and hooked end details should be used in these bents. If headroom permits, it would be advisable to increase the depth of the column line beams in the lower levels. If that is done, the same reinforcing could probably be used in all the beams, with the required additional strength being gained by the depth increase.

3.13   Design of the First Floor, Basement, and Foundations

The lower level construction for the concrete structure will be similar to that for the steel structure, with the exception of the first floor area over the basement and the elimination of the steel columns and base plates at the basement. A slightly different layout may be used for the floor structure over the unexcavated area since it is possible to develop continuity with the framed system over the basement in this structure. The plan in Figure 3.55 shows a layout for this type of system.

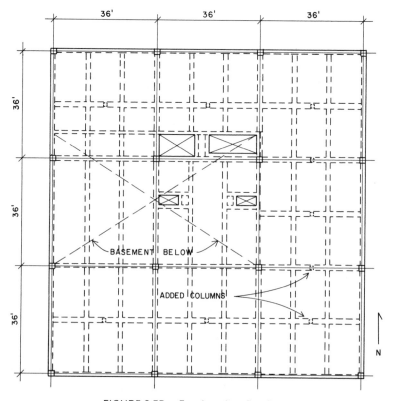

FIGURE 3.55.   Framing plan: first floor.

One problem in the use of a continuous structure over the two first floor areas is that the span length changes abruptly at the edge of the basement area. This causes a condition of moment reversal and high shear in the first span of the short beams. While it is possible to design for this condition, there are some alternatives worth considering.

One alternative consists of using a construction joint between the two areas, effectively interrupting the structural continuity between them. Being thus made independent of the other system, the structure over the unexcavated area could be designed as for the steel structure, as shown in Figure 3.25, or could use a variety of layouts.

If it is possible to introduce some additional columns in the basement area, another alternative would be that shown in the plan in Figure 3.56. The shortened spans in the basement area are now in

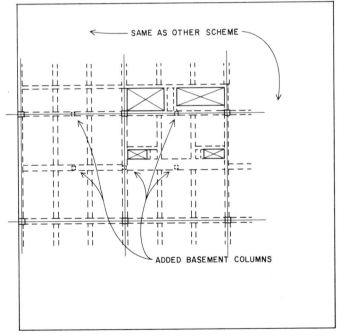

FIGURE 3.56.   Alternate framing plan: first floor.

balance with those over the unexcavated area, which eliminates the problem discussed for the first system. The beams and girders at the basement area would be considerably smaller than those required for the longer spans, although this cost savings would be offset by the need for additional columns and footings.

The three alternatives discussed are reasonably competitive. Assuming that the additional basement columns are not a problem, the author prefers the third solution and has shown it in the construction drawings.

The basement walls, basement floor slab, grade walls, and footings would be essentially similar to those for the steel structure. The continuity of horizontal reinforcing in the walls is somewhat simplified, since the steel columns are not encased in the concrete sections. The tops of the column footings may be slightly higher, since the steel base plates and anchor bolts need not be accommodated.

The column footings will be somewhat larger because of the greater dead loads, making the feasibility of spread footings marginal. If the allowable soil pressure is any less than the 8000 psf assumed, the use of piles or piers would probably be advisable.

One additional consideration in the footing design is the need for a footing depth sufficient to provide for the required dowelling extension of the column bars in the bottom story. Since this length is a function of both the bar size and the f_y value, the choice of these in the column design must be coordinated with the footing design.

3.14   Construction Drawings—Concrete Structure

The illustrations that follow show some of the details for the typical floor and lower level construction for the concrete structure. As with the other examples, the plans and details are essentially illustrative only and do not include all the details and notation that would be required for complete construction documentation.

Partial Basement and Foundation Plan.   (Figure 3.57.) This plan is essentially similar to that for the steel structure, as shown in Figure 3.24. Note the added columns and footings in the basement area to accommodate the first floor system using the scheme shown in Figure 3.56.

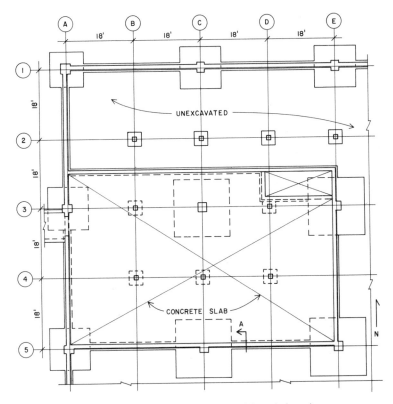

FIGURE 3.57.   Partial basement and foundation plan.

Some of the footing details and wall details would be different because of the ommission of the steel columns, the column base plates and anchor bolts, and the seats for the first floor steel beams. The location of the exterior walls is slightly different because of the different treatment of the skin of the building; see Figures 3.28 and 3.61 for comparison.

Partial Framing Plan—Ground Floor.   (Figure 3.58.) This plan shows the use of a continuous system for the two areas with a basic column module of 18 ft. The location of the north wall of the basement causes some disruption of this system, although the only significant considerations are the change in direction of the slab

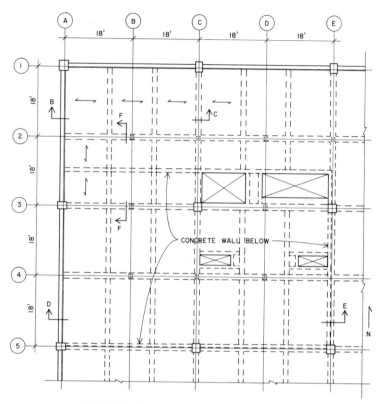

FIGURE 3.58. Partial framing plan: first floor.

spans and the special reinforcing for the beams that are supported by this wall. The latter condition is shown in Figure 3.63.

Partial Framing Plan—Typical Floor. (Figure 3.59.) This shows the typical upper level floor system as designed in the calculations. The core framing at the large openings has been developed to cause the least disruption of the basic system layout.

Detail A. (Figure 3.60.) This shows the typical basement floor slab and wall construction. The detail is essentially the same as that for the steel structure, except that the tops of the column footings

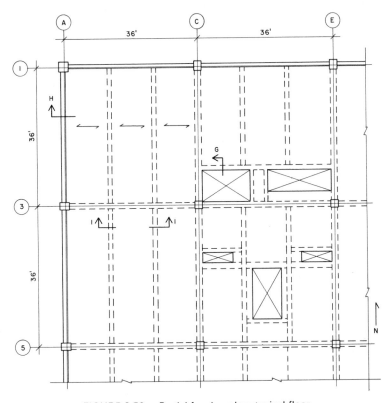

FIGURE 3.59.   Partial framing plan: typical floor.

are raised because of the absence of the steel base plates and anchor bolts. The need for some water sealing of the slab-to-wall joint and a moisture barrier under the slab would depend on specific site conditions.

Detail B.   (Figure 3.28, Section 3.8.) This section is also essentially the same as in the steel structure, with the possible exception of the wall portion above the floor level. If a metal curtain wall is used, the detail is the same as that in Figure 3.28. If the exposed concrete wall is used, the detail is similar to that in Figure 3.61. If a precast concrete skin is used, the detail is some modification of that shown in Figure 3.65 for the typical floor.

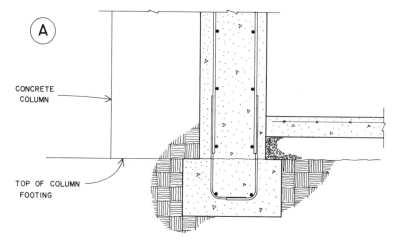

FIGURE 3.60.   Detail A.

Detail C.   (Figure 3.29, Section 3.8.) With the slab and beam system poured on fill the typical details are the same as shown for the steel structure. The precise form and detail of these members would depend on the nature of the fill material and on the need for moisture protection and/or thermal insulation.

The piers for this system would be formed and poured before the backfill is placed. An alternate to poured concrete piers would be to use piers of concrete masonry units with the cores filled with concrete.

Detail D.   (Figure 3.61.) This shows the typical exterior wall condition at the basement area. A pour joint for the walls and columns is made at the level of the bottom of the concrete beam system for the framed floor. The remainder of the walls and columns, up to the top of the floor slab, would be poured with the beam and slab system.

Detail E.   (Figure 3.62.) This shows the transition between the two floor systems and indicates that they are poured monolithically, with the pour joint in the wall at the bottom of the beams. For continuity of the beam reinforcing in the bottom of the beams the detailed position of the bottom of the beams is slightly lower in the

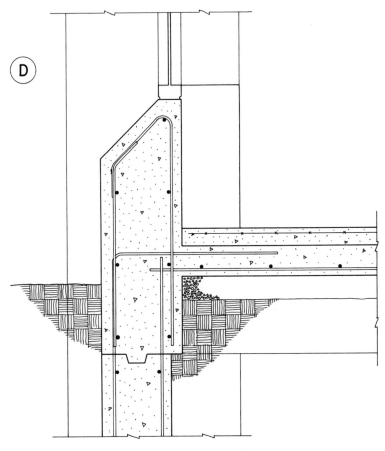

FIGURE 3.61.   Detail D.

system on fill, since additional cover is required for the concrete that is deposited on the soil.

Detail F.   (Figure 3.63.) This shows the condition that occurs where the basement wall causes a disruption of the regular 18 ft span for the floor system. This results in a high shear and a condition of virtually continuous negative moment for these short spans. They would probably be reinforced as shown by extending some of the

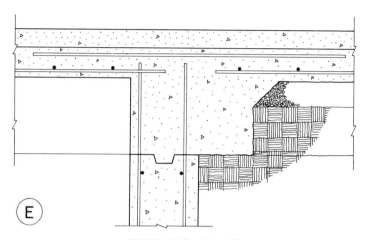

FIGURE 3.62.   Detail E.

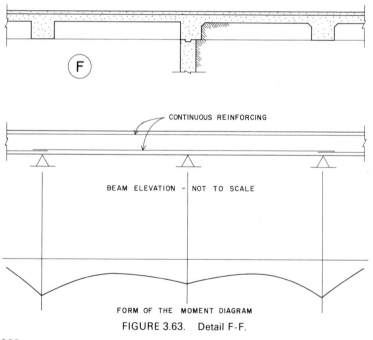

CONTINUOUS REINFORCING

BEAM ELEVATION - NOT TO SCALE

FORM OF THE MOMENT DIAGRAM

FIGURE 3.63.   Detail F-F.

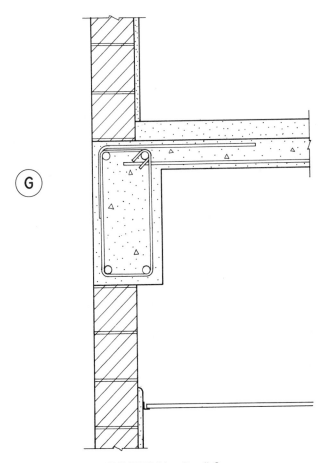

FIGURE 3.64.   Detail G.

bottom bars and by making the negative moment top bars continuous. The high shear stress would probably require a continuous series of closely spaced stirrups.

Detail G.   (Figure 3.64.) This section is similar in some details to that for the steel structure as shown in Figure 3.33. From the point of view of the wall construction, the concrete beam is similar to the concrete encasement for the steel beam. As with the steel structure,

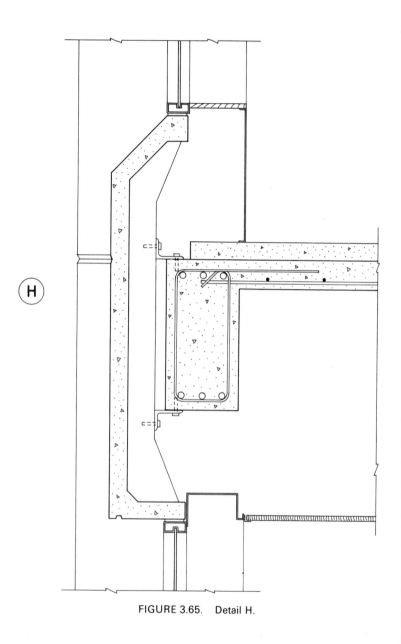

FIGURE 3.65.　Detail H.

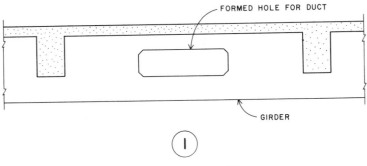

FIGURE 3.66.   Detail I.

it would also be possible to pull the face of the beam back and run the wall past it, if the exposed concrete is not desired.

Detail H.   (Figure 3.65.) This is actually an alternate to the section as shown in Figure 3.41. It indicates the use of a precast concrete facing member that is supported by the spandrel beam in a manner similar to that shown for the metal skin unit with the steel structure, as in Figure 3.32. One advantage of the construction in Figure 3.65 over the solid poured spandrel would be a reduction in dead load and volume of concrete.

It would also be possible to use the metal curtain wall similar to that for the steel structure. Attachment would be similar to that for the precast members, using preset anchors or inserts in the concrete structure.

Detail I.   (Figure 3.66.) This shows the use of an opening through the web of the deep interior girder to accommodate air handling ducts, as was discussed in the design calculations. The usual rule of thumb is to keep these openings within the middle third of the span and within the middle third of the depth. This allows for continuity of the major tension and compression forces due to moment and avoids the highest shear condition near the end of the span. In our floor system layout, the location of the beams must also be considered ; the middle third being conveniently open for this condition.

It is desirable to provide a radius or chamfer at the corners of the openings to help relieve the concentration of stresses at these points.

3.15 Alternate Floor Systems

The design examples for Building Three have illustrated two options for the floor framing of the typical floor—one in steel and the other in poured-in-place concrete. In theory there are a considerable number of options involving variations in materials, system type, form, layout, and specific details of construction. In real design situations the truly feasible choices are often limited by particular dictates of economics, speed of construction, local code requirements and construction practices, and desired architectural details.

If the building plan and the 36 ft square column bay system are adhered to, these factors alone will establish the priority of some solutions over others. Add to these the particular floor live loads, the desire to include wiring in the floors, a demountable partitioning system, and a modular ceiling system, and the need for a particular fire rating for the floor assembly and the choices are narrowed further.

The discussion that follows presents a few other possibilities for the construction of the typical floor.

Poured Concrete Slab on Steel Beams. An alternative to the metal deck used with the steel beams would be a poured-in-place concrete slab. Using welded attachments on the tops of the steel beams would permit the development of composite action of the concrete slab and steel beams, which could result in a reduction in size of the typical beams. This composite action does not aid in the rigid frame action which was a major factor in design of the column line beams and girders.

One advantage of this system would be the elimination of the sprayed-on fireproofing on the underside of the deck, since the concrete slab could develop the necessary fire resistance by itself. The applied fireproofing would therefore be used only on the steel beams and columns.

Dead load of this structure would be higher since the metal deck and fill would be replaced by a structural concrete slab and separate fill. The total dead load of this system would be somewhere between that for the two design examples, since the steel beams weigh less than the concrete beam stems.

The layout of the framing system would be essentially the same as with the metal deck, although the spacing of the beams could be increased, since minimum slab thickness required for fire rating would probably permit longer spans. While this is a structural possibility, the wider spaced, heavier loaded beams would have to be deeper, which may make the change questionable.

A detail for this type of system is shown in Figure 3.67. Design of the slab is essentially the same as was illustrated in the concrete structure example. Design of the composite steel beams is well illustrated in textbooks and handbooks.

Precast Concrete Deck on Steel Beams.   Another alternative with the steel frame is to use precast concrete deck units. A concrete fill would also be used with this system, serving the purposes of leveling and bonding of the units as well as the previous ones of incorporation of wiring. Although the precast units are usually voided the weight reduction would be only slightly below that of the solid concrete slab. While it is possible to use some of the void spaces in the precast units for incorporation of wiring or plumbing and even for air distribution, this requires very careful coordination during the design and detailing processes and is not often done.

These precast units can easily achieve longer spans than those used in the design examples. However, the heavier, deeper beams produced by wider spacing might cause a problem. Effective use of this type of construction would probably require a general revision of the framing layout, with something different than the square bay system.

As with the poured slab, it may be possible to eliminate the sprayed-on fireproofing, depending on the fire rating required. Some details for this type of construction are shown in Figure 3.68. Design of the precast units would be done using the load tables and suggested details and specifications provided by the manufacturer.

One-Way Concrete Joist System.   Figure 3.69 shows a layout and some details for a system using a one-way concrete joist system supported by girders in one direction. While the joist system itself is quite efficient, the loads on the girders are high, making the system less feasible for the square bay layout. A rectangular bay system, with short span girders and long span joists would improve

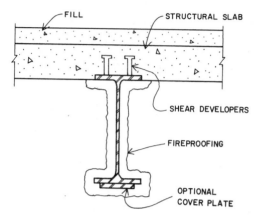

FIGURE 3.67.   Steel frame with poured concrete slab.

the system. If the deep spandrels and the maximum depth interior girders, as illustrated in the design example, are used the system would be workable, although not optimal.

One potential problem is due to the fact that this system is not given a very high fire rating by building codes, making it possible only with some fire protection. This may require the use of a fully plastered ceiling or of some other assembly capable of the higher rating.

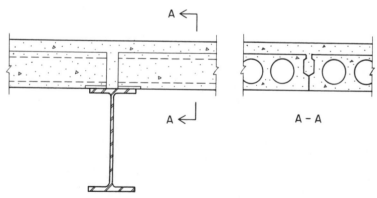

FIGURE 3.68.   Steel frame with precast concrete slab.

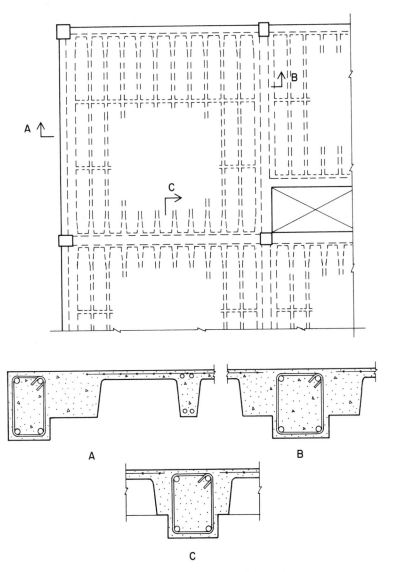

FIGURE 3.69. One-way concrete joist system.

The large girders not withstanding, this system would probably be slightly lower in weight than the beam and slab system in the design example. The joists and slab may theoretically be made quite thin, although fire rating requirements may not permit their optimal reduction.

For purposes of developing the rigid frame action in the direction parallel to the joists, as well as providing for the framing of the large openings, it may be necessary to provide column line beams, as shown in the framing plan in Figure 3.69.

Design of the joist system itself can be done from various handbook tabulations, if the span, load, and concrete strength can be matched to the handbook examples. Even where the match-up is not exact, the handbooks can usually be used to establish an approximate design, eliminating several early approximation stages of the design.

Two-Way Concrete Joist (Waffle) System. The square column bays make it reasonable to consider the use of a two-way spanning concrete system. The size of the span and the relatively low live load make a waffle system, rather than a solid slab system, most feasible. A principal drawback, as with the one-way joists, is the limited fire rating of the system.

Figure 3.70 shows a layout and some details for a system that is analogous to the flat slab system with drop panels. The large openings for stairs and elevators would require a transition to a beam system in part of the plan, with the joists in this area functioning essentially in one-way span action.

Figure 3.71 shows a layout and some details for a system that is analogous to the two-way slab on edge supports. The edge supports in this case consist of the spandrels and the wide column line beams created by the unvoided waffle spaces.

Only a complete design of both systems could demonstrate the relative efficiency and cost of the two alternatives. Both offer the potential advantage of reducing the depth of the floor construction somewhat, since, except for the core framing, the structure does not have the deep beams and girders on the interior which were part of the two design examples.

Design of the typical waffle joists in these two systems may also be done from handbook tables.

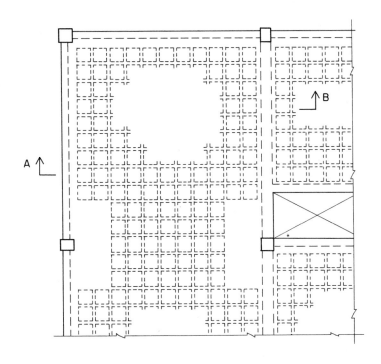

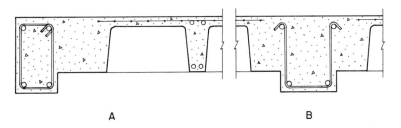

A   B

FIGURE 3.70. Two-way concrete joist system.

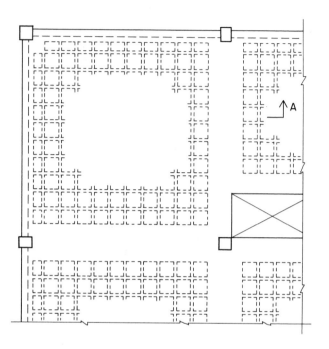

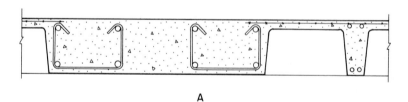

A

FIGURE 3.71.   Two-way concrete joists with edge beams.

References

1. Harry Parker: *Simplified Mechanics and Strength of Materials*, 3rd ed. (prepared by Harold D. Hauf), Wiley, New York, 1977.

2. Harry Parker: *Simplified Engineering for Architects and Builders*, 5th ed. (prepared by Harold D. Hauf), Wiley, New York, 1975.

3. Harry Parker: *Simplified Design of Reinforced Concrete*, 4th ed. (prepared by Harold D. Hauf), Wiley, New York, 1976.

4. Harry Parker: *Simplified Design of Structural Steel*, 4th ed. (prepared by Harold D. Hauf), Wiley, New York, 1974.

5. Harry Parker: *Simplified Design of Structural Wood*, 3rd ed. (prepared by Harold D. Hauf), Wiley, New York, 1979.

6. Charles G. Ramsey and Harold R. Sleeper: *Architectural Graphic Standards*, 6th ed., Wiley, New York, 1970.

7. *Uniform Building Code*, 1976 ed., International Conference of Building Officials, 5360 South Workman Mill Road, Whittier, CA 90601.

8. *Manual of Steel Construction*, 7th ed., American Institute of Steel Construction, 1970.

9. *Building Code Requirements for Reinforced Concrete*, ACI 318-71, American Concrete Institute, 1971.

10. *Concrete Masonry Design Manual*, 1974 ed., Concrete Masonry Association of California, 2550 Beverly Boulevard, Los Angeles, CA 90057.

Appendix

||||||||||||||||||||||||||||||||||||||||||||||||||||||||||||

This section contains some of the tables and charts that have been used in the design examples. These are provided essentially for the convenience of readers to whom the references may not be available. If they are available, however, it is highly recommended that the materials be used directly from the references, which in some cases contain explanations and example illustrations of their use. Some of the items reprinted also have considerable footnotes, not all of which have been shown here. Complete information for these publications is given in the list of references.

Tables 24-H, 25-A-1, 25-C-1, 25-G, 25-H, 25-J, 25-K, 25-P, 25-R-1, 25-R-2, 25-T-J-1, 25-T-J-6, 25-T-R-14, and 47-I are reproduced from the 1976 edition of the *Uniform Building Code*, copyright 1976, with permission of the publisher, The International Conference of Building Officials.

Tables for steel design are reproduced from pages 2-8, 2-44, 2-49, 3-13, 3-14, 3-15, and 3-97 of the *AISC Manual of Steel Construction*, Seventh Edition, with permission of the publisher, the American Institute of Steel Construction.

Tables for masonry design are reproduced from pages III-71 and III-98 of the *Concrete Masonry Design Manual*, 1974 Edition, with permission of the publisher, the Concrete Masonry Association of California.

TABLE 24-H. Maximum Working Stresses in Pounds Per Square Inch for Reinforced Solid and Hollow Unit Masonry

TYPE OF STRESS	SPECIAL INSPECTION REQUIRED	
	Yes	No
1. Compression—Axial, Walls	See Section 2418	One-half of the values permitted under Section 2418
2. Compression—Axial, Columns	See Section 2418	One-half of the values permitted under Section 2418
3. Compression—Flexural	$0.33 f'_m$ but not to exceed 900	$0.166 f'_m$ but not to exceed 450
4. Shear: a. No shear reinforcement, Flexural[2]	$1.1\sqrt{f'_m}$ 50 Max.	25
Shear walls[3] $M/Vd \geq 1$[4]	$.9\sqrt{f'_m}$ 34 Max.	17
$M/Vd = 0$[4]	$2.0\sqrt{f'_m}$ 50 Max.	25
b. Reinforcing taking all shear, Flexural	$3.0\sqrt{f'_m}$ 150 Max.	75
Shear walls[3] $M/Vd \geq 1$[4]	$1.5\sqrt{f'_m}$ 75 Max.	35
$M/Vd = 0$[4]	$2.0\sqrt{f'_m}$ 120 Max.	60
5. Modulus of Elasticity[5]	$1000 f'_m$ but not to exceed 3,000,000	$500 f'_m$ but not to exceed 1,500,000
6. Modulus of Rigidity[5]	$400 f'_m$ but not to exceed 1,200,000	$200 f'_m$ but not to exceed 600,000
7. Bearing on full Area[6]	$0.25 f'_m$ but not to exceed 900	$0.125 f'_m$ but not to exceed 450
8. Bearing on ⅓ or less of area[6]	$0.30 f'_m$ but not to exceed 1200	$0.15 f'_m$ but not to exceed 600
9. Bond —Plain bars	60	30
10. Bond —Deformed	140	100

[1]Stresses for hollow unit masonry are based on net section.

[2]Web reinforcement shall be provided to carry the entire shear in excess of 20 pounds per square inch whenever there is required negative reinforcement and for a distance of one-sixteenth the clear span beyond the point of inflection.

[3]When calculating shear or diagonal tension stresses, shear walls which resist seismic forces shall be designed to resist 1.5 times the forces required by Section 2312 (d) 1.

242

TABLE 25-A-1. Allowable Unit Stresses—Structural Lumber

DOUGLAS FIR – LARCH (Surfaced dry or surfaced green. Used at 19% max. m.c.)
DOUGLAS FIR – LARCH (North)

Grade	Size								Footnotes
Dense Select Structural	2" to 4" thick 2" to 4" wide	2450	2800	1400	95	455	1850	1,900,000	
Select Structural		2100	2400	1200	95	385	1600	1,800,000	
Dense No. 1		2050	2400	1200	95	455	1450	1,900,000	
No. 1		1750	2050	1050	95	385	1250	1,800,000	
Dense No. 2		1700	1950	1000	95	455	1150	1,700,000	25-2
No. 2		1450	1650	850	95	385	1000	1,700,000	25-3
No. 3		800	925	475	95	385	600	1,500,000	and
Appearance		1750	2050	1050	95	385	1500	1,800,000	25-4
Stud		800	925	475	95	385	600	1,500,000	(see footnotes
Construction	2" to 4" thick 4" wide	1050	1200	625	95	385	1150	1,500,000	2 through 13)
Standard		600	675	350	95	385	925	1,500,000	
Utility		275	325	175	95	385	600	1,500,000	
Dense Select Structural	2" to 4" thick 6" and wider	2100	2400	1400	95	455	1650	1,900,000	
Select Structural		1800	2050	1200	95	385	1400	1,800,000	
Dense No. 1		1800	2050	1200	95	455	1450	1,900,000	
No. 1		1500	1750	1000	95	385	1250	1,800,000	
Dense No. 2		1450	1700	950	95	455	1250	1,700,000	
No. 2		1250	1450	825	95	385	1050	1,700,000	
No. 3		725	850	475	95	385	675	1,500,000	
Appearance		1500	1750	1000	95	385	1500	1,800,000	

243

TABLE 25-A-1.   (Continued)

SPECIES AND COMMERCIAL GRADE	SIZE CLASSIFICATION	EXTREME FIBER IN BENDING "F_b"		Tension Parallel to Grain "F_t"	Horizontal Shear "F_v"	Compression perpendicular to Grain "F_c⊥"	Compression Parallel to Grain "F_c"	MODULUS OF ELASTICITY "E"	U.B.C. STDS UNDER WHICH GRADED
		Engineered Uses (Single)	Repetitive-member Uses						
Dense Select Structural	Beams and Stringers[12]	1900	—	1100	85	455	1300	1,700,000	25-2, 25-3 (see footnotes 2 through 9 and 11)
Select Structural		1600	—	950	85	385	1100	1,600,000	
Dense No. 1		1550	—	775	85	455	1100	1,700,000	
No. 1		1300	—	675	85	385	925	1,600,000	
Dense Select Structural	Posts and Timbers[12]	1750	—	1150	85	455	1350	1,700,000	
Select Structural		1500	—	1000	85	385	1150	1,700,000	
Dense No. 1		1400	—	950	85	455	1200	1,700,000	
No. 1		1200	—	825	85	385	1000	1,600,000	
Select Dex	Decking	1750	2000	—	—	385	—	1,800,000	
Commercial Dex		1450	1650	—	—	385	—	1,700,000	
Select	Decking	1750	2000	—	—	385	—	1,800,000	
Commercial		1450	1650	—	—	385	—	1,800,000	
Dense Select Structural	Beams and Stringers[12]	1900	—	1250	85	455	1300	1,700,000	25-2, 25-4 (see footnotes 2 through 11)
Select Structural		1600	—	1050	85	385	1100	1,600,000	
Dense No. 1		1550	—	1050	85	455	1100	1,700,000	
No. 1		1350	—	900	85	385	925	1,600,000	
Dense Select Structural	Posts and Timbers[12]	1750	—	1150	85	455	1350	1,700,000	
Select Structural		1500	—	1000	85	385	1150	1,600,000	
Dense No. 1		1400	—	950	85	455	1200	1,700,000	
No. 1		1200	—	825	85	385	1000	1,600,000	
Selected Decking	Decking	—	1900	—	—	—	—	1,800,000	
Commercial Decking		—	1600	—	—	—	—	1,700,000	
Selected Decking	Decking	—	2150	(Stresses for Decking apply at 15% moisture content)				1,900,000	
Commercial Decking		—	1800					1,700,000	

244

TABLE 25-C-1. Part A—Allowable Unit Stresses for Structural Glued-Laminated Softwood Timber for Normal Loading Duration—Visually Graded

COMBINATION SYMBOL 1	NUMBER OF LAMINATIONS 2	EXTREME FIBER IN BENDING (F_b)' Load Parallel to Wide Face of Laminations 3	Load Perpendicular to Wide Face of Laminations 4	TENSION PARALLEL TO GRAIN (F_t) 5	COMPRESSION PARALLEL TO GRAIN (F_c) 6	HORIZONTAL SHEAR (F_v) WHEN LOADED: Parallel to Wide Face 7	Perpendicular to Wide Face 8	COMPRESSION PERPENDICULAR TO GRAIN ($F_{c\perp}$) 9	MODULUS OF ELASTICITY (E) 10
					ALLOWABLE UNIT STRESSES IN POUNDS PER SQUARE INCH				
				DRY CONDITIONS OF USE'					
				Douglas Fir and Western Larch'					
16F[4]	4 or more	—	1600	1300	1500	—	165	385	1,600,000
18F[4]	4 or more	—	1800	1400	1500	—	165	385	1,700,000
20F[4]	4 or more	—	2000	1600	1500	—	165	385[5]	1,700,000
22F[4]	4 or more	—	2200	1600	1500	—	165	385[5]	1,800,000
24F[4]	4 or more	—	2400	1600	1500	—	165	385[5]	1,800,000
1[7]	4 or more[8]	900	1200	1000	1500	145	165	385	1,600,000
2[7]	4 or more[8]	1500	1800	1400	1800	145	165	385	1,800,000
3[7]	4 or more[8]	1900	2200	1800	2100	145	165	450	1,900,000
4[7]	4 or more[8]	2100	2400	1900	2000	145	165	410	2,000,000
5[7]	4 or more[8]	2400	2600	2100	2200	145	165	450	2,100,000
DOUGLAS FIR AND WESTERN LARCH OUTER LAMINATIONS AND WESTERN WOODS INNER LAMINATIONS'									
				DRY CONDITIONS OF USE'					
16F[4]	11 or more	—	1600	1300	1200	—	145	385[6]	1,500,000
20F[4]	12 or more	—	2000	1350	1250	—	145	450	1,700,000
24F[4]	12 or more	2400	2400	1400	1300	—	145	450	1,800,000
1[9]	4 or more	525	—	—	—	—	—	—	1,000,000

TABLE 25-G. Safe Lateral Strength and Required Penetration of Box and Common Wire Nails Driven Perpendicular to Grain of Wood

SIZE OF NAIL	STANDARD LENGTH (Inches)	WIRE GAUGE	PENETRA-TION REQUIRED (Inches)	LOADS (Pounds)[1][2]	
				Douglas Fir Larch or Southern Pine	Other Species
BOX NAILS					
6d	2	12½	1¼	47	
8d	2½	11½	1½	59	
10d	3	10½	1⅝	71	See
12d	3¼	10½	1⅝	71	U.B.C.
16d	3½	10	1¾	80	Standard
20d	4	9	2⅛	104	No.
30d	4½	9	2¼	116	25-17[3]
40d	5	8	2½	132	
COMMON NAILS					
6d	2	11½	1¼	63	
8d	2½	10¼	1½	78	
10d	3	9	1⅝	94	
12d	3¼	9	1⅝	94	See
16d	3½	8	1¾	107	U.B.C.
20d	4	6	2⅛	139	Standard
30d	4½	5	2¼	154	No.
40d	5	4	2½	176	25-17
50d	5½	3	2¾	202	
60d	6	2	2⅞	223	

[1]The safe lateral strength values may be increased 25 percent where metal side plates are used.
[2]For wood diaphragm calculations these values may be increased 30 percent. (See U.B.C. Standard No. 25-17.)
[3]For other species the lateral strength values of box wire nails shall not exceed 75 percent of the values listed in the Standard.

TABLE 25-H. Safe Resistance to Withdrawal of Common Wire Nails Inserted Perpendicular to Grain of the Wood, in Pounds per Linear Inch of Penetration into the Main Member

KIND OF WOOD	SIZE OF NAIL									
	6d	8d	10d	12d	16d	20d	30d	40d	50d	60d
Douglas Fir, Larch	29	34	38	38	42	49	53	58	63	68
Southern Pine	34	39	44	44	49	57	61	67	73	79
Other Species	See U.B.C. Standard No. 25-17									

TABLE 25-J. Allowable Shear in Pounds per Foot for Horizontal Plywood Diaphragms with Framing of Douglas Fir—Larch of Southern Pine

Plywood Grade	Common Nail Size	Minimum Nominal Penetration in Framing (in inches)	Minimum Nominal Plywood Thickness (in inches)	Minimum Nominal Width of Framing Member (in inches)	Blocked Diaphragms — Nail Spacing at diaphragm boundaries (all cases) and continuous panel edges parallel to load (cases 3, 4, 5 & 6)				Unblocked Diaphragms — Nails spaced 6" max. at supported end	
					6	4	2½	2	Load perpendicular to unblocked edges and continuous panel joints (case 1)	Other configurations (cases 2, 3, 4)
					Nail spacing at other plywood panel edges					
					6	6	4	3		
STRUCTURAL I	6d	1¼	5/16	2	185	250	375	420	165	125
				3	210	280	420	475	185	140
	8d	1½	3/8	2	270	360	530	600	240	180
				3	300	400	600	675	265	200
	10d	1⅝	½	2	320	425	640²	730²	285	215
				3	360	480	720	820	320	240
C-D, C-C, STRUCTURAL II and other grades covered in U.B.C. Standard No. 25-9	6d	1¼	5/16	2	170	225	335	380	150	110
				3	190	250	380	430	170	125
			3/8	2	185	250	375	420	165	125
				3	210	280	420	475	185	140
	8d	1½	3/8	2	240	320	480	545	215	160
				3	270	360	540	610	240	180
			½	2	270	360	530	600	240	180
				3	300	400	600	675	265	200
	10d	1⅝	½	2	290	385	575²	655²	255	190
				3	325	430	650	735	290	215
			5/8	2	320	425	640²	730²	285	215
				3	360	480	720	820	320	240

TABLE 25-J. (Continued)

[1] These values are for short time loads due to wind or earthquake and must be reduced 25 percent for normal loading. Space nails 10 inches on center for floors and 12 inches on center for roofs along intermediate framing members.

Allowable shear values for nails in framing members of other species set forth in Table No. 25-17-J of U.P.C. Standards shall be calculated for all grades by multiplying the values for nails in STRUCTURAL I by the following factors: Group III, 0.82 and Group IV, 0.65.

[2] Reduce tabulated allowable shears 10 percent when boundary members provide less than 3-inch nominal nailing surface.

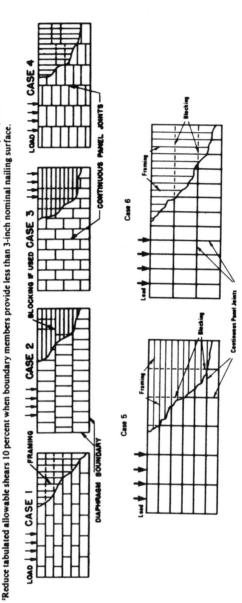

NOTE: Framing may be located in either direction for blocked diaphragms.

248

TABLE 25-K. Allowable Shear for Wind or Seismic Forces in Pounds per foot for Plywood Shear Walls with framing of Douglas Fir—Larch or Southern Pine

PLYWOOD GRADE	NAIL SIZE (Common or Galvanized Box)	MINIMUM NAIL PENETRATION IN FRAMING (Inches)	MINIMUM NOMINAL PLYWOOD THICKNESS (Inches)	PLYWOOD APPLIED DIRECT TO FRAMING — Nail Spacing at Plywood Panel Edges				NAIL SIZE (Common or Galvanized Box)	PLYWOOD APPLIED OVER ½-INCH GYPSUM SHEATHING — Nail Spacing at Plywood Panel Edges			
				6	4	2½	2		6	4	2½	2
STRUCTURAL I	6d	1¼	5/16	200	300	450	510	8d	200	300	450	510
	8d	1½	3/8	230[3]	360[3]	530[3]	610[3]	10d	280	430	640[2]	730[2]
	10d	1⅝	1/2	340	510	770[2]	870[2]	—	—	—	—	—
C-D, C-C, STRUCTURAL II and other grades covered in U.B.C. Standard No. 25-9	6d	1¼	5/16	180	270	400	450	8d	180	270	400	450
	8d	1½	3/8	220[3]	320[3]	470[3]	530[3]	10d	260	380	570[2]	640[2]
	10d	1⅝	1/2	310	460	690[2]	770[2]	—	—	—	—	—
	NAIL SIZE (Galvanized Casing)							NAIL SIZE (Galvanized Casing)				
Plywood Panel Siding in Grades Covered in U.B.C. Standard No. 25-9	6d	1¼	5/16	140	210	320	360	8d	140	210	320	360
	8d	1½	3/8	130[3]	200[3]	300[3]	340[3]	10d	160	240	360	410

[1] All panel edges backed with 2-inch nominal or wider framing. Plywood installed either horizontally or vertically. Plywood installed with face grain parallel to studs spaced 24 inches on center for other conditions and plywood thicknesses. These values are for short time loads due to wind or earthquake and must be reduced 25 percent for normal loading.

Allowable shear values for nails in framing members of other species set forth in Table No. 25-17-J of U.B.C. Standards shall be calculated for all grades by multiplying the values for common and galvanized box nails in STRUCTURAL I and galvanized casing nails in other grades by the following factors: Group III, 0.82 and Group IV, 0.65.

[2] Reduce tabulated allowable shears 10 percent when boundary members provide less than 3-inch nominal nailing surface.

[3] The values for ⅜-inch thick plywood applied direct to framing may be increased 20 percent provided studs are spaced a maximum of 16 inches on center or plywood is applied with face grain across studs.

249

TABLE 25-P. Nailing Schedule

CONNECTION	NAILING[1]
Joist to sill or girder, toe nail	3-8d
Bridging to joist, toe nail each end	2-8d
1" x 6" subfloor or less to each joist, face nail	2-8d
Wider than 1" x 6" subfloor to each joist, face nail	3-8d
2" subfloor to joist or girder, blind and face nail	2-16d
Sole plate to joist or blocking, face nail	16d at 16" o.c.
Top plate to stud, end nail	2-16d
Stud to sole plate, toe nail	4-8d
Doubled studs, face nail	16d at 24" o.c.
Doubled top plates, face nail	16d at 16" o.c.
Top plates, laps and intersections, face nail	2-16d
Continuous header, two pieces	16d at 16" o.c. along each edge
Ceiling joists to plate, toe nail	3-8d
Continuous header to stud, toe nail	4-8d
Ceiling joists, laps over partitions, face nail	3-16d
Ceiling joists to parallel rafters, face nail	3-16d
Rafter to plate, toe nail	3-8d
1" brace to each stud and plate, face nail	2-8d
1" x 8" sheathing or less to each bearing, face nail	2-8d
Wider than 1" x 8" sheathing to each bearing, face nail	3-8d
Built-up corner studs	16d at 24" o.c.

(Continued)

TABLE 25-P. *(Continued)*

CONNECTION	NAILING[1]
Built-up girder and beams	20d at 32″ o.c. at top and bottom and staggered 2-20d at ends and at each splice
2″ planks	2-16d at each bearing
Particleboard:[5]	
Wall Sheathing (to framing):	
⅜″-½″	6d[3]
⅝″-¾″	8d[3]
Plywood:[5]	
Subfloor, roof and wall sheathing (to framing):	
½″ and less	6d[2]
⅝″-¾″	8d[3] or 6d[4]
⅞″-1″	8d[2]
1⅛″-1¼″	10d[3] or 8d[4]
Combination Subfloor-underlayment (to framing):	
¾″ and less	6d[4]
⅞″-1″	8d[4]
1⅛″-1¼″	10d[3] or 8d[4]
Panel Siding (to framing)	
½″ or less	6d[6]
⅝″	8d[6]
Fiberboard Sheathing:[7]	
½″	No. 11 ga.[8]
	6d[3]
	No. 16 ga.[9]
25/32″	No. 11 ga.[8]
	8d[3]
	No. 16 ga.[9]

[1]Common or box nails may be used except where otherwise stated.

[2]Common or deformed shank.

[3]Common.

[4]Deformed shank.

[5]Nails spaced at 6 inches on center at edges, 12 inches at intermediate supports (10 inches at intermediate supports for floors), except 6 inches at all supports where spans are 48 inches or more. For nailing of plywood diaphragms and shear walls refer to Section 2514 (c). Nails for wall sheathing may be common, box or casing.

[6]Corrosion resistant siding and casing nails.

[7]Fasteners spaced 3 inches on center at exterior edges and 6 inches on center at intermediate supports.

[8]Galvanized roofing nails with 7/16-inch diameter head and 1½-inch length for ½-inch sheathing and 1¾ inch for 25/32-inch sheathing.

[9]Galvanized staple with 7/16-inch crown and 1⅛-inch length for ½-inch sheathing and 1½-inch length for 25/32-inch sheathing.

TABLE 25-R-1. Allowable Spans for Plywood Subfloor and Roof Sheathing Continuous over Two or More Spans and Face Grain Perpendicular to Supports

PANEL IDENTIFICATION INDEX[3]	PLYWOOD THICKNESS (Inch)	ROOF[2]				FLOOR MAXIMUM SPAN[4] (In inches)
		MAXIMUM SPAN (In Inches)		LOAD (IN POUNDS PER SQUARE FOOT)		
		Edges Blocked	Edges Unblocked	Total Load	Live Load	
12/0	$\frac{5}{16}$	12		155	150	0
16/0	$\frac{5}{16}$, $\frac{3}{8}$	16		95	75	0
20/0	$\frac{5}{16}$, $\frac{3}{8}$	20		75	65	0
24/0	$\frac{3}{8}$, $\frac{1}{2}$	24	16	65	50	0
30/12	$\frac{5}{8}$	30	26	70	50	12[5]
32/16	$\frac{1}{2}$, $\frac{5}{8}$	32	28	55	40	16[7]
36/16	$\frac{3}{4}$	36	30	55	50	16[7]
42/20	$\frac{5}{8}$, $\frac{3}{4}$, $\frac{7}{8}$	42	32	40[6]	35[6]	20[7]
48/24	$\frac{3}{4}$, $\frac{7}{8}$	48	36	40[6]	35[6]	24

[1] These values apply for Structural I and II, C-C and C-D grades only. Spans shall be limited to values shown because of possible effect of concentrated loads.

[2] Uniform load deflection limitation: 1/180th of the span under live load plus dead load, 1/240th under live load only. Edges may be blocked with lumber or other approved type of edge support.

[3] Identification index appears on all panels in the construction grades listed in Footnote No. 1.

[4] Plywood edges shall have approved tongue and groove joints or shall be supported with blocking, unless ¼-inch minimum thickness underlayment is installed, or finish floor is $\frac{25}{32}$-inch wood strip. Allowable uniform load based on deflection of 1/360 of span is 165 pounds per square foot.

[5] May be 16-inch if $\frac{25}{32}$-inch wood strip flooring is installed at right angles to joists.

[6] For roof live load of 40 pounds per square foot or total load of 55 pounds per square foot, decrease spans by 13 percent or use panel with next greater identification index.

[7] May be 24 inch if $\frac{25}{32}$-inch wood strip flooring is installed at right angles to joists.

TABLE 25-R-2. Allowable Loads for Plywood Roof Sheathing Continuous over Two or More Spans and Face Grain Parallel to Supports

	THICKNESS	NO. OF PLIES	SPAN	TOTAL LOAD	LIVE LOAD
STRUCTURAL I	$\frac{1}{2}$	4	24	35	25
	$\frac{1}{2}$	5	24	55	40
Other grades covered in UBC Standard 25-9	$\frac{1}{2}$	5	24	30	25
	$\frac{5}{8}$	4	24	40	30
	$\frac{5}{8}$	5	24	60	45

[1] Uniform load deflection limitations: 1/180 of span under live load plus dead load, 1/240 under live load only. Edges shall be blocked with lumber or other approved type of edge supports.

TABLE 25-T-J-1. Allowable Spans for Floor Joists 40 Lbs. Per Square Foot Live Load

DESIGN CRITERIA: Deflection - For 40 lbs. per sq. ft. live load. Limited to span in inches divided by 360. Strength - Live load of 40 lbs. per sq. ft. plus dead load of 10 lbs. per sq. ft. determines the required fiber stress value.

JOIST SIZE (IN)	SPACING (IN)	Modulus of Elasticity, "E", in 1,000,000 psi													
		0.8	0.9	1.0	1.1	1.2	1.3	1.4	1.5	1.6	1.7	1.8	1.9	2.0	2.2
2x6	12.0	8-6 / 720	8-10 / 780	9-2 / 830	9-6 / 890	9-9 / 940	10-0 / 990	10-3 / 1040	10-6 / 1090	10-9 / 1140	10-11 / 1190	11-2 / 1230	11-4 / 1280	11-7 / 1320	11-11 / 1410
	16.0	7-9 / 790	8-0 / 860	8-4 / 920	8-7 / 980	8-10 / 1040	9-1 / 1090	9-4 / 1150	9-6 / 1200	9-9 / 1250	9-11 / 1310	10-2 / 1360	10-4 / 1410	10-6 / 1460	10-10 / 1550
	24.0	6-9 / 900	7-0 / 980	7-3 / 1050	7-6 / 1120	7-9 / 1190	7-11 / 1250	8-2 / 1310	8-4 / 1380	8-6 / 1440	8-8 / 1500	8-10 / 1550	9-0 / 1610	9-2 / 1670	9-6 / 1780
2x8	12.0	11-3 / 720	11-8 / 780	12-1 / 830	12-6 / 890	12-10 / 940	13-2 / 990	13-6 / 1040	13-10 / 1090	14-2 / 1140	14-5 / 1190	14-8 / 1230	15-0 / 1280	15-3 / 1320	15-9 / 1410
	16.0	10-2 / 790	10-7 / 850	11-0 / 920	11-4 / 980	11-8 / 1040	12-0 / 1090	12-3 / 1150	12-7 / 1200	12-10 / 1250	13-1 / 1310	13-4 / 1360	13-7 / 1410	13-10 / 1460	14-3 / 1550
	24.0	8-11 / 900	9-3 / 980	9-7 / 1050	9-11 / 1120	10-2 / 1190	10-6 / 1250	10-9 / 1310	11-0 / 1380	11-3 / 1440	11-5 / 1500	11-8 / 1550	11-11 / 1610	12-1 / 1670	12-6 / 1780
2x10	12.0	14-4 / 720	14-11 / 780	15-5 / 830	15-11 / 890	16-5 / 940	16-10 / 990	17-3 / 1040	17-8 / 1090	18-0 / 1140	18-5 / 1190	18-9 / 1230	19-1 / 1280	19-5 / 1320	20-1 / 1410
	16.0	13-0 / 790	13-6 / 850	14-0 / 920	14-6 / 980	14-11 / 1040	15-3 / 1090	15-8 / 1150	16-0 / 1200	16-5 / 1250	16-9 / 1310	17-0 / 1360	17-4 / 1410	17-8 / 1460	18-3 / 1550
	24.0	11-4 / 900	11-10 / 980	12-3 / 1050	12-8 / 1120	13-0 / 1190	13-4 / 1250	13-8 / 1310	14-0 / 1380	14-4 / 1440	14-7 / 1500	14-11 / 1550	15-2 / 1610	15-5 / 1670	15-11 / 1780
2x12	12.0	17-5 / 720	18-1 / 780	18-9 / 830	19-4 / 890	19-11 / 940	20-6 / 990	21-0 / 1040	21-6 / 1090	21-11 / 1140	22-5 / 1190	22-10 / 1230	23-3 / 1280	23-7 / 1320	24-5 / 1410
	16.0	15-10 / 790	16-5 / 860	17-0 / 920	17-7 / 980	18-1 / 1040	18-7 / 1090	19-1 / 1150	19-6 / 1200	19-11 / 1250	20-4 / 1310	20-9 / 1360	21-1 / 1410	21-6 / 1460	22-2 / 1550
	24.0	13-10 / 900	14-4 / 980	14-11 / 1050	15-4 / 1120	15-10 / 1190	16-3 / 1250	16-8 / 1310	17-0 / 1380	17-5 / 1440	17-9 / 1500	18-1 / 1550	18-5 / 1610	18-9 / 1670	19-4 / 1780

NOTES:

(1) The required extreme fiber stress in bending, F_b, in pounds per square inch is shown below each span.

(2) Use single or repetitive member bending stress values (F_b) and modulus of elasticity values (E), from Tables Nos. 25-A-1, and 25-A-2.

(3) For more comprehensive tables covering a broader range of bending stress values (F_b) and Modulus of Elasticity values (E), other spacing of members and other conditions of loading, see U.B.C. Standard No. 25-21.

(4) The spans in these tables are intended for use in covered structures or where moisture content in use does not exceed 19 percent.

TABLE 25-T-J-6.   Allowable Spans for Ceiling Joists 10 Lbs. Per Square Foot Live Load (Drywall Ceiling)

DESIGN CRITERIA: Deflection - For 10 lbs. per sq. ft. live load. Limited to span in inches divided by 240. Strength - Live load of 10 lbs. per sq. ft. plus dead load of 5 lbs. per sq. ft. determines required fiber stress value.

JOIST SIZE (IN)	SPACING (IN)	Modulus of Elasticity, "E", in 1,000,000 psi													
		0.8	0.9	1.0	1.1	1.2	1.3	1.4	1.5	1.6	1.7	1.8	1.9	2.0	2.2
2x4	12.0	9-10 710	10-3 770	10-7 830	10-11 880	11-3 930	11-7 980	11-10 1030	12-2 1080	12-5 1130	12-8 1180	12-11 1220	13-2 1270	13-4 1310	13-9 1400
2x4	16.0	8-11 780	9-4 850	9-8 910	9-11 970	10-3 1030	10-6 1080	10-9 1140	11-0 1190	11-3 1240	11-6 1290	11-9 1340	11-11 1390	12-2 1440	12-6 1540
2x4	24.0	7-10 900	8-1 970	8-5 1040	8-8 1110	8-11 1170	9-2 1240	9-5 1300	9-8 1360	9-10 1420	10-0 1480	10-3 1540	10-5 1600	10-7 1650	10-11 1760
2x6	12.0	15-6 710	16-1 770	16-8 830	17-2 880	17-8 930	18-2 980	18-8 1030	19-1 1080	19-6 1130	19-11 1180	20-3 1220	20-8 1270	21-0 1310	21-8 1400
2x6	16.0	14-1 780	14-7 850	15-2 910	15-7 970	16-1 1030	16-6 1080	16-11 1140	17-4 1190	17-8 1240	18-1 1290	18-5 1340	18-9 1390	19-1 1440	19-8 1540
2x6	24.0	12-3 900	12-9 970	13-3 1040	13-8 1110	14-1 1170	14-5 1240	14-9 1300	15-2 1360	15-6 1420	15-9 1480	16-1 1540	16-4 1600	16-8 1650	17-2 1760
2x8	12.0	20-5 710	21-2 770	21-11 830	22-8 880	23-4 930	24-0 980	24-7 1030	25-2 1080	25-8 1130	26-2 1180	26-9 1220	27-2 1270	27-8 1310	28-7 1400
2x8	16.0	18-6 780	19-3 850	19-11 910	20-7 970	21-2 1030	21-9 1080	22-4 1140	22-10 1190	23-4 1240	23-10 1290	24-3 1340	24-8 1390	25-2 1440	25-11 1540
2x8	24.0	16-2 900	16-10 970	17-5 1040	18-0 1110	18-6 1170	19-0 1240	19-6 1300	19-11 1360	20-5 1420	20-10 1480	21-2 1540	21-7 1600	21-11 1650	22-8 1760
2x10	12.0	26-0 710	27-1 770	28-0 830	28-11 880	29-9 930	30-7 980	31-4 1030	32-1 1080	32-9 1130	33-5 1180	34-1 1220	34-8 1270	35-4 1310	36-5 1400
2x10	16.0	23-8 780	24-7 850	25-5 910	26-3 970	27-1 1030	27-9 1080	28-6 1140	29-2 1190	29-9 1240	30-5 1290	31-0 1340	31-6 1390	32-1 1440	33-1 1540
2x10	24.0	20-8 900	21-6 970	22-3 1040	22-11 1110	23-8 1170	24-3 1240	24-10 1300	25-5 1360	26-0 1420	26-6 1480	27-1 1540	27-6 1600	28-0 1650	28-11 1760

(1) The required extreme fiber stress in bending F_b, in pounds per square inch is shown below each span.

(2) Use single or repetitive member bending stress values (f_b) and modulus of elasticity values (E), from Tables Nos. 25-A-1, and 25-A-2.

(3) For more comprehensive tables covering a broader range of bending stress values (F_b) and Modulus of Elasticity values (E), other spacing of members and other conditions of loading, see U.B.C. Standard No. 25-21.

(4) The spans in these tables are intended for use in covered structures or where moisture content in use does not exceed 19 percent.

TABLE 25-T-R-14. Allowable Spans for High Slope Rafters Slope Over 3 in 12, 30 Lbs. Per Square Foot Live Load (Light Roof Covering)

DESIGN CRITERIA: Strength - 7 lbs. per sq. ft. dead load plus 30 lbs. per sq. ft. live load determines required fiber stress. **Deflection** - For 30 lbs. per sq. ft. live load. Limited to span in inches divided by 180. **RAFTERS:** Spans are measured along the horizontal projection and loads are considered as applied on the horizontal projection.

Allowable Extreme Fiber Stress in Bending, "F_b" (psi).

RAFTER SIZE	SPACING (IN)	500	600	700	800	900	1000	1100	1200	1300	1400	1500	1600	1700	1800	1900
2x4	12.0	5-3 / 0.27	5-9 / 0.36	6-3 / 0.45	6-8 / 0.55	7-1 / 0.66	7-5 / 0.77	7-9 / 0.89	8-2 / 1.02	8-6 / 1.15	8-9 / 1.28	9-1 / 1.42	9-5 / 1.57	9-8 / 1.72	10-0 / 1.87	10-3 / 2.03
	16.0	4-7 / 0.24	5-0 / 0.31	5-5 / 0.39	5-9 / 0.48	6-1 / 0.57	6-5 / 0.67	6-9 / 0.77	7-1 / 0.88	7-4 / 0.99	7-7 / 1.11	7-11 / 1.23	8-2 / 1.36	8-5 / 1.49	8-8 / 1.62	8-10 / 1.76
	24.0	3-9 / 0.19	4-1 / 0.25	4-5 / 0.32	4-8 / 0.39	5-0 / 0.47	5-3 / 0.55	5-6 / 0.63	5-9 / 0.72	6-0 / 0.81	6-3 / 0.91	6-5 / 1.01	6-8 / 1.11	6-10 / 1.21	7-1 / 1.32	7-3 / 1.43
2x6	12.0	8-3 / 0.27	9-1 / 0.36	9-9 / 0.45	10-5 / 0.55	11-1 / 0.66	11-8 / 0.77	12-3 / 0.89	12-9 / 1.02	13-4 / 1.15	13-10 / 1.28	14-4 / 1.42	14-9 / 1.57	15-3 / 1.72	15-8 / 1.87	16-1 / 2.03
	16.0	7-2 / 0.24	7-10 / 0.31	8-5 / 0.39	9-1 / 0.48	9-7 / 0.57	10-1 / 0.67	10-7 / 0.77	11-1 / 0.88	11-6 / 0.99	12-0 / 1.11	12-5 / 1.23	12-9 / 1.36	13-2 / 1.49	13-7 / 1.62	13-11 / 1.76
	24.0	5-10 / 0.19	6-5 / 0.25	6-11 / 0.32	7-5 / 0.39	7-10 / 0.47	8-3 / 0.55	8-8 / 0.63	9-1 / 0.72	9-5 / 0.81	9-9 / 0.91	10-1 / 1.01	10-5 / 1.11	10-9 / 1.21	11-1 / 1.32	11-5 / 1.43
2x8	12.0	10-11 / 0.27	11-11 / 0.36	12-10 / 0.45	13-9 / 0.55	14-7 / 0.66	15-5 / 0.77	16-2 / 0.89	16-10 / 1.02	17-7 / 1.15	18-2 / 1.28	18-10 / 1.42	19-6 / 1.57	20-1 / 1.72	20-8 / 1.87	21-3 / 2.03
	16.0	9-5 / 0.24	10-4 / 0.31	11-2 / 0.39	11-11 / 0.48	12-8 / 0.57	13-4 / 0.67	14-0 / 0.77	14-7 / 0.88	15-2 / 0.99	15-9 / 1.11	16-4 / 1.23	16-10 / 1.36	17-4 / 1.49	17-11 / 1.62	18-4 / 1.76
	24.0	7-8 / 0.19	8-5 / 0.25	9-1 / 0.32	9-9 / 0.39	10-4 / 0.47	10-11 / 0.55	11-5 / 0.63	11-11 / 0.72	12-5 / 0.81	12-10 / 0.91	13-4 / 1.01	13-9 / 1.11	14-2 / 1.21	14-7 / 1.32	15-0 / 1.43
2x10	12.0	13-11 / 0.27	15-2 / 0.36	16-5 / 0.45	17-7 / 0.55	18-7 / 0.66	19-8 / 0.77	20-7 / 0.89	21-6 / 1.02	22-5 / 1.15	23-3 / 1.28	24-1 / 1.42	24-10 / 1.57	25-7 / 1.72	26-4 / 1.87	27-1 / 2.03
	16.0	12-0 / 0.26	13-2 / 0.34	14-3 / 0.43	15-2 / 0.53	16-2 / 0.63	17-0 / 0.74	17-10 / 0.85	18-7 / 0.97	19-5 / 1.09	20-1 / 1.22	20-10 / 1.35	21-6 / 1.49	22-2 / 1.63	22-10 / 1.78	23-5 / 1.93
	24.0	9-10 / 0.19	10-9 / 0.25	11-7 / 0.32	12-5 / 0.39	13-2 / 0.47	13-11 / 0.55	14-7 / 0.63	15-2 / 0.72	15-10 / 0.81	16-5 / 0.91	17-0 / 1.01	17-7 / 1.11	18-1 / 1.21	18-7 / 1.32	19-2 / 1.43

(1) The required modulus of elasticity, E, in 1,000,000 pounds per square inch is shown below each span.

(2) Use single or repetitive member bending stress values (F_b) and modulus of elasticity values (E), from Tables Nos. 25-A-1, and 25-A-2. For duration of load stress increases, see Section 2504 (c) 4.

(3) For more comprehensive tables covering a broader range of bending stress values (F_b) and Modulus of Elasticity values (E), other spacing of members and other conditions of loading, see U.B.C. Standard No. 25-21.

(4) The spans in these tables are intended for use in covered structures or where moisture content in use does not exceed 19 percent.

TABLE 47-I. Allowable Shear for Wind or Seismic Forces in Pounds per Foot for Vertical Diaphragms of Lath and Plaster, Gypsum Sheathing Board, and Gypsum Wallboard Wood Framed Wall Assemblies

TYPE OF MATERIAL	THICKNESS OF MATERIAL	WALL CONSTRUCTION	NAIL SPACING[2] MAXIMUM (in Inches)	SHEAR VALUE	MINIMUM NAIL SIZE
Woven or Welded Wire Lath and Portland Cement Plaster	$\frac{7}{8}''$	Unblocked	6	180	No. 11 gauge, $1\frac{1}{2}''$ long with $\frac{7}{16}''$ diameter head nail or No. 16 gauge staples having $\frac{7}{8}''$ long legs.
Gypsum Lath, Plain or Perforated	$\frac{3}{8}''$ Lath and $\frac{1}{2}''$ Plaster	Unblocked	5	100	No. 13 gauge, $1\frac{1}{8}''$ long, $\frac{19}{64}''$ head, plaster-board blued nail
Gypsum Sheathing Board	$\frac{1}{2}'' \times 2' \times 8'$	Unblocked	4	75	No. 11 gauge, $1\frac{3}{4}''$ long, $\frac{7}{16}''$ head, diamond-point, galvanized
	$\frac{1}{2}'' \times 4'$	Blocked	4	175	
	$\frac{1}{2}'' \times 4$	Unblocked	7	100	
Gypsum Wallboard	$\frac{1}{2}''$	Unblocked	7	100	5d cooler nails
			4	125	
		Blocked	7	125	
			4	150	
	$\frac{5}{8}''$	Blocked	4	175	6d cooler nails
		Blocked Two-ply	Base Ply 9 Face Ply 7	250	Base Ply—6d cooler nails Face Ply—8d cooler nails

[1] These vertical diaphragms shall not be used to resist loads imposed by masonry or concrete walls. Values are for short-time loading due to wind or earthquake and must be reduced 25 percent for normal loading.
[2] Applies to nailing at all studs, top and bottom plates, and blocking.

S$_x$ ALLOWABLE STRESS DESIGN SELECTION TABLE
For shapes used as beams

$F_y = 50$ ksi			S_x	Shape	F_y'	F_y''	$F_y = 36$ ksi		
L_c	L_u	M_R					L_c	L_u	M_R
Ft.	Ft.	Kip-ft.	In.³		Ksi	Ksi	Ft.	Ft.	Kip-ft.
8.9	9.9	825	300	W 30 × 108	57.3	57.3	11.1	12.4	600
9.0	11.5	825	300	W 27 × 114	—	—	10.6	15.9	600
10.8	15.4	825	300	W 24 × 120	64.5	—	12.8	21.4	600
11.7	20.2	781	284	W 21 × 127	62.0	—	13.8	28.1	568
10.8	14.2	759	276	W 24 × 110	54.9	—	12.7	19.7	552
7.9	9.8	738	270	W 30 × 99	44.7	52.6	10.9	11.6	540
9.0	10.2	734	267	W 27 × 102	—	62.2	10.6	14.2	534
7.2	12.3	693	252	S 24 × 120	—	—	8.5	17.1	504
10.7	12.9	684	250	W 24 × 100	45.5	64.5	12.7	17.9	500
11.6	17.8	686	250	W 21 × 112	48.3	—	13.7	24.8	500
8.9	9.6	668	243	W 27 × 94	60.9	56.3	10.5	12.8	486
7.1	12.0	649	236	S 24 × 105.9	—	—	8.3	16.7	472
8.1	10.9	608	221	W 24 × 94	—	—	9.6	15.1	442
10.6	21.1	605	220	W 18 × 114	—	—	12.5	29.3	440
7.9	9.5	579	212	W 27 × 84	44.4	51.1	10.5	11.2	424
10.6	19.5	556	202	W 18 × 105	—	—	12.4	27.1	404
6.5	8.8	547	199	S 24 × 100	—	—	7.6	12.2	398
8.1	13.3	545	198	W 21 × 96	—	—	9.5	18.5	396
8.1	9.6	542	197	W 24 × 84	—	64.6	9.5	13.4	394
13.1	31.4	516	189	W 14 × 119	44.7	—	15.5	43.7	378
6.4	8.6	514	187	S 24 × 90	—	—	7.5	12.0	374
10.5	17.9	509	185	W 18 × 96	54.5	—	12.4	24.9	370
8.0	8.7	484	176	W 24 × 76	62.8	57.5	9.5	11.9	352
13.1	29.5	477	176	W 14 × 111	38.9	—	15.4	41.0	352
6.3	8.5	481	175	S 24 × 79.9	—	—	7.4	11.8	350
8.0	11.4	465	169	W 21 × 82	—	—	9.5	15.8	338
10.3	20.6	457	166	W 16 × 96	62.7	—	12.2	28.6	332
13.1	27.8	440	164	W 14 × 103	33.9	—	15.4	38.6	324
6.4	11.0	443	161	S 20 × 95	—	—	7.6	15.3	322
7.9	14.6	432	157	W 18 × 85	—	—	9.3	20.3	314
7.3	8.6	419	153	W 24 × 68	46.0	52.3	9.5	10.2	306
6.3	10.8	418	152	S 20 × 85	—	—	7.4	15.0	304
7.4	9.6	415	151	W 21 × 73	—	—	8.8	13.4	302
10.3	18.8	415	151	W 16 × 88	52.1	—	12.1	26.2	302
13.0	25.6	401	151	W 14 × 95	28.8	—	15.4	35.6	295
7.9	13.4	391	142	W 18 × 77	—	—	9.3	18.6	284
7.4	8.9	385	140	W 21 × 68	—	—	8.7	12.4	280
13.0	23.8	362	138	W 14 × 87	24.5	—	15.3	33.1	267
10.8	21.9	358	131	W 14 × 84	45.6	—	12.7	30.5	262
$F_y = 50$ ksi							$F_y = 36$ ksi		

$F_y = 36$ ksi	BEAMS — W shapes	W 12

Allowable uniform loads in kips for beams laterally supported

For beams laterally unsupported, see page 2 - 84

Designation		W12			W12				
Weight per Foot		36	31	27	22	19	16.5	*14	Deflection Inches
Flange Width		6⅝	6½	6½	4	4	4	4	
L_c		6.9	6.9	6.9	4.3	4.2	4.1	3.5	
L_u		13.4	11.6	10.1	6.4	5.3	4.3	4.2	
	3						80.0	68.4	0.02
	4				92.8	83.6	70.4	58.5	0.03
	5				81.0	68.2	56.3	46.8	0.05
	6	108.3	92.9	82.2	67.5	56.8	46.9	39.0	0.07
	7	105.1	90.3	78.2	57.8	48.7	40.2	33.4	0.10
	8	92.0	79.0	68.4	50.6	42.6	35.2	29.2	0.13
	9	81.8	70.2	60.8	45.0	37.9	31.3	26.0	0.17
	10	73.6	63.2	54.7	40.5	34.1	28.2	23.4	0.21
	11	66.9	57.5	49.7	36.8	31.0	25.6	21.3	0.25
	12	61.3	52.7	45.6	33.7	28.4	23.5	19.5	0.30
	13	56.6	48.6	42.1	31.1	26.2	21.7	18.0	0.35
$F_y = 36$ ksi — Span in Feet	14	52.6	45.1	39.1	28.9	24.3	20.1	16.7	0.41
	15	49.1	42.1	36.5	27.0	22.7	18.8	15.6	0.47
	16	46.0	39.5	34.2	25.3	21.3	17.6	14.6	0.53
	17	43.3	37.2	32.2	23.8	20.0	16.6	13.8	0.60
	18	40.9	35.1	30.4	22.5	18.9	15.6	13.0	0.67
	19	38.7	33.3	28.8	21.3	17.9	14.8	12.3	0.75
	20	36.8	31.6	27.4	20.2	17.0	14.1	11.7	0.83
	21	35.0	30.1	26.1	19.3	16.2	13.4	11.1	0.91
	22	33.5	28.7	24.9	18.4	15.5	12.8	10.6	1.00
	23	32.0	27.5	23.8	17.6	14.8	12.2	10.2	1.09
	24	30.7	26.3	22.8	16.9	14.2	11.7	9.7	1.19
	25	29.4	25.3	21.9	16.2	13.6	11.3	9.4	1.29
								(23.7)	

Properties and Reaction Values

	36	31	27	22	19	16.5	*14	
S in.³	46.0	39.5	34.2	25.3	21.3	17.6	14.8	For explanation of deflection see page 2 - 23
V kips	54.1	46.5	41.1	46.4	41.8	40.0	34.2	
R kips	37.6	32.2	28.4	31.2	28.0	26.8	22.7	
R_i kips	8.2	7.2	6.4	7.0	6.4	6.2	5.3	
N_e in.	5.5	5.5	5.5	5.7	5.7	5.6	5.6	

Load above heavy line is limited by maximum allowable web shear.

* Tabulated loads for this shape are computed with the allowable stress (ksi) shown in parentheses at the bottom of the allowable load column.

M 14-12-10-8-7-6

I

BEAMS
M shapes

$F_y = 36 \text{ ksi}$

**Allowable uniform loads in kips
for beams laterally supported**

For beams laterally unsupported, see page 2 - 84

Designation	M14	M12	M10	M10	M10	M8	M7	M6
Weight per Foot	17.2	11.8	29.1	22.9	9	6.5	5.5	4.4
Flange Width	4	3⅛	5⅞	5¾	2¾	2¼	2⅛	1⅞
L_c	3.6	2.7	6.3	6.1	2.6	2.4	2.2	1.9
L_u	4.1	3.1	10.8	10.5	2.7	2.5	2.5	2.4
1								19.8
2					45.5	31.3	26.0	19.2
3	85.3	61.6	122.3		41.4	24.6	18.3	12.8
4	84.4	48.0	106.4		31.0	18.5	13.8	9.6
5	67.5	38.4	85.1	69.3	24.8	14.8	11.0	7.7
6	56.3	32.0	70.9	62.9	20.7	12.3	9.2	6.4
7	48.2	27.4	60.8	53.9	17.7	10.6	7.9	5.5
8	42.2	24.0	53.2	47.2	15.5	9.2	6.9	4.8
9	37.5	21.3	47.3	42.0	13.8	8.2	6.1	4.3
10	33.8	19.2	42.6	37.8	12.4	7.4	5.5	3.8
11	30.7	17.5	38.7	34.3	11.3	6.7	5.0	3.5
12	28.1	16.0	35.5	31.5	10.3	6.2	4.6	3.2
13	26.0	14.8	32.7	29.0	9.6	5.7	4.2	3.0
14	24.1	13.7	30.4	27.0	8.9	5.3	3.9	
15	22.5	12.8	28.4	25.2	8.3	4.9	3.7	
16	21.1	12.0	26.6	23.6	7.8	4.6		
17	19.9	11.3	25.0	22.2	7.3	4.3		
18	18.8	10.7	23.6	21.0	6.9			
19	17.8	10.1	22.4	19.9	6.5			
20	16.9	9.6	21.3	18.9	6.2			
21	16.1	9.1	20.3	18.0	5.9			
22	15.3	8.7						
23	14.7	8.3						
24	14.1	8.0						
25	13.5	7.7						
26	13.0							
27	12.5							
28	12.1							
29	11.6							
30	11.3							

(Left margin: $F_y = 36 \text{ ksi}$ — Span in Feet*)*

Properties and Reaction Values

	M14	M12	M10	M10	M10	M8	M7	M6
S in.³	21.1	12.0	26.6	23.6	7.8	4.6	3.4	2.4
V kips	42.6	30.8	61.2	34.7	22.8	15.7	13.0	9.9
R kips	23.4	19.4	50.4	28.6	17.0	14.6	**13.6**	**11.9**
R_i kips	5.7	4.8	11.5	6.5	4.2	3.6	3.5	3.1
N_e in.	6.9	5.9	4.4	4.4	4.9	3.8	3.3	2.8

Load above heavy line is limited by maximum allowable web shear.
Values of R in **bold face** exceed maximum web shear V.

COLUMNS
W shapes

TABLE I

Allowable axial loads in kips

$F_y = 36\ ksi$

W 14

Designation					W14				
Nominal Depth and Width					14 × 16				
Weight per Foot	342	320	314	287	264	246	237	228	219
6	2099	1954	1917	1752	1611	1500	1446	1392	1336
7	2082	1938	1901	1738	1597	1488	1434	1380	1324
8	2064	1921	1885	1723	1583	1474	1421	1368	1312
9	2045	1903	1868	1707	1568	1461	1408	1355	1300
10	2026	1885	1850	1690	1553	1446	1394	1342	1287
11	2006	1865	1831	1673	1537	1431	1379	1328	1273
12	1985	1845	1812	1655	1520	1416	1364	1313	1259
13	1963	1825	1792	1637	1503	1400	1349	1298	1245
14	1941	1804	1771	1618	1486	1383	1333	1282	1230
15	1918	1782	1750	1598	1467	1366	1316	1266	1214
16	1894	1759	1728	1578	1448	1348	1299	1250	1198
17	1870	1736	1705	1557	1429	1330	1281	1233	1182
18	1845	1712	1682	1535	1409	1311	1263	1215	1165
19	1819	1687	1658	1513	1389	1292	1245	1197	1148
20	1793	1662	1634	1491	1368	1272	1226	1179	1130
22	1738	1610	1583	1444	1324	1231	1186	1141	1093
24	1681	1555	1530	1395	1278	1189	1145	1101	1054
26	1621	1498	1475	1344	1231	1144	1102	1059	1014
28	1559	1439	1417	1291	1182	1098	1057	1016	972
30	1495	1377	1357	1235	1130	1049	1010	971	928
32	1428	1313	1295	1178	1077	999	961	924	883
34	1358	1247	1231	1118	1021	947	911	875	836
36	1286	1178	1164	1056	964	893	859	824	787
38	1212	1107	1095	992	904	837	805	772	736
40	1135	1033	1023	926	842	779	748	718	684

Left side vertical labels: $F_y = 36\ ksi$ — Effective length in ft. KL with respect to least radius of gyration r_y

Properties

Area A (in.²)	101	94.1	92.3	84.4	77.6	72.3	69.7	67.1	64.4
I_x (in.⁴)	4910	4140	4400	3910	3530	3230	3080	2940	2800
I_y (in.⁴)	1810	1640	1630	1470	1330	1230	1170	1120	1070
Ratio r_x/r_y	1.65	1.59	1.64	1.63	1.63	1.62	1.62	1.61	1.62
r_y (in.)	4.24	4.17	4.20	4.17	4.14	4.12	4.11	4.10	4.08
L_c (ft.)	17.3	17.7	17.2	17.1	17.0	16.9	16.8	16.8	16.8
L_u (ft.)	106.5	96.3	99.8	93.0	87.2	82.4	79.9	77.6	75.0
B_x Bending	.181	.191	.181	.182	.182	.183	.183	.183	.183
B_y factors	.458	.481	.460	.464	.468	.470	.471	.473	.474
a_x Multiply	735	616	655	583	525	481	459	438	417
a_y values by 10⁶	271	244	243	219	198	183	175	168	160

$F_y = 36$ ksi W 14	COLUMNS W shapes TABLE I Allowable axial loads in kips								

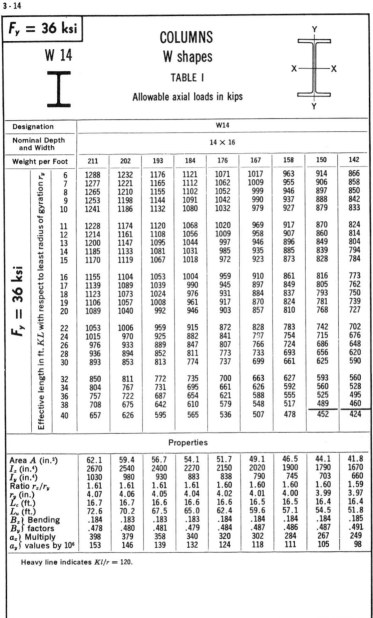

Designation	W14								
Nominal Depth and Width	14 × 16								
Weight per Foot	211	202	193	184	176	167	158	150	142
6	1288	1232	1176	1121	1071	1017	963	914	866
7	1277	1221	1165	1112	1062	1009	955	906	858
8	1265	1210	1155	1102	1052	999	946	897	850
9	1253	1198	1144	1091	1042	990	937	888	842
10	1241	1186	1132	1080	1032	979	927	879	833
11	1228	1174	1120	1068	1020	969	917	870	824
12	1214	1161	1108	1056	1009	958	907	860	814
13	1200	1147	1095	1044	997	946	896	849	804
14	1185	1133	1081	1031	985	935	885	839	794
15	1170	1119	1067	1018	972	923	873	828	784
16	1155	1104	1053	1004	959	910	861	816	773
17	1139	1089	1039	990	945	897	849	805	762
18	1123	1073	1024	976	931	884	837	793	750
19	1106	1057	1008	961	917	870	824	781	739
20	1089	1040	992	946	903	857	810	768	727
22	1053	1006	959	915	872	828	783	742	702
24	1015	970	925	882	841	797	754	715	676
26	976	933	889	847	807	766	724	686	648
28	936	894	852	811	773	733	693	656	620
30	893	853	813	774	737	699	661	625	590
32	850	811	772	735	700	663	627	593	560
34	804	767	731	695	661	626	592	560	528
36	757	722	687	654	621	588	555	525	495
38	708	675	642	610	579	548	517	489	460
40	657	626	595	565	536	507	478	452	424

(Left vertical labels: $F_y = 36$ ksi — Effective length in ft. KL with respect to least radius of gyration r_y)

Properties									
Area A (in.²)	62.1	59.4	56.7	54.1	51.7	49.1	46.5	44.1	41.8
I_x (in.⁴)	2670	2540	2400	2270	2150	2020	1900	1790	1670
I_y (in.⁴)	1030	980	930	883	838	790	745	703	660
Ratio r_x/r_y	1.61	1.61	1.61	1.61	1.60	1.60	1.60	1.60	1.59
r_y (in.)	4.07	4.06	4.05	4.04	4.02	4.01	4.00	3.99	3.97
L_c (ft.)	16.7	16.7	16.6	16.6	16.6	16.5	16.5	16.4	16.4
L_u (ft.)	72.6	70.2	67.5	65.0	62.4	59.6	57.1	54.5	51.8
B_x } Bending	.184	.183	.183	.183	.184	.184	.184	.184	.185
B_y } factors	.478	.480	.481	.479	.484	.487	.486	.487	.491
a_x } Multiply	398	379	358	340	320	302	284	267	249
a_y } values by 10⁶	153	146	139	132	124	118	111	105	98

Heavy line indicates $Kl/r = 120$.

COLUMNS
W shapes
TABLE I
Allowable axial loads in kips

$$F_y = 36 \text{ ksi}$$

W 14

Designation				W14			
Nominal Depth and Width				14 × 14½			
Weight per Foot	136	127	119	111	†103	†95	†87

Effective length in ft. KL with respect to least radius of gyration r_y		136	127	119	111	†103	†95	†87
	6	826	770	723	675	625	576	528
	7	818	763	716	668	619	570	523
	8	810	755	709	662	613	564	518
	9	801	747	701	654	606	558	512
	10	792	739	693	647	599	552	506
	11	783	730	685	639	592	545	500
	12	773	721	676	631	585	538	493
	13	763	711	667	623	577	531	487
	14	753	702	658	614	569	523	480
	15	742	691	648	605	560	516	473
	16	731	681	639	596	552	508	465
	17	719	670	628	586	543	499	458
	18	707	659	618	576	534	491	450
	19	695	648	607	566	524	482	442
	20	683	636	596	556	515	473	434
	22	657	612	574	535	495	455	417
	24	630	587	550	512	474	436	399
	26	602	560	525	489	452	416	381
	28	572	533	499	464	429	394	361
	30	542	504	472	439	405	372	341
	32	510	474	444	412	381	350	320
	34	476	443	414	384	355	326	298
	36	442	410	384	356	328	301	275
	38	406	377	352	326	300	275	251
	40	368	342	319	295	272	249	227

Properties

	136	127	119	111	†103	†95	†87
Area A (in.²)	40.0	37.3	35.0	32.7	30.3	27.9	25.6
I_x (in.⁴)	1590	1480	1370	1270	1170	1060	967
I_y (in.⁴)	568	528	492	455	420	384	350
Ratio r_x/r_y	1.67	1.67	1.67	1.67	1.67	1.66	1.66
r_y (in.)	3.77	3.76	3.75	3.73	3.72	3.71	3.70
L_c (ft.)	15.6	15.6	15.5	15.5	15.4	15.4	15.4
L_u (ft.)	49.2	46.5	43.7	41.0	38.6	35.7	33.1
B_x ⎫ Bending	.186	.185	.186	.186	.185	.185	.186
B_y ⎭ factors	.520	.520	.522	.526	.527	.529	.532
a_x ⎫ Multiply	237	220	204	189	174	158	144
a_y ⎭ values by 10⁶	85	79	73	68	62	57	52

Heavy line indicates $Kl/r = 120$.
† Flange is non-compact; see discussion preceding column load tables.

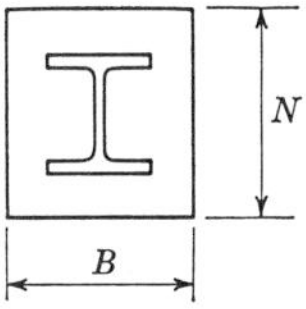

COLUMN BASE PLATES
Dimensions for maximum column loads

Base plates, F_b = 27 ksi to 8" thick
Base plates, F_b = 24 ksi over 8" thick
Concrete, f'_c = 3000 psi

$F_y = 36$ ksi
Columns

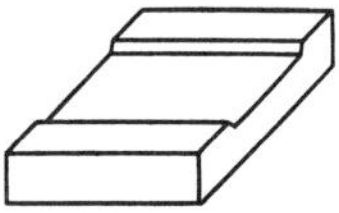

Column			Unit Pressure on Support F_p = 0.25 f'_c = 750 psi						Unit Pressure on Support F_p = 0.375 f'_c = 1125 psi					
Designation	Max. Load	Dimensions		Thickness of Plate			Gross Wt.	Dimensions		Thickness of Plate			Gross Wt.
		B	N	Calc.	Fin.	Rolled		B	N	Calc.	Fin.	Rolled	
	Kips	In.	In.	In.	In.	In.	Lb.	In.	In.	In.	In.	In.	Lb.
W 14 × 730	4315	72	80	8.98	9	9½	15502	59	65	8.38	8½	9	9778
665	3928	69	76	8.48	8½	9	13371	56	63	7.46	7½	8	7996
605	3562	66	72	7.52	7½	8	10770	54	59	7.06	7	7½	6769
550	3237	62	70	7.31	7¼	7¾	9529	51	57	6.64	6¾	7¼	5971
500	2933	60	66	6.79	6¾	7¼	8134	49	54	6.21	6¼	6¾	5060
455	2670	57	63	6.45	6½	7	7121	47	51	5.90	5⅞	6¼	4244
W 14 × 426	2489	55	61	6.21	6¼	6¾	6416	45	50	5.65	5⅝	6	3825
398	2328	54	58	5.85	5⅞	6¼	5546	44	48	5.38	5⅜	5¾	3440
370	2167	52	56	5.60	5⅝	6	4950	42	46	5.11	5⅛	5½	3010
342	2099	51	55	5.52	5½	5⅞	4669	41	46	5.15	5⅛	5½	2939
314	1917	49	53	5.25	5¼	5⅝	4138	40	43	4.75	4¾	5⅛	2497
287	1752	47	50	4.91	4⅞	5¼	3495	38	41	4.44	4½	4⅞	2152
264	1611	45	48	4.65	4⅝	5	3060	36	40	4.29	4¼	4⅝	1887
246	1500	43	47	4.53	4½	4⅞	2791	35	39	4.12	4⅛	4½	1740
237	1446	43	45	4.36	4⅜	4¾	2604	34	38	4.00	4	4	1464
228	1392	42	45	4.26	4¼	4⅝	2476	34	37	3.82	3⅞	3⅞	1381
219	1336	41	44	4.15	4⅛	4½	2300	33	36	3.70	3¾	3¾	1262
211	1288	40	43	4.04	4⅛	4½	2193	33	35	3.58	3⅝	3⅝	1186
202	1232	40	42	3.91	3⅞	3⅞	1844	32	35	3.52	3½	3½	1111
193	1176	39	41	3.78	3¾	3¾	1699	31	34	3.39	3⅜	3⅜	1008
184	1121	38	40	3.65	3⅝	3⅝	1561	31	33	3.22	3¼	3¼	942
176	1071	37	39	3.52	3½	3½	1431	30	32	3.08	3⅛	3⅛	850
167	1017	36	38	3.40	3⅜	3⅜	1308	29	32	3.08	3⅛	3⅛	822
158	963	35	37	3.27	3¼	3¼	1192	29	30	2.90	2⅞	2⅞	709
150	914	34	36	3.15	3⅛	3⅛	1084	28	30	2.76	2¾	2¾	654
142	866	33	35	3.03	3	3	982	27	29	2.63	2⅝	2⅝	582
W 14 × 320	1954	50	53	5.30	5¼	5⅝	4223	40	44	4.92	4⅞	5¼	2618
W 14 × 136	826	32	35	3.00	3	3	952	26	29	2.61	2⅝	2⅝	561
127	770	31	34	2.86	2⅞	2⅞	858	25	28	2.47	2½	2½	496
119	723	30	33	2.74	2¾	2¾	771	24	27	2.33	2⅜	2⅜	436
111	675	30	30	2.64	2⅝	2⅝	669	24	25	2.18	2¼	2¼	382
103	625	28	30	2.37	2⅜	2⅜	565	23	25	1.99	2	2	326
95	576	27	29	2.23	2¼	2¼	499	22	24	1.84	1⅞	1⅞	280
87	528	26	28	2.09	2⅛	2⅛	438	21	23	1.69	1¾	1¾	239
W 14 × 84	503	24	28	2.09	2⅛	2⅛	405	19	24	1.84	1⅞	1⅞	242
78	466	23	28	2.08	2⅛	2⅛	388	19	22	1.65	1¾	1¾	207
W 14 × 74	436	22	27	1.99	2	2	337	17	23	1.68	1¾	1¾	194
68	400	21	26	1.85	1⅞	1⅞	290	16	23	1.67	1¾	1¾	182
61	358	20	24	1.73	1¾	1¾	238	16	20	1.41	1½	1½	136
W 14 × 53	302	17	24	1.54	1⅝	1⅝	188	13	21	1.36	1⅜	1⅜	106
48	273	16	23	1.42	1½	1½	156	12	21	1.37	1⅜	1⅜	98
43	244	15	22	1.29	1⅜	1⅜	129	12	19	1.04	1⅛	1⅛	73

Note: Rolled plate thicknesses above 4 inches are based on finished thickness plus suggested allowances for finishing one side, and may be modified to suit fabricating plant practice. When it is required to finish both surfaces of base plates, additional allowance must be made.

FLEXURAL COEFFICIENT K-CHART

Example: Given: h = 16.7′, t = 7.63″, d = 3.8″,
n = 40, f_m = 250 psi x 1.33 = 333 psi.

Lateral force = w = 20 psf

$$M = \frac{wl^2}{8} \times 12 = \frac{20 \times 16.7^2}{8} \times 12 = 8367''\#$$

$$K = \frac{M}{bd^2} = \frac{8367}{12 \times 3.8^2} = 48$$

Enter diagram with K = 48, proceed to right to
intersect f_m = 333 psi, read np = 0.070

$$p = \frac{.07}{40} = .0018$$

A_s = pbd = .0018 x 12 x 3.8 = .08 sq. in./ft
use #5 @ 48″

$$\text{Check } f_s = \frac{M}{A_s \, jd} = \frac{8367}{.08 \times .9 \times 3.8} = 30,580 \text{ psi}$$

Decrease spacing to #5 @ 40″

$$f_s = \frac{8367 \times 40/12}{.31 \times .9 \times 3.8} = 26,300 \text{ psi}$$

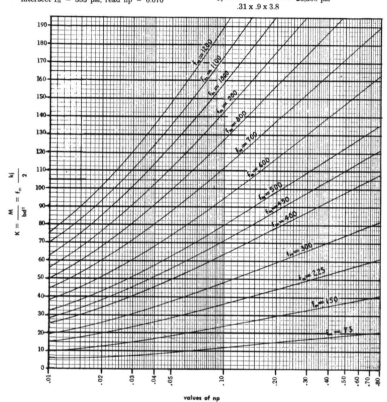

$$K = \frac{M}{bd^2} = f_m \frac{kj}{2}$$

values of np

DISTRIBUTION OF HORIZONTAL FORCES ALONG
A FIXED MASONRY WALL—AVERAGE RIGIDITIES

h/d	R_f	h/d	R_f	h/d	R_f	h/d	R_f	h/d	R_f	h/d	R_f
9.90	.0025	5.20	.0160	1.85	.2104	1.38	.3694	0.91	.7177	0.45	1.736
9.80	.0026	5.10	.0169	1.84	.2128	1.37	.3742	0.90	.7291	0.44	1.779
9.70	.0027	5.00	.0179	1.83	.2152	1.36	.3790	0.89	.7407	0.43	1.825
9.60	.0027	4.90	.0189	1.82	.2176	1.35	.3840	0.88	.7527	0.42	1.874
9.50	.0028	4.80	.0200	1.81	.2201	1.34	.3890	0.87	.7649	0.41	1.924
9.40	.0029	4.70	.0212	1.80	.2226	1.33	.3942	0.86	.7773	0.40	1.978
9.30	.0030	4.60	.0225	1.79	.2251	1.32	.3994	0.85	.7901	0.39	2.034
9.20	.0031	4.50	.0239	1.78	.2277	1.31	.4047	0.84	.8031	0.38	2.092
9.10	.0032	4.40	.0254	1.77	.2303	1.30	.4100	0.83	.8165	0.37	2.154
9.00	.0033	4.30	.0271	1.76	.2330	1.29	.4155	0.82	.8302	0.36	2.219
8.90	.0034	4.20	.0288	1.75	.2356	1.28	.4211	0.81	.8442	0.35	2.287
8.80	.0035	4.10	.0308	1.74	.2384	1.27	.4267	0.80	.8585	0.34	2.360
8.70	.0037	4.00	.0329	1.73	.2411	1.26	.4324	0.79	0.873	0.33	2.437
8.60	.0038	3.90	.0352	1.72	.2439	1.25	.4384	0.78	0.888	0.32	2.518
8.50	.0039	3.80	.0377	1.71	.2468	1.24	.4443	0.77	0.904	0.31	2.605
8.40	.0040	3.70	.0405	1.70	.2497	1.23	.4504	0.76	0.920	0.30	2.697
8.30	.0042	3.60	.0435	1.69	.2526	1.22	.4566	0.75	0.936	0.29	2.795
8.20	.0043	3.50	.0468	1.68	.2556	1.21	.4628	0.74	0.952	0.28	2.900
8.10	.0045	3.40	.0505	1.67	.2586	1.20	.4692	0.73	0.969	0.27	3.013
8.00	.0047	3.30	.0545	1.66	.2617	1.19	.4757	0.72	0.987	0.26	3.135
7.90	.0048	3.20	.0590	1.65	.2648	1.18	.4823	0.71	1.005	0.25	3.265
7.80	.0050	3.10	.0640	1.64	.2679	1.17	.4891	0.70	1.023	0.24	3.407
7.70	.0052	3.00	.0694	1.63	.2711	1.16	.4959	0.69	1.042	0.23	3.560
7.60	.0054	2.90	.0756	1.62	.2744	1.15	.5029	0.68	1.062	0.22	3.728
7.50	.0056	2.80	.0824	1.61	.2777	1.14	.5100	0.67	1.082	0.21	3.911
7.40	.0058	2.70	.0900	1.60	.2811	1.13	.5173	0.66	1.103	0.20	4.112
7.30	.0061	2.60	.0985	1.59	.2844	1.12	.5247	0.65	1.124	.195	4.220
7.20	.0063	2.50	.1081	1.58	.2879	1.11	.5322	0.64	1.146	.190	4.334
7.10	.0065	2.40	.1189	1.57	.2914	1.10	.5398	0.63	1.168	.185	4.454
7.00	.0069	2.30	.1311	1.56	.2949	1.09	.5476	0.62	1.191	.180	4.580
6.90	.0072	2.20	.1449	1.55	.2985	1.08	.5556	0.61	1.216	.175	4.714
6.80	.0075	2.10	.1607	1.54	.3022	1.07	.5637	0.60	1.240	.170	4.855
6.70	.0078	2.00	.1786	1.53	.3059	1.06	.5719	0.59	1.266	.165	5.005
6.60	.0081	1.99	.1805	1.52	.3097	1.05	.5804	0.58	1.292	.160	5.164
6.50	.0085	1.98	.1824	1.51	.3136	1.04	.5889	0.57	1.319	.155	5.334
6.40	.0089	1.97	.1844	1.50	.3175	1.03	.5977	0.56	1.347	.150	5.514
6.30	.0093	1.96	.1864	1.49	.3214	1.02	.6066	0.55	1.376	.145	5.707
6.20	.0097	1.95	.1885	1.48	.3245	1.01	.6157	0.54	1.407	.140	5.914
6.10	.0102	1.94	.1905	1.47	.3295	1.00	.6250	0.53	1.438	.135	6.136
6.00	.0107	1.93	.1926	1.46	.3337	0.99	.6344	0.52	1.470	.130	6.374
5.90	.0112	1.92	.1947	1.45	.3379	0.98	.6441	0.51	1.504	.125	6.632
5.80	.0118	1.91	.1969	1.44	.3422	0.97	.6540	0.50	1.539	.120	6.911
5.70	.0124	1.90	.1991	1.43	.3465	0.96	.6641	0.49	1.575	.115	7.215
5.60	.0130	1.89	.2013	1.42	.3510	0.95	.6743	0.48	1.612	.110	7.545
5.50	.0137	1.88	.2035	1.41	.3555	0.94	.6848	0.47	1.651	.105	7.908
5.40	.0144	1.87	.2058	1.40	.3600	0.93	.6955	0.46	1.692	.100	8.306
5.30	.0152	1.86	.2081	1.39	.3647	0.92	.7065				

Index

||||||||||||||||||||||||||||||||||||||||||||||||||||||||||||

Anchorage, 35, 40, 83

Basement wall, *see* Concrete

Composite construction, 232
Concrete:
  basement wall, 24, 175, 222
  column, 205
  column footing, 26, 74, 116, 173,
    222
  floor beam, 193
  floor girder, 201
  floor slab, 191, 232
  joist, 233
  precast floor deck, 233
  rigid frame, 198, 211, 217
  waffle slab, 236
  wall footing, 26, 73, 115, 175

Diaphragm:
  chord, 29, 80
  horizontal, 27, 31, 78, 116
  nailing schedule, 59
  vertical, *see* Shear wall
Deflection of:
  concrete beam, 193
  concrete slab, 192
  steel floor structure, 172
  steel roof beam, 101
  wood ceiling joist, 16
  wood floor joist, 18
  wood rafter, 15

Earthquake, *see* Seismic load

Fire protection of steel, 141,
  170
Footing, *see* Concrete

Masonry:
  bearing wall, 103
  column, 107, 112
  header, 110
  shear wall, 118

Overturning moment, 35, 40, 83,
  86, 123, 159

Plywood:
  horizontal diaphragm, 27, 31, 78
  floor deck, 17
  roof deck, 10, 66
  shear wall, 33, 82

Reduction of live load, 19, 67

Seismic load, 78, 116
Shear wall:
  gypsum drywall, 37
  masonry, 118
  plaster, 37
  plywood, 33, 82
Sill bolts:
  for lateral resistance, 40, 83
  for tie down, 35, 41, 83

Sliding:
  due to seismic load, 83
  due to wind, 40
Steel:
  column for axial load only, 23, 72, 102, 146
  column base plate, 169
  column with combined load, 150, 165
  column splice, 149
  floor beam, 142
  floor deck, 141
  horizontal diaphragm, 117
  open web joist, 123
  rigid frame:
    combined load, 150, 163
    gravity load, 143
    wind load, 155
  roof deck, 100
  roof girder, 101
  roof joist, 101

Tie down, 35, 83
Torsion due to lateral load, 85, 119

Wind:
  direct pressure on wall, 32, 104, 107, 249
  load, 27, 155
  moments in rigid frame, 159, 217
Wood:
  beam, 19, 69, 72
  ceiling joist, 15
  column, 22, 71
  diaphragm chord, 29, 80
  floor joist, 17
  glue laminated beam, 21, 67, 70
  header, 72
  purlin, 69
  rafter, 10, 66
  roof joist, 66
  stud, 23, 32, 70
  truss, 42, 97